The Kaiser's
Confidante

The Kaiser's Confidante

Mary Lee, the First American-Born Princess

RICHARD JAY HUTTO

McFarland & Company, Inc., Publishers
Jefferson, North Carolina

LIBRARY OF CONGRESS CATALOGUING-IN-PUBLICATION DATA

Names: Hutto, Richard Jay, author.
Title: The Kaiser's confidante : Mary Lee, the first American-born princess / Richard Jay Hutto.
Other titles: Mary Lee, the first American-born princess
Description: Jefferson, North Carolina : McFarland & Company, Inc., Publishers, 2017 | Includes bibliographical references and index.
Identifiers: LCCN 2017000244 | ISBN 9781476665726 (softcover : acid free paper) ∞
Subjects: LCSH: Waldersee, Mary Esther, Gräfin von, 1837 or 1838–1914. | Princesses—Germany—Biography. | Americans—Germany—Biography. | Noer, Frederick von, Prince, 1800–1865. | Waldersee, Alfred, Graf von, 1832–1904. | William II, German Emperor, 1859–1941. | Germany—Court and courtiers—Biography.
Classification: LCC DD219.W32 H87 2017 | DDC 943.08/4092 [B] —dc23
LC record available at https://lccn.loc.gov/2017000244

BRITISH LIBRARY CATALOGUING DATA ARE AVAILABLE

ISBN (print) 978-1-4766-6572-6
ISBN (ebook) 978-1-4766-2808-0

© 2017 Richard Jay Hutto. All rights reserved

No part of this book may be reproduced or transmitted in any form or by any means, electronic or mechanical, including photocopying or recording, or by any information storage and retrieval system, without permission in writing from the publisher.

Front cover image *Von Klarheit zu Klarheit*, Grafin Elisabeth Waldersee, 1918

Printed in the United States of America

McFarland & Company, Inc., Publishers
Box 611, Jefferson, North Carolina 28640
www.mcfarlandpub.com

For Katy and Martin

Table of Contents

Preface	1
Introduction	7
1. New Opportunities in the Old World	11
2. Married into the Royal Mob	21
3. A Princess in Her Own Right	33
4. Another Chance at Love	45
5. Mentoring a Future Empress	55
6. Religion and Philanthropy	71
7. A Clear Path to the Throne	83
8. Ensconced in Power	93
9. Father Figure	105
10. "The Empress' American Rival"	115
11. Distaff Diplomacy	129
12. Command in the Boxer Rebellion	137
13. Alfred's Return from China	160
14. The Long-Delayed Visit to America	166
15. Death and Solitude	174
Epilogue	182
Chapter Notes	193
Bibliography	213
Index	219

Preface

Mary Lee, the first American-born princess, is known primarily, if at all, for her two marriages. At the age of 27, in 1864, she married Prince Friedrich of Schleswig-Holstein-Sonderburg-Augustenburg, who was 64 and a brother of the queen of Denmark and of the Duke of Schleswig-Holstein. Widowed on her extended honeymoon in the Holy Land and left a large fortune to add to her own modest one, Mary then married, in 1874, Count Alfred von Waldersee, who would become chief of the German General Staff (1888–1891), field marshal (1900), and the commander-in-chief of the Eight-Nation Alliance (including the United States) that suppressed China's Boxer Rebellion (1900–1901). The long-coveted chancellorship was often dangled in front of him like a precious jewel but was always pulled from his fingertips at the last moment. His wife was deservedly given much of the credit for his success at court, where she enjoyed a great deal of influence as the mentor and friend of the kaiserin, wife of Wilhelm II. The reach and intensity of that influence is the subject examined here.

In 2008, I included Mary von Waldersee in my book *Crowning Glory: American Wives of Princes and Dukes*. Her entry was only three pages long, but the memory of her remained with me. It seemed inconceivable that a woman of her supposed influence at the German court—she continued to be listed in the authoritative *Almanach de Gotha* (the official guide to royal families) as a princess even after her remarriage—would have so little written about her. A year after her death, her husband's niece, Countess Elisabeth von Waldersee, wrote what amounted to a hagiography concentrating upon her religious activities and philanthropy.[1] According to her, Mary did not want her diaries to be made public, and they are presumed to have been destroyed.

In 1962, one of Mary's cousins, Alson J. Smith, wrote a rather odd book[2] that made use of the voluminous correspondence of Mary and her mother. Although written as fact, there is more than a little fiction to his work. Not only was Smith very selective in his reliance upon primary sources in the family correspondence, he deliberately ignored or misstated those that did not agree with his opinions (even alleging a sexual relationship between Mary and Kaiser Wilhelm II, for which there is no supporting evidence of any kind). The earlier information he provides about Mary's family background is on much firmer ground (his mother was a great-niece of Mary's father), and every effort has been made to verify any of his statements relied upon in this work.

Mary von Waldersee strongly disliked publicity and wrote only one article about her life,[3] explaining "newspaper editors in America" had published "extraordinary and at the same time foolish stories about me and my influence in the political affairs of my adopted country, Germany." She sat for one newspaper interview for the *San Francisco Call*[4] by Miss Marian Watts, who met her while playing as a member of the orchestra as a pupil at Berlin's Königliche Hochschule (Conservatory of Music). Watts was able to secure the interview after learning that her aunt in America was a childhood friend of Mary's. In her lengthy article (which revealed nothing of importance other than Mary's tact), she complained of the difficulty she encountered in arranging the interview, declaring, "It is easier to meet Queen Victoria than the Countess von Waldersee."[5]

Mary's second husband, Count Alfred von Waldersee, faithfully kept a diary for decades and those have been published in an abridged version in English[6] as well as a much more complete version in German. He comes across as a man whose undoubted military expertise is equaled only by his own vanity and self-promotion. The esteemed historian John Röhl calls von Waldersee a "reactionary anti–Semite and war fanatic."[7]

The treasure trove of information, however, is in 17 uncatalogued boxes of correspondence and memorabilia in Harvard's Houghton Library given, along with a modest bequest for their maintenance, in 1922 by Mary Perkins Quincy (who visited Mary in Hanover in March of 1907), a niece of Mary Hoppin, to whom most of the letters were written. Although arranged roughly (but not wholly) chronologically, they beg for an authoritative and scholarly cataloguing. While quite a few of the letters are written by Mary von Waldersee, the great majority were written by her indefatigable mother, Ann D. Lee, who lived with Mary for most of her adult life until her death at the age of 96. Her frequent letters, usually written to her cousin in America, Mary Hoppin (whose husband was a professor at Yale), were then circulated among other family members so that everyone would know of her life in Germany. There are also dried flowers from Chancellor Bismarck's private garden, seating charts, calling cards, newspaper clippings, and other memorabilia Mrs. Lee sent with explanatory notes.

When the gift of the collection was announced, the Harvard Alumni Bulletin boasted that the letters had been bound in "black German leather, made from the hide of an Indian goat, tanned and finished in Germany. The sides are finished in Japanese hand-made, laid paper, designed and hand-printed in France. The color scheme is the black, red, and white of the old empire, and the Hohenzollern Eagle is used as a design."[8] The gift followed that of HRH Prince Henry of Prussia, younger brother of Emperor Wilhelm II, who donated "a valuable historical collection relating to the history of the empire."[9]

Mrs. Lee was a woman of good lineage and fine education who possessed an excellent observer's eye for detail and understatement. Unfortunately, she also exhibited the prejudices of her day, strongly disliking Jews as well as Catholics in general and Jesuits in particular. Occasionally, the date of her multi-page letters may be misleading, since Mrs. Lee often started a letter on which she would write the date on the first page only to continue it over the next several days or even weeks before completing and posting it to America.

Mrs. Lee wrote with usual frankness, "I have always spoken my opinion freely—that it could only be the *devil* that leads the Jesuits—their time of reckoning is sure to come and God will be the avenger. He has not suffered the blood of martyrs to flow like a river without noting it."[10] When she learned that William R. Grace had been elected the first Roman Catholic mayor of New York City, she wrote,

> How is it possible our people "to the manor born" and one would think should feel love of country higher than party, how can they rest in such apathy, yes stupidity and see the R.C. [Roman Catholic] power gaining such sway. It is startling to know what headway they have made.... [I]f our country is destroyed it will be by the Papacy. To every reflecting mind it is evident the Pope and the Jesuits are doing their utmost to gain the control of America.[11]

On another instance she wrote, "I have charity that sympathizes with all who love Christ Jesus and take His teaching as their standard. But none for the Papacy or Jesuits unless they repent."[12]

In speaking of how the crown prince [Wilhelm II] was viewed in America, she warned, "As you know—all the world over Jews have money—which is a power in the press—no doubt they send their papers to countrymen in America and thus a false opinion will be formed of the present Crown Prince—who in reality has noble qualities."[13] She seemed blind to any imperfections in Wilhelm, writing after he succeeded to the throne,

"What a wonderfully wise idea it was for the Emperor to go to Russia! You will see now his whole aim is for *peace*—blessed thing for all countries—and you will join us in thanking God it is so."[14]

Mrs. Lee's prejudices were not limited to Jews and Catholics, however. When she related the official visit by the Sultan of Morocco, she wrote, "The Moors have been here…. They were received by their Majesties in Throne Room surrounded by their court. Alfred too was there and also at the Dinner to which Emperor invited them—being Mahametans [Mohammedans] they were so afraid of eating something prepared with *pigs fat* they sent their own cook to the Castle to look after their dinner!"[15] Similarly when the shah of Persia and his retinue visited, she wrote, "He and his 70—women and men—are to be placed at Bellevue Palace—suburb of Berlin—by themselves—they are so uncivilized it is necessary."[16]

When Mrs. Lee read in the *Tribune* that her husband had left her "a small fortune," she was offended,[17] as she didn't consider $1 million (in 1853) to be modest at all. In one letter, she told of a centerpiece of a "pyramid of cake" which one attendee referred to as "Cupid!" to which the long-widowed Mrs. Lee wrote, "But it had been so long since he and I met, I did not recognize him."[18] In another, she decreed, "The Germans beat every thing for eating—they can't go to a committee without thinking they must stop a while to eat."[19] Her hearing completely left her in her last years, and when she fell and broke her right hand, she taught herself to write with her left. Without her correspondence it would be impossible to reconstruct Mary von Waldersee's life as well as a privileged view of the inner world of the Prussian court.

It is particularly difficult to refer consistently to the characters by the name protocol should dictate, especially since their names would evolve over time (e.g., Prince Wilhelm of Prussia became the crown prince who became the kaiser/emperor, etc.). Within his family, he was often referred to as Willy or Willie but sometimes as Wilhelm or William. In those instances in which I have directly quoted someone else, I have used the name and spelling in the original. When there is any question as to whom I am referring, I have often placed within brackets a one-name descriptor. This is particularly necessary when speaking of Queen Victoria; her daughter the Empress Victoria [Vicky], formerly the princess royal and the crown princess; the Kaiserin/Empress Augusta Victoria [Dona]; and Queen Victoria's many granddaughters named Victoria. I mean no disrespect by doing so, but it would often be difficult for the reader to comprehend to whom I'm referring without the use of short descriptors. Fortunately, the family used nicknames for most of Queen Victoria's granddaughters who were also named Victoria, such as "Ena" (later Queen of Spain), "Sissy," "Moretta," "Toria," "Ducky," and "Thora." A genealogical chart is provided for the major characters.

My largest debt of gratitude is to John Röhl, the undisputed expert on the life and reign of Wilhelm II. His scholarship is exceeded only by his generosity, and I am truly grateful for his wisdom and counsel. Any conclusions based on his sources with which he might disagree are entirely my own. My long-time friend, royal biographer Hugo Vickers, has been consistently supportive through this extended process, and I thank him for his friendship.

I am also grateful to the staff and resources at the Houghton Library of Harvard University; Kenneth Henke at the Princeton Theological Seminary Library; Carolyn Sautter at the Musselman Library of Gettysburg College; HSH Princess Elisabeth zu Ysenburg at Schloß Glücksburg; Dr. Peter Schiffer at Hauptstaatsarchiv Stuttgart; Dr. Malte Bischoff at Landesarchiv Schleswig-Holstein; Jette Renneberg Elkjær at the Royal Danish Embassy in Washington; HE Christopher Smith, Honorary Consul of the kingdom of Denmark; Belle Bush at the Central Georgia Technical College Library; Arturo Beeche; Candace Metz; Mitchell Owens; Marlene Eilers Koenig; Nash Rambler; Katie Tice; Ilana Miller, Sam Lester; and especially Mary Pearson for her expert professional assistance.

I am particularly grateful to my daughter, Katy Hutto, for her expertise in assembling and preparing the accompanying photos and genealogical chart and also for returning to the Houghton Library at Harvard University to retrieve something I missed on my visits there. Of course, I am deeply indebted to my wife, Katherine, and our son, Martin, for their patience and forbearance. Katherine is quite correct that I was born in the wrong century and has become accustomed to my speaking of Queen Victoria's family members as though they might walk in the door at any moment.

Introduction

If one man can be blamed for the carnage of "the Great War," surely Kaiser Wilhelm II, German emperor and king of Prussia, deserves to have that burden laid at his feet. Nine million combatants were killed in that conflict (thought at the time to be "the war to end all wars") largely due to technological advances that made human annihilation more efficient as well as more clinical when soldiers were less likely to face one another at the point of a bayonet.[1] In Britain alone, one-fifth of all peers and their immediate heirs were killed.[2] "In the first sixteen months of operations no less than eight hundred men of title were killed in action, or died of their wounds, and over a thousand more were serving with the land or sea forces."[3] Britain suffered 673,375 deaths (with some estimates as high as 723,000)—more than twice their number of deaths in World War II—with 1,643,469 wounded, while the German Empire suffered more than two million deaths.[4] The idle young titled and landed classes of Britain welcomed the advent of war as a way to prove they deserved their heritage. "Frequently, the young lords were given junior commissions on the battlefront, leading their men with bravery in their hearts but only a pistol or a baton in their hands. They were first in the German machine-gunners' sights. While one in eight British soldiers perished during the four-year conflict, the ratio was one in five for the nobility."[5] In the July 1916 battle against the Germans near the Somme River in France, more than 21,000 British soldiers died in a single day, a number that exceeded one-third the total United States deaths suffered in the entire Viet Nam War.[6]

In some grotesque way, the misguided and neurotic kaiser would have thought it entirely fitting that Britain pay for his imagined slights. Wilhelm hated his mother, the Empress Vicky, eldest child of Queen Victoria; he even referred to her as "that English princess who is my mother."[7] During childbirth, his arm was so mangled (no one noticed the injury for several days) that it forever hung limp and lifeless as a constant reminder of his imperfection. The arm, like his mother's expectations of him, always came up short.

Throughout childhood Wilhelm's mother subjected him to medical treatments he considered little more than deliberate torture. He suffered from a painful disease of the inner ear that greatly affected his balance, making riding with only one arm even more difficult. According to him, his riding instructor sadistically placed him back in the saddle each time he fell from it until finally he could balance himself astride a horse.[8] When his mother eventually gave up hope of healing the arm, a constant reminder of his deficiencies, she also relinquished any affection for her first-born son and heir.

The kaiser also loathed his mother's brother, England's King Edward VII, because of his louche lifestyle. In fact, his grandmother was the only thing he liked about England. Even as a boy, he ordered his handlers to leave him alone when he suffered a nosebleed, protesting, "Now maybe all the English blood will drain out of me!"[9] As Victoria's eldest grandchild, Wilhelm was certain he was the true heir of the great queen. His own mother and father, the enfeebled emperor who reigned for only 99 days before succumbing to cancer, dangerously tried to steer their empire toward a liberal cabinet-style monarchy envisioned by Queen Victoria's long-dead and much-adored German husband, Prince Albert. Vicky had been schooled by her father for just such a purpose. Only divine providence, as far as the son was concerned, interceded by ending the suffering of the man whose heir considered him such an unworthy successor to the kaiser's illustrious ancestor, Frederick the Great.

Even during his father's short reign, Wilhelm attempted to supplant his parents' authority by insisting upon ruling himself through an official regency. Within minutes of his father's death, the kaiser broke into his mother's office and stole her papers, ordered her effectively locked in her rooms, and forbade any member of the staff to have any correspondence or files, no matter how personal, leave the palace, nor could any telegrams be sent. Vicky's short-term hollow victory over her son during her husband's brief reign was particularly bitter as her subsequent downfall quickly brought back to power the one woman who had been able to steal her son's love and allegiance and use it, as far as the empress was concerned, not for the good of the country but for her own personal gain. The woman was surely not the kaiser's weak-willed and simple wife, Augusta Victoria, who never deserved such a lofty union but had been elevated to her position with the help of the same American woman, now restored to power, who was the new empress's closest advisor and confidante. As one observer wrote at the time, "Gradually the American girl became the power behind the throne. She helped to make and unmake Imperial Chancellors. She assisted in the drawing up of important dispatches. It was even rumoured that she actually wrote out speeches for the kaiser to deliver."[10]

This woman, the unlikeliest of candidates to be called "the power behind the throne," was rumored to share the kaiser's bed, although his mother never would have given credence to such Oedipal implications (nor is there any support for such a rumor). He came so frequently to her lavish apartment overlooking the river Spree that it was said the kaiser wouldn't make a move without the woman's approval. She wore her piety both as sword and shield and was referred to by some as "a sanctified Pompadour," although Vicky, the Empress Frederick, called her a "parvenue, intriguante adventuress."[11] A contemporary account agreed that the appeal to Wilhelm was not sexual, but "by her cleverness and intellectual brilliancy, rather than by her looks, for she is a woman already well-advanced in years."[12]

No one could have envisioned the meteoric rise to power of this wealthy and powerful but common-born American. As a court insider wrote of her at the time, she was "cordially disliked" by the kaiser's mother, Empress Vicky, "who is both jealous and incensed" at the woman's "influence over her son and daughter-in-law."[13] Even a New York newspaper, acknowledging that she was "a woman of queenly presence," wrote, "For a long time there has been a social feud between the Empress Frederick [Vicky] ... and it is said that the American woman has more influence with the emperor than his mother."[14] Another American newspaper, calling her "the woman Roosevelt," wrote, "She chose a husband—at first a pawn, now a gallant knight—whom she could move forward along the chessboard of life."[15] A San Francisco journalist, calling her "the most ambitious woman in Europe," wrote after a long-sought interview, "It is easier to meet Queen Victoria.... Very few Americans have had the honor and, indeed, very few of them know that this extraordinary woman is an American."[16] One contemporary even called her "the female Metternich," comparing her skills to those of the legendary 19th-century Austrian diplomat.[17]

No one did more to turn Wilhelm toward militarism and anti–Semitism in the guise of religious fervor than she and her husband. Her wealth, social position, and political connections at court enabled her to exact a terrible toll as a price for the kaiser's dysfunctional family. Had she not eventually overstepped her bounds and tried to temper the kaiser's increasingly harsh pronouncements and public stances, perhaps she would have been in a position to save her young charge from the homosexual cabal that finally caused his downfall and eventual exile. (He was no longer able to keep those activities quiet after one of his generals died of a heart attack while dancing in a tutu for the kaiser and his friends.) It is no exaggeration to say that the "sanctified Pompadour" and her husband helped the kaiser lead his nation—and thus the world—away from the liberal cabinet-style monarchy envisaged by his parents and thus down the path to destruction and the brand of anti–Semitism that gave birth to Hitler's Nazism.

Chapter 1

New Opportunities in the Old World

David Lee lived a classic Horatio Alger life decades before the character was conceived and written. Born in Ridgefield, Connecticut, in the foothills of the Berkshire Mountains, Lee left the family farm for New York City in 1810 at the age of 18 and secured a position at a grocery store at 125 Front Street, just above Wall Street, that included a small room over the shop. He worked hard, volunteered for the militia when Manhattan was threatened by the British in the War of 1812, and learned his trade well. After the war, Lee saved enough money to buy into partnership with the store's owner, David Leavitt, establishing Leavitt and Lee.[1]

It was an opportune time to enter the merchant grocery business since sailing lines were just beginning to ship wares to Liverpool and the European markets. The senior partner, Leavitt, sold his grocery interests in 1822 to Luman Reed then amassed a large fortune as a New York City banker. Leavitt eventually became president of the Fulton Bank of New York City and assumed the presidency of the American Exchange Bank during the financial panic of 1837 when he successfully financed the completion of the Illinois and Michigan Canal. For his role in linking the Midwest with the East Coast, Chicago's Leavitt Street was named for him. Leavitt also owned and operated the Fulton Street Ferry and built a lavish mansion in Brooklyn Heights, which stood until 1904. He developed a 300-acre estate, called Brookside, in Great Barrington, Massachusetts, where he displayed his impressive art collection, including *The Battle of Monmouth*, a painting he commissioned from artist Emanuel Leutze (who also painted *Washington Crossing the Delaware*). Leavitt's son, David Jr., moved to Dresden, Germany, where his daughters were among the earliest of American heiresses to marry titled husbands. Louise married Baron Franz Oswald Trützschler von Falkenstein, Helen married Baron Adolf von Strahlenheim, and Josephine married Max Erwin von Arnim. One of the von Arnim descendants was the wife of Ernst August, Prince of Lippe, a claimant as head of household of the Principality of Lippe.[2]

In 1822, after the senior Leavitt's departure, the firm became Reed and Lee.

> It made an admirable partnership. Reed was dashing, bold, and liberal; he would take a country customer in a frank manner: "Now, sir, this is our price; you just go and take a walk around among other grocer houses, and if you can get the article for less, buy it. If you can't, then come back and get it from us." Lee was close, sharp, a good accountant, and not afraid of work. Sometimes he would stop at the store until long after midnight, writing up the books. He attended to the in-door business and Mr. Reed to the out-door.[3]

When the Erie Canal opened in 1825, the firm of Reed and Lee prospered greatly and expanded to the Midwest. All those late nights poring over the books, however, took a toll on David Lee.

> In 1827, Mr. Lee went out of the house [grocery partnership], with the distinct understanding that he was never to go into the grocery business again. His health was broke down. He had almost lost the use of his eyes, when Elliott the Eye Doctor undertook his case. He used calomel and other powerful medicine until he cured the eyes of Mr. Lee, but lost him the use of his limbs. Mr. Reed had paid him liberally for his share of the business. He was horror-struck a few months after when he found that the greediness for gain of his old partner had made him go back again into the business.[4]

Lee's financial needs must have been great to force him back into business while suffering such terrible infirmities, but in 1827 two other partners bought into the newly named firm of Lee, Dater & Miller and operated a "mammoth store in Front Street, between Maiden Lane and Burling Slip, on the corner of Fletcher Street."[5] Their modest fortunes were greatly increased when clipper ships began racing around Cape Horn to San Francisco, where flour was selling for $44 a barrel during the California gold rush. Daniel Miller, the third partner, had been a young clerk at Reed's firm, and his joining Lee and Dater "was a severe blow to Mr. Reed. He felt it to be ungrateful."[6] His daughter, Helen Day Miller, would have a unique vantage point to view the Gilded Age as the wife of the much-maligned financier Jay Gould.[7]

David Lee did what every upwardly mobile young man is taught to do—he married above himself. His bride, Ann Duryee Phillips, born on August 5, 1803, in Middletown, Connecticut, was proud of her distinguished lineage as a granddaughter of Governor Saltonstall as well as her descent from the Winthrops (her daughters would proudly retain their memberships in the Daughters of the American Revolution even though they lived abroad all their adult lives). Her father died when Ann was only three, so she spent a great deal of time with her great-uncle, William Cushing, the longest-serving member of the original U.S. Supreme Court. Cushing, who administered the oath of office for George Washington's second term of office, and his wife, Hannah Phillips, were close friends of the Washingtons (Cushing turned down his offer to serve as Chief Justice), whom they visited twice yearly at Mount Vernon.

David Lee and Ann Phillips were married in 1827, the same year he went back into business as head of his own firm, and the couple moved into a newly constructed mansion on College Place (now West Broadway) between Barclay and Chambers streets. As his wife later wrote, "When we were first engaged he decided to retire and I wanted him to buy one of the old places near the City on the Hudson River and I could live in country and have garden ... but I was disappointed by retirement lasting but 3 weeks."[8] Their location near what was then the site of Columbia College, north of the noise of much of the business area, was perfect for rearing a family. Their first-born, George, died as an infant. Their grief was overcome when Anna was born in 1830, followed by Josephine Louisa "Josie" in 1833, David in 1834, Abigail "Abby" in 1836, and finally Mary Esther Lee, who was to become internationally known, on October 3, 1837.

A large family pressed the need for space at the same time the city was marching northwards. In 1848, they purchased a new three-storey home on increasingly fashionable Union Square. It was just a short walk from David Lee's club, the Union, where his fellow members included J. P. Morgan, Cornelius Vanderbilt, and Ulysses S. Grant. In April of 1861, soon after the fall of Fort Sumter, 250,000 people—the largest assembled in the United States up to that time—gathered in Union Square to show their support for the Union forces. But David Lee and his family would not see their domestic privacy so publicly invaded. Long in ill health, he died in 1853 leaving his widow and children an impressive estate of $1 million (approximately $28 million in today's equivalent[9]). This didn't place him in the pantheon of John Jacob Astor, who left a fortune of $20 million at his death in 1848 (making him the fourth wealthiest American in history according to *Forbes* magazine),[10] but it was certainly sufficient to ensure a comfortable life for his widow and children.

Though Mary was the baby of the family at her father's death, one relation later described her as a "child-woman of fifteen [with] a deep and sincere natural piety, a profound human sympathy, and an unalterable sense of her own moral righteousness. It was a formidable combination—sincere piety and human sympathy yoked with ambition, cleverness, and a way with men—and one that was destined to baffle and frustrate those who opposed her throughout life."[11] Mary had received a much better education than most young women of her era, with five years at Bolton Priory School, run until 1882 by Nanette Bolton,[12] in New Rochelle, New York, where one of her schoolmates was Mary Custis Lee, daughter of Robert E. Lee, although the two families were not related. Then, in preparation for her all-important debut, she was given three years of preparatory training at Mrs. McCauley's School for Young Ladies in Manhattan.

Mary, an ardent Presbyterian, avidly followed the well-known abolitionists of her day and was peculiarly pious even in her youth. Her siblings did not share her religious interests, her brother being particularly drawn to a leisurely life afforded by his inheritance. Her mother, now a wealthy widow, was still of marriageable age and looked to Europe for her prospects and those of her four lovely daughters. The eldest, Anna, was headstrong and had no interest in her mother's plans. She took her share of the inheritance, moved to France to study art and write poetry, and established her own independence for the remainder of her life.

Years later Mary was to write of the conditions under which their lives changed so dramatically. Although many would later claim that Mrs. Lee took her daughters to Europe in order to marry titled husbands, Mary wrote to her cousin in America, "Now, dear cousin, you see how we have been led, step by step, to make our homes in Europe, and not, as some might think, did my mother bring us abroad with such an object!"[13]

At a ball in New York, Mary's next elder sister, Abby, met a handsome young British Navy captain, Augustus Charles Murray (1815–1902), who was a grandson of the 4th Earl of Dunmore, the last British governor of Virginia. Murray, a Naval attaché at the British embassy in Washington, was not only a tall and handsome Scot, but he also had a unique royal connection. His father's sister, Lady Augusta Murray (1768–1830), married as his first wife in 1793 Prince Augustus Frederick, later Duke of Sussex, sixth son of King George III. Their first wedding was a secret one in a Church of England ceremony in the Hotel Sarmiento in Rome. Several months later they were married again in a religious ceremony at St. George's Church in London's Hanover Square. As their marriage was in contravention of the Royal Marriages Act of 1772, it was considered invalid and she was not afforded the style of Duchess. They had two children, Sir Augustus d'Este and Emma Augusta d'Este, a lady-in-waiting to her first cousin, Queen Victoria. Emma Augusta married Baron Truro, Great Britain's Lord Chancellor from 1850 to 1852. Although they lived together in Berlin and London until 1801, their union was annulled in 1794 and he was created a royal

1. New Opportunities in the Old World

duke and received a parliamentary grant of £12,000. She was given by her husband a pension of £4,000 per year, custody of their children, and assumed with royal consent the style of Countess de Ameland (whom Lady Blessington referred to in writing as an "ill-used woman"). The Duke of Sussex married again after his first wife's death in 1830 and was an attentive father to his two children but did not compete with his brothers in the royal race to provide a legitimate heir to the throne.[14]

Mary described to her cousin the meeting between her sister and the groom:

> My brother-in-law Captain Augustus Charles Murray, grandson of the Earl of Dunmore, met my sister [Abby] at our father's house in New York, and, although he was on the eve of quitting the city, to look after some western lands, he felt himself so attracted to her that he postponed his departure for some time—in fact, did not leave until he had demanded her hand in marriage. The wedding took place in our American home, on 14th August, 1851; and they left for a European tour, accompanied by my sister Josie.[15]

After the lavish wedding and reception at the Lee mansion on Union Square, the couple honeymooned in Canada then left for Paris where the groom had been assigned. There, his sister, another Augusta, proved to be a perfect complement to their plans. She had married in 1834, becoming the second wife of Prince Louis Stanislas de la Tremouille (46 years her senior), son of the 7th Duc de Thouars and 6th Duc de la Tremouille. They had two daughters before her husband died in 1837 and she remained a widow for 40 years. The princess would become of great benefit to the Lee sisters. Mary continued in her letter written years later:

> During their stay in Paris my brother-in-law's sister, the Princess de la Tremouille, showed them every attention, and they became mutually attached, and remained lifelong friends. At one of the soirees given by the Princess my sister Josie made the acquaintance of her future husband, Baron de Waechter, the Württemberg Minister at the Court of the Tuileries. He was a friend of the Princess, and she was much pleased at the impression which my sister made upon him. This resulted, as you know, in their marriage in Paris; and in the following year, when I came out of school, my sister and brother-in-law both kindly invited me to come over and make them a visit. This I so much enjoyed that it was prolonged much more than I had dreamed of in leaving my native land, which I always regarded as my home, for there lived my dear mother, as well as brother.

When Mary and her mother learned that Josie's wedding date had been set for December 19, 1855, Mary left for Paris at the age of 17. She traveled with a family friend, Mrs. Winfield Scott, as chaperone. Mrs. Scott's husband was a hero of the Mexican War and served as commanding general of the U.S. Army longer than anyone in history—a successful 20 years. He was the first man since George Washington to hold the rank of lieutenant general. Scott, who served under every president from Jefferson to Lincoln, was the Whig nominee for President in 1852.[16] His wife, Maria de Hart Mayo Scott (1817–1862), a famous beauty in her youth, was from an influential family in Richmond, Virginia, and her name opened many doors in Paris for young Mary. The two took an apartment at Rue de Resberg 6 and immediately launched into the social world in which Mary's sisters ensured they were included.

There is one note from Abby's marriage to her handsome Scotsman, and Josie's to her baron, however, that Mary failed to mention. It seems to be the first time she openly encountered anti–Semitism, but it would not be the last. It may also have helped shape her opinions on the subject. According to Mary's cousin and biographer,

> American and English Puritans and their descendants had been delighted to name their children after Biblical characters—Rebecca, Abigail, Aaron, Hezekiah, Ezekiel. But that had never been true in Europe. In Europe, to have a surname of Hebrew derivation was considered a certain indication of Jewish ancestry. And now it was discreetly whispered that while Anna, Josephine, and Mary were all good Aryan names, it was misleading—in Europe—for a non–Jew to be named Abigail.[17]

The eldest Lee daughter, Anna, who was always the independent one, refused to consider such a ridiculous point of view. Josie was then engaged to a baron from an old established Lutheran family and begged her sister Abby to change her name before Josie's planned wedding. Mary sided—supposedly with reluctance—with Josie, and thus Abby's name was changed to "Blanche," even though her mother refused for the remainder of her life to call her anything but Abby. In fact, in 1889, when an American friend, Professor Edward Salisbury, wanted to name his daughter for Abby, Mrs. Lee replied to him, "It should be her Baptismal name, Abby Mumford, and *not* Blanche."[18]

Paris society at the time of Mary's arrival was presided over by the famously beautiful Spanish-born Empress Eugénie, wife of Napoleon III. Another young American woman, Lillie Greenough, arrived at the court in Paris at approximately the same time as Mary. Lillie would marry an American banker, Charles Moulton, who had long lived in Paris, and, after his death, as a wealthy widow she married the Danish minister to the United States. She wrote of her first encounter with the empress dressed for an evening fete: "I was completely dazed by her loveliness and beauty. I can't imagine a more beautiful apparition than she was. Her delicate coloring, the pose of her head, her hair, her expressive mouth, her beautiful shoulders, and wonderful grace made a perfect ensemble."[19]

1. New Opportunities in the Old World

Another American, Mrs. Burton Harrison, wrote of her first glimpse of the empress when she joined friends ice-skating:

> On a pond in the Bois de Boulogne, where there were coronetted carriages, powdered and plushed footmen, and Tom Thumb grooms waiting on all the grand people of the Tuileries society. There I had my first view of the Empress Eugénie, skating slowly, holding on to a bâton supported between two gentlemen of her court. She wore a short costume of sapphire blue velvet, trimmed with grèbe, with a toque of the same plumage. I lost my heart to her instantly, such beauty, grace, distinction were hers, and her smile adorable.[20]

The empress was also far less socially exclusive than the English or German courts, and beautiful young American women—particularly those with large inheritances—were welcome at the French court. The empress's wealthy grandfather, the Scottish-born William Kirkpatrick, was a naturalized U.S. citizen who served as the United States Consul at Malaga. Several sets of American heiresses, including the three Jerome sisters ("the beautiful, the good, and the witty,"[21] the first of whom was Winston Churchill's mother) and the Yznagas (exotic Catholics known as "the little sisters of the rich"), made their debut in London society only after first having been favorites of Napoleon III and his empress. The French court also welcomed prominent Jews, a practice that would have been unthinkable in London, Berlin, or Vienna. The fabulously wealthy Rothschilds were mainstays of the French court, and the Jewish Achille Fould had worked for the Rothschilds prior to his service as the powerful minister of state and of the imperial household. Fould also was a trusted art advisor to Eugénie and counseled her to make several of her wisest purchases.

Years later, in the only personal account Mary Lee wrote of her life, she gave credit to the Empress Eugénie, declaring,

> Paris was at that period the centre of the world's gayety and brilliancy.... The Empress Eugénie was lovely, and the most graceful apparition I ever saw. There were wonderful fetes at the Tuileries, and the empress was a charming hostess, greeting every one with friendliness. She was full of animation, a bright smile generally accompanying her words. I often had the opportunity of seeing her, and she frequently showed me particular attention. The Emperor rarely spoke to ladies at these fetes; his eyes were usually half closed, and his face showed no emotion.[22]

The emperor fully realized, however, that his wife's glittering evenings made his court popular. He is quoted in memoirs of his wife as having quipped, "Somebody has said: 'Let me write the songs of a nation and the rest will take care of itself.' I would add: 'Let me conduct the dancing in Paris and I will be willing to leave the songs to the poetasters of Montmartre.'"[23]

Mary spent her days studying languages and music at the Sorbonne[24] and her evenings with her sisters at various social events that would have impressed someone twice her age. Even then, Mary evinced a religious fervor that would seem to be at odds with evenings spent at court. She wrote,

> My mother had brought us up religiously, so that although at first, with the ardor of a schoolgirl, it seemed to me that the splendor of Parisian society could not have been more pleasing, I soon discovered that much of it was merely on the surface. There was at that time, as now, a great deal in Paris which is serious and genuinely religious, and in this I came to take a deep and active interest. Then in the winter of 1857 came the great revival in America through those extraordinary gatherings known as the Fulton Street prayer-meetings, and even in Paris the influence was felt.

Mary's mother, who had remained in New York to deal with matters of her late husband's estate, leased their Union Square home and arrived in Paris just in time to celebrate Thanksgiving with her daughters. On December 19, 1855, Josie Lee married the Baron de Waechter in a Lutheran ceremony held at the Württemberg legation in Paris. The groom's service to his independent kingdom was duly recognized, and he eventually served ably as its minister of foreign affairs and finally chamberlain to the king.[25] Perhaps their mother's presence in Paris was a bit too much for the headstrong eldest daughter, Anna. She took her own inheritance and moved to Bordeaux where she lived happily amid her artistic pursuits. For all practical purposes she was never to return to her family nor did

Mary Lee in Hamburg, 1857 (*Von Klarheit zu Klarheit*, **Grafin Elisabeth Waldersee, 1918**).

she marry, dying in France in 1882.²⁶ As her mother wrote to American cousins at the time when she was informed by telegram, "This time I come stricken with grief blinded by tears while I write."²⁷ Mary and her mother had colds and so did not travel to Bordeaux, but a suitable memorial was later erected.

Not long afterwards, when Mary and her mother were out walking on a Sunday afternoon, "who should we meet but the Crown Princess [Vicky], her two youngest daughters, and Lady of Honor, followed by a footman in showy Court livery. The Princess came over, shook hands with us both, and expressed such sympathy with us in our sorrow. She has lost several children. I told her she

Mary Lee standing behind her sisters, Blanche, left, and Josie, in Paris, 1859 (*Von Klarheit zu Klarheit*).

could understand what I felt from her own experiences. After a little chat she again shook hands with us in the most friendly manner."²⁸

At the time of the Lees' arrival, all Paris was lit in celebration at the birth of the royal heir, the prince imperial, on March 16, 1856. One account insists that, after a long delivery, the empress whispered to her husband, "C'est une fille?" He answered, "Non," and she asked, "C'est un garçon?" This time, when he replied, "Non," she asked in fear, "Mais alors, qu-est-ce que c'est?"²⁹

Later that same year, Josie also gave birth to her first child and named her Blanche in appreciation for the sister who changed her own name to deflect anti–Semitic criticism. It had been a difficult birth, however, and when Josie learned in 1860 that she was pregnant again, she decided to move to her husband's family estate in Württemberg to wait for the birth.

Both Mary and her mother would accompany Josie and live with her in anticipation at Lautenbach in the Black Forest at Baden-Württemberg on the Neckar River. It was their first trip to Germany, and, for Mary, it would become life changing.

Chapter 2

Married into the Royal Mob

A map of Germany reveals a large body of land abutting Denmark extending into the North Sea above Hamburg. The southernmost portion of that land, extending up to Kiel, was historically the Duchy of Holstein. Above Holstein was Schleswig, which had been a Danish duchy since the 12th century. In 1848, King Frederick VII of Denmark proclaimed that Schleswig would become an integral part of Denmark while maintaining its autonomy. Schleswig-Holstein's large German majority rebelled in favor of independence from Denmark and expressed their desire to become instead part of the German federation. As a result, the Prussian army drove Danish troops from Schleswig and Holstein in the First Schleswig War of 1848–1851. Denmark's King Christian IX tried again in 1863 to integrate Schleswig-Holstein into Denmark, precipitating the Second Schleswig War of 1864. Because of complicated laws of succession, King Christian IX's death in 1864 created a crisis over the question of whether Schleswig and Holstein would remain Danish or become German.[1]

Denmark was forced to cede all rights to both duchies on August 1, 1864, to Austria's Emperor Franz Joseph I and Prussia's King William I. A treaty stipulated that the inhabitants would be given six years to decide whether to be citizens of Denmark. However, in 1866 Prussia forcibly regained Holstein from Austria and the two duchies became the Province of Schleswig-Holstein. (Today Holstein and the southern part of Schleswig comprise the northernmost of the 16 states of Germany.) The Schleswig-Holstein succession issue was so convoluted that Britain's prime minister, Lord Palmerston, said, only half in jest, "Only three people … have ever really understood the Schleswig-Holstein business—the Prince Consort, who is dead—a German professor, who has gone mad—and I, who have forgotten all about it."[2] Prince Albert, after careful consideration, came to the conclusion that Denmark had no right to the duchies.

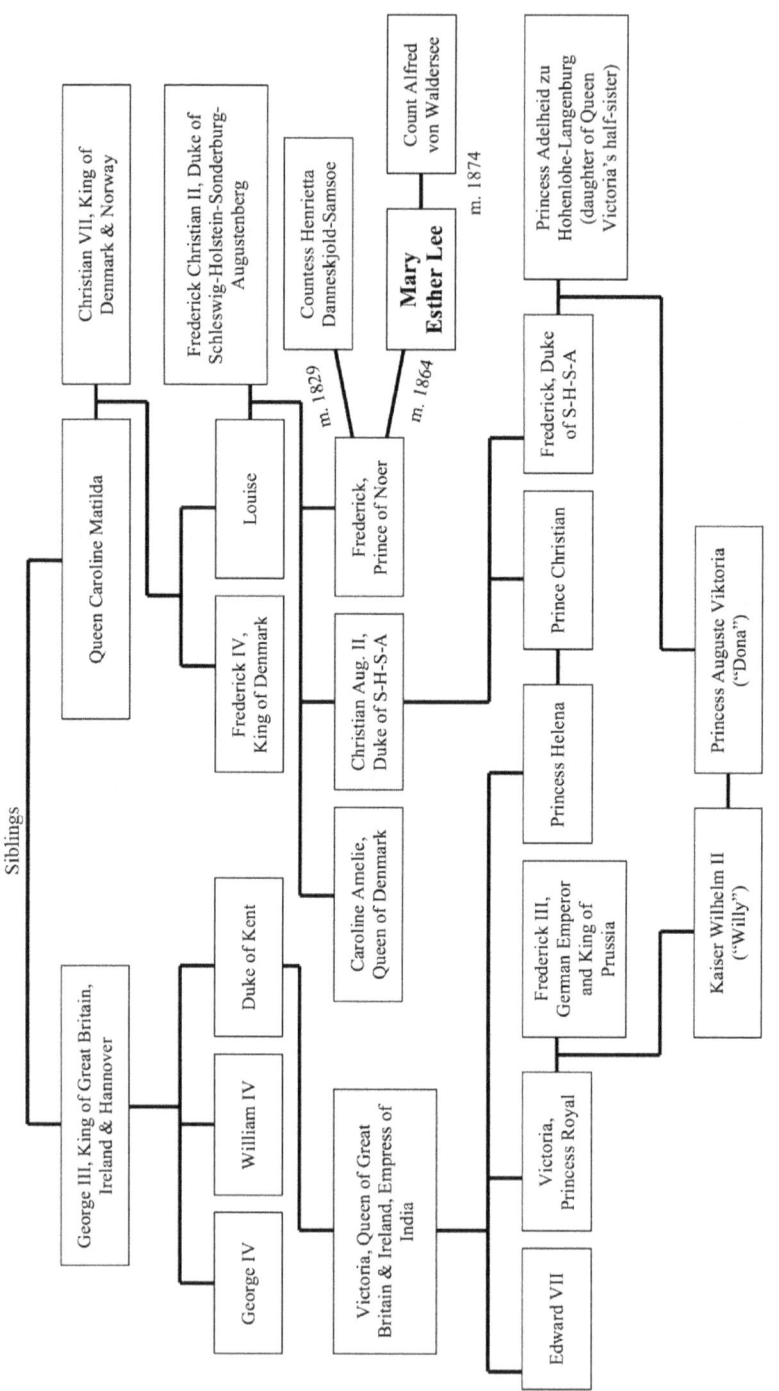

Genealogy chart.

2. Married into the Royal Mob

The dynastic issue of succession was a particularly thorny one that would have a vital impact on Mary Lee's future. According to the line of succession, after King Frederick VII of Denmark died in 1863 without an heir, the crowns of both Denmark and Schleswig passed to Duke Christian of Glücksburg (the future King Christian IX). The crown of Holstein was considered a thornier issue. A decision that it should also pass to the Glücksburg branch was challenged by a rival pro–German branch of the Danish royal family, the House of Augustenburg, who demanded, as they previously had in 1848, the crowns of both Schleswig and Holstein.

The House of Augustenburg (technically Schleswig-Holstein-Sonderburg-Augustenburg) had been, since 1764, the next senior agnatic line of the royal house directly after the main line of the kings of Denmark. They were descended from Princess Louise, only sister of Denmark's King Frederick VI, who married at her brother's urging in 1786 the then-hereditary Prince of Augustenburg, Frederick Christian II. When in 1863 the senior royal line of Denmark died out, the Augustenburgs should have been the next male-line heir. Although the Augustenburgs played a vital role in the Schleswig-Holstein question and claimed to be next in line for the Danish throne, they lost their claim when Christian IX was chosen to become Denmark's king. His great-granddaughter, Queen Margrethe II, still holds the Danish throne.

Back in 1848, during the First Schleswig War, the Duke of Schleswig-Holstein was Prince Christian, whose mother was Princess Louise. The duke's sister, Princess Caroline Amelie, had created yet another strong tie to the Danish throne by becoming the second wife of the philandering King Christian VIII of Denmark. Although not the mother of the heir, Caroline Amelie served for decades as Queen of Denmark and became very popular. Duke Christian and Queen Caroline had a younger brother, Prince Frederick Emil August, who would first bring Mary Lee to prominence. As sons of a royal duke, Christian and Frederick were entitled to the style of "Highness," and their sister was now "Her Majesty." Their family ties to the royal houses of Europe were extensive as their paternal grandmother, Queen Caroline Matilda, was a sister of Britain's King George III. Because of their descent from her, who was born a princess of Great Britain as a daughter of Frederick Prince of Wales, they were in line for the British throne, although admittedly far down the list.

Prince Frederick, who was born at Kiel on August 23, 1800, had been governor of Holstein, and, in the 1848 uprising, he and his brother sided with Prussia and sought to keep Holstein from Danish rule. "More than one-third of Denmark's population were Germans, living in the duchies of

Schleswig, Holstein, and Lauenburg [which] made up about one half of the monarchy's economic power."[3]

Denmark's King Christian VIII, the brother-in-law of Prince Frederick, at first attempted to walk a middle road in the Schleswig-Holstein debate. He later "expressly confirmed the ancient privileges of Schleswig-Holstein and appointed Prince Frederick ... to the honorary position of Governor of the duchies."[4] In 1842, the king gave Prince Frederick the rank of Stadtholder (defacto head of state) and

> raised him to the rank of ... commander-in-chief in Slesvig [sic] and Holstein and made him president of the government of the duchies. As the queen, Caroline Amalia, was a sister of the Augustenburg princes, this appointment was thought to be due to her influence, and was looked upon as so injurious to the cause of the Danes in the Slesvig-Holstein provinces, that it drew forth violent and angry remonstrances in every part of the Danish islands.[5]

The king held steadfast, however, declaring faith in his brothers-in-law, and then gave the posts of chancellor and foreign secretary for the duchies to two of their loyal friends and allies.

In 1848, Prince Frederick led troops into Rendsburg, in the heart of the duchies, and took its defenders by surprise. No blood was shed and the Danish officers were allowed to depart after hearing a patriotic speech by Prince Frederick then pledging not to fight against Schleswig-Holstein in the future. Weeks later Prince Frederick led forces at the Battle of Bov, but he arrived two hours after the fighting began and the Danes won the disorganized engagement.[6] As a result of his efforts to retain independent control of Schleswig-Holstein for himself and his brother, Prince Frederick was then exiled from Denmark in 1848 for anti–Danish political activity. The London Treaty of 1852 between Germany and Denmark would deprive them of their rights although they would be very well compensated.[7]

Long before his attempt at military heroics, Prince Frederick married in 1829 Countess Henriette von Daneskjold-Samsoe, his second cousin, who was a descendant of King Christian V of Denmark, belonging to an illegitimate branch of the House of Oldenburg. Henriette's elder sister, Countess Luisa-Sophie, married Prince Frederick's elder brother, Christian August II, Duke of Augustenburg. Frederick and Henriette had a son and daughter (as well as two children who died as infants), and Henriette died in Paris on September 10, 1858. Their daughter, Princess Louisa, would become the person who introduced Mary Lee to this complicated maze of Danish royals.[8]

Mary and her mother, who were awaiting Josie's child's delivery at Lautenbach, decided when Baron de Waechter was called back to Paris on official business they would take an apartment in nearby Stuttgart, where there was an excellent hospital and medical care, should the birth be difficult. They moved to Königstrasse 35, which everyone found to their liking. Mrs. Lee, who, to her surprise, adjudged the Germans delightful, wrote to American relatives that the apartment "is on a principal street ... the guard passes every day, and the bands play."[9]

In Paris, Josie had known the yet-unmarried Princess Louisa of Schleswig-Holstein, who was born in 1836, only two years before Mary (making her the same age as Mary's sister Abby). Princess Louisa visited Josie in Stuttgart, and, as Josie's activities were limited because of her pregnancy, Mary played the role of hostess. She and the young princess became friendly. They had a mutual fondness for horses and often went riding together.[10] When Louisa left to return to her father's home in France, she and Mary promised to see one another after the baby's birth when Mary and her mother returned to Paris.

Josie's healthy son, Johann August, was delivered at the Stuttgart hospital on March 9, 1861, only one month before the United States broke into war when Confederate troops fired on Charleston's Fort Sumter. After seeing Josie and the baby safely at home, Mary and her mother returned to their apartment in Paris. Mrs. Winfield Scott, Mary's earlier chaperone, had moved on to Rome, where she died on June 15, 1862.

Mary was now 23 and unmarried, and there was no shortage of eligible bachelors who would benefit from a marriage to her, although she evidently did not deem them worthy of her hand. Mary was charming and well educated.

> There could be no doubt of the fact that, apart from her fortune, she was worth wooing for her own sake, and within a couple of months of her introduction to Berlin society she had a dozen men courting her. They were rich and poor, good-looking and the reverse, some shady adventurers; others genuinely in love with her.... To all of them, however, Mary had but one answer, accompanied by a laughing glance from her eloquent eyes, and followed by a few tactful words she managed to retain their friendship despite her refusal.[11]

As her kinsman wrote of her, "The man she married must be not only a proper and devout Protestant, but also powerful and respected enough to open a door into that larger world for which she longed."[12]

While the war at home seemed distant, it was to affect Mary in an unexpected manner. On November 8, 1861, two Confederate diplomats, James Mason and John Slidell, were aboard the RMS *Trent*, a British ship regularly scheduled to deliver mail, official packets, and freight to British outposts and colonies. Mason and Slidell were traveling to London and

Paris seeking official diplomatic recognition for the Confederate states. The USS *Jacinto* seized the RMS *Trent*, boarded it, and took them and their male secretaries into custody. Britain was outraged and demanded a public apology for this affront to her sovereignty.[13]

Privately, Queen Victoria, whose realm depended upon Southern cotton and textiles, had been leaning in favor of official recognition of the Confederacy, but her husband, Prince Albert, counseled against doing so. In Paris, where the textile industry would be crippled without imports of Southern cotton, Empress Eugénie was very fond of several Southerners who were American wives of titled members of the French nobility. As the *New York Times*' London correspondent reported, "In France the Empress Eugénie is believed to control the Imperial policy.... 'The English are now beginning to see that the Southern people are a much superior people to their quondam associates of the North.' These are the words of one of the most enlightened men in England, and a liberal in politics."[14] No less an authority than Chancellor Bismarck said that the empress was "the only man in Paris."[15]

In the spring of 1862, the Empress Eugénie gave a ball in honor of the "Secessionist Belles" who were friends and relatives of Mason and Slidell. The women were trying to persuade Napoleon III to grant official recognition to the Confederacy as well as to allow Confederate ships to be outfitted and loaded at French ports. One of the most prominent women who asked the empress to host the event was the New Orleans-born "Creole beauty" Marie Louise Pilié. She married in 1862 the much older Marquis de Chasseloup-Laubat, who served as Napoleon III's naval minister.[16] Her dowry at their marriage was reported to be $200,000.[17]

Another American woman who was an integral component of the empress's inner circle was the Baroness de Pierres (1821–1873), whose husband was the equerry in charge of Eugénie's stables as well as her afternoon riding partner. The baroness was born Jane Thorne, whose father, Colonel Herman Thorne, was an early New York City millionaire with particular influence during the reign of Louis Philippe. Jane was a superb rider, and her face is considered the most beautiful in the famous Winterhalter portrait of the empress and her ladies of honor (to Eugénie's right in white with a large blue bow at the back of her hair and on her arm), yet she incongruously and secretly smoked a clay pipe and her American slang delighted the empress.[18]

Although Mary's allegiance was to the Union, she feared angering the empress, who had been so hospitable to her, if she refused to accept her invitation to the ball. She attended "attractively gowned in one of M.

2. Married into the Royal Mob 27

Worth's latest creations, escorted by a young British officer, one of Captain Murray's [her brother-in-law] friends from the embassy. And here, between waltzes, her friend the Princess Louisa introduced her to her father. He was a tall, still handsome, very distinguished gentleman of sixty-two who wore sideburns. He had intelligent gray-blue eyes and was worldly wise, polished, urbane."[19]

Mary would have been aware that his sister, Caroline Amelie, was at the time the popular Dowager Queen of Denmark whose stepson, Frederick VII, was the current king. She may even have known that he was a second cousin of Queen Victoria, then in widow's mourning for less than a year. Mary also showed wisdom in wearing a dress made by Charles Worth, the British-born father of French haute couture first made famous by the empress.

During their ensuing conversation, Prince Frederick spoke admiringly of the evening's support for the South and its struggle against the Union. "His sympathy was misplaced, Mary informed him tartly. He was somewhat taken aback. Ah so, well, he actually did not know much about the subject, and he would be greatly honored if Miss Lee would permit him to call upon her mother and herself and receive further enlightenment on the matter."[20]

And so began a regular round of royal visits to the Rue de Resberg. As the prince was born in 1800, he was three years older than Mrs. Lee, who, rather understandably, thought his attentions were directed at her. While Mary and Princess Louisa rode in the Bois du Boulogne, the prince and Mrs. Lee played chess.

Mary and her mother were somewhat taken aback when the prince asked them to accompany him and his daughter to Italy in December of 1862, accompanied by the Baroness Zeuthen from Copenhagen. Mary and Princess Louisa thought the trip would promote the budding relationship between their parents and were delighted to act as chaperones for the older couple. As Mrs. Lee related of their journey, "The Prince preferred and so traveled under one of his minor titles, Baron de Grenwald. He is a most excellent man and has long been an intimate friend of my children. Formerly the Prince was Governor of Holstein and was exiled in the political troubles of '48–'50."[21]

They were too late to book the Simplon and thus traveled via Geneva, "but gained much by crossing the beautiful Cornice [Corniche] Road from Nice to Geneva. Oh, it was grand as well as beautiful!"[22] The group arrived at Rome on Christmas Eve just in time "to go to the Sistine Chapel—full of curiosity to see the Pope and the imposing ceremony of that evening, but were disappointed—no Pope came—so after looking at the superb chapel and listening *unedified* to the chants of gorgeously dressed priests in an unknown tongue we were glad to get back to our hotel and to bed perfectly 'used up!'"[23] It seems that her avid anti–Catholicism did not prevent her disappointment that the pope did not officiate. After making the most of Rome, they visited the ruins of Pompeii, inspected the art galleries in Florence, and sailed on Lake Maggiore.[24] Mrs. Lee was even delighted that she was fit enough to ascend Mount Vesuvius. One thing became clear on the trip, however; Prince Frederick's amatory interest was directed at Mary and not her mother. Although she admired him, a surprised Mary told him that the disparity in their ages (63 and 24) made marriage unlikely.

Ernst II, the Duke of Saxe-Coburg & Gotha, was Queen Victoria's first cousin as well as the brother of her beloved husband, Prince Albert. He knew Prince Frederick well, recalling of him, "His commanding personal appearance increased the effect of his critical manner. He was a tall man, powerfully and symmetrically built, altogether a handsome and proud figure." Evidently Prince Frederick's elder brother, although head of the family, suffered by comparison with his brother. Duke Ernst II wrote, "As he was everywhere far more conspicuous and assertive than the Head of the House, he unintentionally appeared as the leader of the small party, which might then be called the Augustenburg one." His opinion of Prince Frederick and his elder brother was not entirely positive, as he also remembered them as "highly aristocratic and hostile to the people. Noër [the prince] lived among the most astounding illusions concerning the esteem felt for him and his power in the land." On the whole, though, the Duke of Saxe-Coburg & Gotha found him and his brother, "excellent, amiable men, as regarded their personal character valiant, honourable, upright and trustworthy, but stubborn in their opinions and convictions."[25]

Among Prince Frederick's appeal to Mary

> was his innate courtesy to women. She had, of course, seen for herself how badly Germans, high and low, treat their womenfolk, and she had guessed that her money and her beauty were the only reasons for the exaggerated and unnatural, because forced, politeness of the Prussians she met in society. Without them she knew that she would have experienced the insolent contempt with which the officer-class endeavour to prove that they are the salt of the earth.[26]

Unlike many titled husbands of wealthy Americans, Prince Frederick did not need Mary's inheritance. "He himself owned some of the Danish crown jewels. He was immensely rich, the owner of several thousand acres of land near Kiel and half a dozen chateaux."[27] One of the pieces of jewelry he eventually gave to Mary was "the sizable diamond Anchor of hope …

and also the souvenir so valued, in shape of [a] locket owned and worn by his Grandmother, the famed Caroline Matilda."[28] The Augustenburg branch had always been the wealthiest of the Schleswig-Holsteins, and he and his brother's family had been handsomely recompensed 2,500,000 thalers for the loss of their independent duchy when Prussia's wily Chancellor, Otto von Bismarck, wrested it from Frederick's nephew.

Mrs. Lee was understandably disappointed by the prince's choice but pleased for Mary, so the visits continued. Unfortunately, the most immediate opposition came from his daughter. "Princess Louisa was distinctly unhappy about this unexpected turn of events—she had heard from her brother, Prince Frederick August, and other members of the Augustenburg clan back home in the duchies."[29] Her brother was particularly devoted to the memory of their late mother and was appalled at the news that was relayed to him. "It was inevitable that the son of a mother so beloved as had been the Princess Henriette should resent such a marriage and not unnatural that its announcement should decide him to put half the world between himself and its perpetrators."[30] The two would never reconcile and the young prince would incur heavy debts in his subsequent international travel. He had reluctantly followed his father into military service and later wrote, "I tried to do my duty as a German but it was not always easy. My mother was born a Daneskjold and how many dear friends and kinsmen we knew in Denmark. Besides I was seventeen, and up to that time a stranger to politics."[31] This latest development marked a permanent break with his father. The young man "wandered through the whole of Northern India" where he became an expert in Hindustani history and later wrote a biography of the Emperor Akbar.[32] Young Prince Frederick August eventually married a commoner (his steward's son's governess) and, relinquishing his royal title, became Count von Noër.[33] At his death in 1881 he left his valuable collection of Oriental and Indian books and manuscripts to Cambridge University, where he had been a student for two years.[34]

Although the family of his father, Prince Frederick, opposed his own planned match, they were not prepared for the force of nature that was Mary.

> It was characteristic of the brood that after one of them had tackled Mary Lee upon the subject and been routed they should avoid her like the plague. The Yankee girl's tongue was too clever and quick for them; she was a mistress in the art of repartee, and her common-sense arguments were too much for their out-of-date lectures about the sacredness of royalty and the necessity for the preservation of the princely caste. Mary Lee simply told them that she would be a far better wife to the prince than any of his stolid and unimaginative relatives could be.[35]

Other suitors had certainly courted Mary but they lacked several of Prince Frederick's superior qualities. She was also uniquely aware that he could offer a rank and station that none of the others could. Finally, she made her choice in the fall of 1864 in a decision she explained much later in a letter to an American cousin: "During these years I learned to know and appreciate the Prince ... and his love finally overpowered the three great obstacles to our marriage—his rank, his age and his children."[36] She was to write of her own changing opinion, "We were first drawn together through our religious interests, and his attachment overcame all other obstacles."[37]

Perhaps Mary had inherited some of her late father's business skills, for she showed remarkable negotiating ability in what transpired next. It was accurately written of her, "Her father was a wholesale grocer, a man who weighed cheese and coffee, just as his brilliant daughter afterwards weighed pros and cons in the German court."[38] The prince was fully aware that he was marrying a commoner and assumed that their marriage would be a morganatic one in which the wife does not share the husband's royal rank. Any children born of the marriage, although fully legitimate, could not inherit their father's titles or any personal property except what he personally owned and specifically willed to them.[39] Mary informed her fiancé that she did not consider herself to be inferior and would not agree to a morganatic marriage. Although he could not have been pleased at this development, evidently he was not prepared to walk away from their planned marriage. Prince Frederick "had not been unaffected by the charm and beauty of the unconventional American girl.... For Mary Lee was a startling contrast to the Prussian princesses who were deemed eligible brides for him."[40]

Mary had a suggestion. One of the prince's subsidiary titles was Duke of Noër, a property he owned near Rendsburg in Schleswig-Holstein, described by his son as "a long

Mary's first husband, Prince Friedrich of Schleswig-Holstein-Sonderburg-Augustenburg (Noër) (Wikimedia Commons).

stretch of wood, arable and pasture land which lies some fourteen miles west of Kiel, along Eckernfjorde, an inlet of the Baltic ... [a] brooding place of fancy."[41] Since Prince Frederick would be surrendering his proud royal title as a prince of Schleswig-Holstein as well as his place in the Danish line of succession, he could ask his friend the emperor of Austria, Franz Joseph, to raise him to the dignity of Prince of Noër, a style his wife could share. The emperor was favorably disposed since Frederick had tried to wrest control of his family's duchies from Denmark and place them closer to German and Prussian control where they would have no greater ally than the Austrian emperor. He replied that he would be happy to comply, and, on September 28 (or October 6), 1864,[42] Prince Frederick, Duke of Noër, was proclaimed the Prince of Noër "by patent of the Austrian Kaiser."[43] Mary could not be a princess or Duchess of Schleswig-Holstein, nor a royal highness, but she could enjoy the style of Princess of Noër.

The *New York Times* reported on December 3, 1864:

> It is stated that the uncle of Prince Frederick of Augustenburgh [sic]—Prince Noër—has married an American lady named Lee, and in consequence has been forced to renounce his rights as a member of a sovereign house, his pride having refused to consent to a morganatic marriage. At the solicitation of the bridegroom, the emperor of Austria has conferred on him the title of Prince and the children born of the marriage will bear the title of Counts of Noër. The Prince can no longer lay claim to the title of "Highness," and his agnatic rights will devolve on his only son by his first marriage.

The groom's family suffered the loss of their duchies in 1864, and now they were to lose their wealthiest member to an American woman they considered little more than an adventuress. Even though her friendship with Mary had diminished, Princess Louisa, who loved her father, was the only member of her family to support the marriage. Mary and the Prince of Noër were married civilly at the U.S. legation in Paris on November 3, 1864, in the presence of her mother and her sister and brother-in-law, Baron and Baroness Waechter. A more formal wedding followed in the Protestant oratory opposite the Louvre presided over by the Rev. Dr. Sutherland, minister of the American church in Paris.

> Mary Lee and Prince Frederick were married, and those who only knew her late in life can have no idea of the beautiful bride she made as she stood beside her handsome love in the Protestant Church and proudly took him to be her husband. She was perfectly happy. It did not worry her that the prince had been compelled to drop his royal rank and had agreed to call himself Prince von Noër. She could not see any difference between Princess Frederick and Princess von Noër.[44]

After a quick ride through the Bois in a carriage decorated with orange blossoms, the newlyweds returned to the prince's Paris home in preparation for an extended honeymoon fully planned by Mary. Neither the husband nor his wife had any idea that the trip would become infamous and would launch Mary onto the world stage. Nor that she would become an extremely wealthy widow within eight months.

CHAPTER 3

A Princess in Her Own Right

The United States newspapers enthusiastically reported on Mary's marriage, "which was up to then the greatest match a Yankee girl had achieved, and it was a common saying in the States that 'if Mary Lee was given half a chance she would turn her Prince into a King.'"[1] Later, in writing about her sisters' and her own marriages, she wrote, "As far as I know, we are the only American family of sisters who have all married *Protestant* Europeans—and I am glad that we make this exception to the pretty general rule."[2] Characteristically, she was correct. The three Caton sisters of Baltimore, whose grandfather, Charles Carroll of Carollton, was the last living signer of the Declaration of Independence, married the 7th Duke of Leeds, the 8th Baron Stafford, and the 1st Marquess of Wellesley, brother of the great Duke of Wellington (whose mistress she had been before marrying his brother). They, however, were Catholic and had been baptized by their cousin, the first Catholic bishop in the United States.[3]

Back in Paris, although Mary now lived with her husband at his home on Rue Balzac, near the Arc de Triomphe, she also spent a great deal of time with her mother at their apartment on Rue de Resberg. Her stepdaughter, Princess Louisa, who was two years older than she, returned to her Augustenburg family in Holstein, where a great deal of conversation centered upon Mary's supposed snaring of their wealthiest member.

Mary took full responsibility for the honeymoon she was planning as a religious pilgrimage.

> They would go to the Holy Land and visit all the sacred places of the Old and New Testaments. They would take Communion in Jerusalem, follow St. Paul's route to Damascus, bow in reverence at the site of the sacred stable at Bethlehem in Judea, and bottle water from the Jordan River for the christening of their future children. Then they would go into the desert to live for a month in a tent like John the Baptist, eating

figs and dates and perhaps even locusts and wild honey. Following this pilgrimage and chastisement of the flesh they would proceed to Egypt and honeymoon after the manner of Cleopatra and the Pharaohs on a luxurious barge, which would journey up the Nile toward its source (only just discovered by John Speke) in Lake Victoria.[4]

Prince Friedrich of Schleswig-Holstein-Sonderburg-Augustenburg (Noër) in 1861 (The Royal Library, National Library of Denmark and Copenhagen University Library).

After ending in Beirut and Smyrna, the couple would return to Frederick's estate at the Chateau de Noër near Kiel. It was certainly an ambitious itinerary for a 65-year-old groom.

Queen Victoria, early in her widowhood, expressed a strong desire to visit the Holy Land accompanied by her spiritual advisor, Dean Stanley. She postponed the trip so often she eventually no longer had the physical stamina to undertake it. After modes of transportation were greatly improved, it became something of a trend for royals to undertake the pilgrimage.[5] But those advances in transportation were still in the future, and, at the time of the honeymoon Mary planned with her prince, there were still slave traders and ivory hunters throughout the area, and roads were primitive at best.

Mary's mother and sister Abby saw them off at the Gare de Lyon, accompanied by their servants, on their way to Marseilles. They made a stop in Smyrna (now Izmir, Turkey) on the trip out instead of during the return as originally planned. From there they continued the itinerary and were thrilled to visit the biblical sites that had so transfixed Mary since her youth. They lived in a tent in the desert for a month before boarding their well-appointed barge at Cairo. After weeks of sparse accommodations, the barge was luxurious by comparison.

News reached them of the defeat of the Confederacy and the assassination of President Lincoln. They heard that their old friend, the Emperor Maximilian, whom they had known as the Austrian Archduke "Maxl," had accepted the proffered throne of Mexico (an idea of the Empress Eugénie), where he and his bride, Carlotta, found the situation much worse than they had been led to expect. But there was other disturbing news as well. Prince Frederick's family was reported to have claimed that his marriage to Mary was, in fact, morganatic after all, thereby making the assertion that his existing children would be his only heirs, eliminating Mary and any future children born from their union from any claim upon his estate. Frederick was concerned enough in Cairo to summon solicitors before departing for their last stop in Beirut. He wrote a new will, leaving the great bulk of his large estate, as well as some of the Danish crown jewels in his personal possession, to Mary.[6] There later was speculation as to whether it was his idea or Mary's, but now the question of whether their marriage was morganatic was moot, since he could leave his property by will to the recipient of his choice.

Years later, Mary's mother recalled a particular moment from the honeymoon: "They were in Palestine—a gentleman finding out who she was— gave her his card—saying he could not resist telling her how intimately he had known her father—how greatly he had respected him and much more—the Prince was present and fully joined in the pleasure of Mary on hearing her beloved father so highly spoken of."[7]

Upon their arrival in Beirut, which was to be the last stop on their storybook honeymoon, Prince Frederick became very ill. The French doctor who was summoned determined that nothing could be done except to make his last hours as comfortable as possible.

> Prince Frederick, never very strong, had been growing steadily worse up to the date of his wedding. His doctors had dosed him with false hopes of ultimate recovery, and while Mary Lee knew that he was very ill she believed that with careful nursing and attention she could save him. But he was too far gone to recover. They had been married on the last day of a cheerless and cold November, and, although the prince struggled bravely through the winter, he was a dead man on the second day of the following July.[8]

The medical report attributed the death to "a complication of fevers with old, chronic difficulties," while Mrs. Lee wrote to her cousin in America of her son-in-law's death,

He was taken at Caesarea Phillippi with, what is plain to us now, an inflammation of the bladder—in a few days he seemed better and insisted on leaving for Beyrout and was anxious to reach that place. They arrived at Beyrout June 26th where they found a good French physician who, in reply to Mary's anxious enquiry, told her she had no cause for alarm, that the Prince would be well again in a short time. He again was better and on the evening of the 30th he sat at the tea table in his room, with Mary who was so rejoiced that, as she thought the danger was over—but alas, delusive hope![9]

Their hope was misplaced, as the prince's illness was fatal. As Mrs. Lee wrote, "He passed a bad night, the next day he failed rapidly and about 3 o'clock on the afternoon of Sunday the 2nd July, without suffering, he expired—leaving his poor wife horror stricken by this overpowering affliction."[10] Mary's later account merely stated, "the Prince was taken suddenly ill and died, and as cholera broke out in the districts, it was not until some time had elapsed that he was buried upon his estate of Noër on the Baltic."[11]

When the news reached the assembled Augustenburg family, they were certain that the wealthy prince had been murdered. His new will leaving everything to Mary, written only days before his unexpected death, was all the evidence they needed. When the Beirut police and the prince's French doctor officially denied there had been any evidence of foul play, the family quickly settled on a second theory. All Mary needed was to tire the older man sufficiently to cause his death, and the seductive wiles of a much younger bride on their honeymoon would have given her every opportunity to assure he remained fatigued. "The poor Prince, who deserved a better fate, received a certain ribald immortality."[12] For Mary's part, she was later to write of her short marriage and the death of her husband, "Then followed those eight happy months of our union, ending with the terrible affliction of his loss, in Beyrouth [Beirut], Syria, July 2d, 1865. He had wound himself so around my heart that happiness for me seemed to have died with him."[13] The *New York Times* reported (with errors) on August 14, 1865:

> A recent mail from Beyrout brings intelligence of the death in that town, on the 2d instant, of Prince Frederick of Schleswig-Holstein-Noër, brother of the Queen Dowager of Denmark and of Duke Christian of Schleswig-Holstein. Prince Frederick, in company with his wife, had been for eight months traveling in the East, and had visited nearly all the celebrated spots in the Holy Land. When at Jerusalem he was seized with an indisposition, which gradually grew worse, and ended in death.

Mary was fortunate that the Schleswig-Holsteins were unpopular at the time, as the majority of royal sentiment seemed to side with her. The Prince of Wales's wife, Alexandra, was a Danish princess who despised the Schleswig-Holsteins for taking the duchies from her father. The Austrian emperor had already shown he was fond of Prince Frederick, but he, too, disliked the rest of the family. Chancellor Bismarck had often evinced his contempt for them as well. The *New York Times*' Paris correspondent, signed only as "Malakoff," defended the young widow, including this passage:

> Some servants who had long been in the family of the Prince and who perhaps were not pleased at seeing him marry again and were therefore more or less hostile to their new mistress, gave out the impression when they came home that the Princess, by pushing the Prince to voyages and fatigues which were dangerous to a man his age, had purposely killed him. This charge, which has gone abroad, is doing the Princess great harm, and has naturally caused her great grief. I happened to meet the other day the doctor who attended the Prince in his last illness, Dr. Soquet, Chief of the Hospitals at Beyrouth, Member of the Council of Hygiene of the French Empire, and in Arabia a Bey [chieftan], who contradicts in the strongest terms these injurious reports. He says ... that nothing could surpass the kindness and affection shown by the Princess to her dying husband, and that his death was as much a visitation of Providence as the death of any man could be.[14]

Surely it took courage for Mary to face her husband's family after the venom with which they had attacked her. A lesser woman might have steered clear of them, but that was not Mary's way. When the funeral was planned at the Chateau de Noër, 14 miles west of Kiel, along Eckernfjörde (an inlet of the Baltic), she was determined to attend, supported by her mother and her brother-in-law, the Baron de Waechter. If she had misgivings, she was given a much-needed boost by an unexpected gift. Waiting for her upon her arrival at Noër was a beautiful triple-strand pearl necklace with a diamond clasp, which her late husband bought for her as a surprise in Jerusalem and had shipped for their return. As her mother wrote, "Dear Mary had not a suspicion of it and was deeply moved when she heard of such another evidence of the love of her devoted husband. Prince Frederick [Mary's stepson] presented her the necklace—she could only weep over it."[15] It is comforting to imagine that she might have worn this tactile reminder of his love as she prepared for his burial.

It is necessary at this point to make note of the fact that Mary's cousin and early biographer, Alson J. Smith, deliberately misstated Mary's treatment by her late husband's family. All writers make judicious use of sources to bolster their version of events, but Smith did far more than that. Ignoring primary sources clearly at his disposal, he instead concocted a hostile Schleswig-Holstein family who did everything in their power to abuse Mary, including their excluding her from sitting in the family pews at her husband's funeral then attacking her viciously afterwards for her supposed "snaring" of her much older husband.

Mary's mother, Mrs. Lee, however, was a first-hand observer and paints a much different picture. The first time she saw her grieving daughter after her return from the honeymoon, "we could not speak but fell on each other's neck, perfectly overpowered."[16] After a brief rest, the sad group left for the funeral accompanied by Mary's sister's husband, Baron Waechter, as well as by Prince Handjeri, the fiancé of Mary's stepdaughter. When they arrived at Kiel, "the young Duke of Schleswig Holstein, claimant to the throne of the Duchies," (his father had renounced his right in his son's favor) had a carriage waiting for them at the station and invited them to come immediately to his chateau for dinner. Her exhausted mother begged off, but Mary and Baron Waechter accepted the gracious invitation and were received with warmth and kindness. Smith, however, wrote of the same encounter, "Realizing that the atmosphere at the Chateau would be somewhat frosty, they politely declined his offer and went to a hotel instead."[17]

His version of the next day was even bleaker.

> The funeral ... was an ordeal. The proud, grieving black-shrouded young widow, her mother, and her brother-in-law were not invited to sit in the Augustenburg family pew. But the American women and the German [sic] baron ignored the ushers who were trying to seat them in an inconspicuous part of the church and pushed firmly into the section reserved for the family of the deceased to sit among a score of frozen-faced Augustenburgs. After the funeral.... Mary insisted on going into the tomb alone to pray.[18]

Actually, on the morning of the service the Duke sent a carriage pulled by four horses for the group, who were officially accompanied by Mary's stepson, young Prince Frederick, and by his soon-to-be brother-in-law, Prince Handjeri. As they drove to the church, "many friends of the late Prince followed in carriages." Once there, young Prince Frederick, "led us to the family pew, in the gallery and near the pulpit—reminding one of a stage box at a theatre—a separate staircase led to it. It is not the custom in the Duchies for a woman to go to the grave, but Prince Frederick knew Mary insisted on the privilege and he had, as he said, the pew hung with black expressly for us."[19]

The funeral was held on "a dark stormy day—quite in sympathy with our feelings." The service was "solemn and impressive," and the minister, "delivered an oration on the noble and Christian qualities of the deceased—he alluded most feelingly to his desolate widow." Not only was the family not unwelcoming, but the late Prince of Noër's sister, the Queen Dowager of Denmark, sent a representative who "brought an affectionate letter from the Queen, written by herself—sympathizing most kindly with Mary and mourning the necessity that prevented her from being present. There were many guests at the Chateau—among them the Princess Amelie of Holstein, sister of the Duke. I shall never forget her taking so much interest in me and mine."[20] Mary's stepson, the young Prince Frederick, "performed a last duty to his parents and laid their bodies in their final resting place. His father had died in Beyrut, his mother in Paris: now both lay under the northern sky of their early wedded home."[21]

Afterwards Mary entered the tomb—alone—to pay her respects to her late husband.[22] His body then joined that of his first wife in the cemetery at Friedhof Krusendorf, in view of the local church. Mrs. Lee, who may perhaps have once harbored hopes for her own marriage to the prince, always remembered him fondly, writing years later of "our dear Prince, Mary's husband. He was a true Christian—just such as you would have liked—they were devotedly attached—but God took him."[23] Earlier she had written of her son-in-law's immediate plans upon returning from his Holy Land honeymoon,

> By express desire of the Prince, after a short visit here [Lautenbach], Josie and I were to go with them to Paris, attend the marriage of his daughter the Princess Louise and then go to his beautiful estate in Schleswig where he had set his heart on celebrating Mary's birthday and the anniversary of their marriage. Mary he idolized—was always writing to me of her goodness and how happy she was—said he "never could have wished a nobler or truer heart tied to his." He and I were great friends—told me he had already selected my room at the Chateau of Noër where I should have a sea view.[24]

Smith would have us believe that what came after the funeral ordeal was even worse—a family united in vitriol against Mary and determined to take back the large inheritance left to her by her husband. He claimed that Mary had to face "the late Prince's family and servants, filled with helpless rage at the woman whom they considered little better than a murderess."[25] But Smith doesn't stop concocting there. By his account, worse was yet to come:

> Then after the funeral, there were the legal amenities—which were far from amiable. Prince Christian, the late Prince's nephew, spoke for the Augustenburg family. He insisted that the Prince's marriage to Mary had in fact been morganatic.... He announced that the family would sue in the Kiel courts to have the marriage declared morganatic and the will made at Cairo null and void because his uncle, already a dying man, had not been legally responsible for his actions.[26]

Yet in Mrs. Lee's voluminous recording of her son-in-law's death and funeral there is not only nothing to support that view but much to refute it. On their first day, her stepson, the young Prince Frederick, presented Mary with the "splendid necklace of three rows of pearls with a diamond clasp"[27] that his father had purchased for her. On the day after the funeral, Mary returned to visit her husband's burial place then left with her family for Kiel.

The Duke called immediately upon our arrival and invited us to dinner, but we were to leave in the 6 p.m. train for Hamburg, so he insisted on our coming to lunch and had his carriage ready for us—his chateau is beautifully situated on the Elbe—about 20 minutes from Kiel. We found the Duchess charming and she received us so kindly. She was expecting her confinement and has since had a daughter. We saw their 3 sweet little children—2 girls and a boy. The Duchess' mother is half sister of Queen Victoria.[28]

One of those "sweet little children," Augusta Viktoria, was only six years old. She would become, with assistance from Mary, the wife of Kaiser Wilhelm II. Her next sister, Karoline Mathilde, would marry Prince Friedrich Ferdinand, Duke of Schleswig-Holstein, and their descendant is the current duke. The little girl born after Mary's visit, Luise Sophie, would marry Prince Friedrich Leopold of Prussia.

Mary did, with her brother-in-law's help, enlist the services of the best attorney in Schleswig-Holstein, but not in opposition to the family, as Smith claimed. An attorney would have been necessary to probate such an extensive estate. Mary saw her mother and the baron on to their train for Paris then went immediately to Vienna. It was easy for her to obtain a private audience with the Emperor Franz Joseph, who had been a good friend of her late husband's. He would have been completely sympathetic to the wife of his close friend and, no doubt, had heard her vilified as having inadvertently caused the premature death of her husband. He gave Mary his sincere sympathy then asked for her help in his own matter. Knowing that she had excellent contacts in America, he asked whether she might be able to intercede with the American government to support his brother, the Emperor Maximilian, who was in great danger in Mexico.

Mary agreed to do all she could for the beleaguered Maximilian. To her great delight, the Emperor Franz Joseph, in appreciation for her assistance and in memory of his friend, the Prince of Noër, named Mary Princess of Noër in her own right.[29] Now there would be no legal arguments that her marriage had been morganatic. As the *New York Tribune* pointed out in 1888, Mary married her prince "not by a morganatic marriage, which every American must abhor, but one by which she became his equal in rank."[30] Years later when the issue arose in a newspaper account that referred to Mary's first marriage, Mrs. Lee wrote,

> She never was "Countess Noër." She was at once Princess on marrying Prince Frederic Augustus—neither was it a morganatic marriage—for she shared his title—his family also accorded her the title of "Highness"—the Duke his Nephew—Father of the present Empress of Germany—was devotedly kind to Mary after his Uncle's death and they corresponded—the Duke mourned greatly for his Uncle and he knew perfectly how sincerely he was attached to Mary. She retained her title Princess of Noër until she married Count Alfred [her second husband].[31]

In Mary's second husband's obituary, one newspaper took pains to explain that her first husband "married her, not morganatically, as has been reported, but with all due formality, thereby dropping his title of Most Serene Highness and becoming plain Prince Noër."[32]

Not until 1909 would this same Emperor Franz Joseph, who gave Mary her own title (he always appreciated a pretty face), create another American bride, Anita Stewart, a princess in her own right just before her marriage to Prince Miguel de Braganza. In 1920, Greece's King George II created another American, Nancy Stewart Leeds, Princess Anastasia in her own right when she married his uncle, Prince Christopher. Both of those women, however, were great heiresses, and it was their bank accounts that created their opportunities.[33] The same was not true for Mary Lee, Princess of Noër, whose husband clearly held the superior financial position in their relationship.

Mary and her expert attorneys had little trouble probating the will drawn in Cairo. His intentions were clear and there were many people who could attest that he was competent and eager to protect his wife against his family's calumnies. Mary received outright a fortune of $4,000,000 (about $61 million in today's equivalent[34]) plus thousands of acres of land and several of her late husband's chateaux.[35]

Mary's stepson, who had been created Count of Noër when he married morganatically a Venezuelan wife, inherited two of the other chateaux, and, after his early death in 1881, his widow and two daughters had to fight his cousin in Britain, Prince Christian (a son-in-law of Queen Victoria's), to retain them. The royal branch of the family insisted that since his marriage was morganatic, the properties reverted to them at his death. Queen Victoria wrote to her daughter, the Princess Royal (who would become so well known to Mary), on February 27, 1882, "I have taken no part whatever in the matter beyond expressing much sympathy for the unfortunate Countess Noër in her affliction, who in addition to her great sorrow has most unexpectedly found her children's inheritance threatened and who cannot be expected to take their part as you or any other widowed mother would do? My position prevents my taking any part in this unfortunate affair."[36] Mary's stepdaughter, Princess Louisa, who had supported her throughout her difficulties, married in London in 1865 only three months after her father's death Prince Michael Vlangali-Handjeri and remained Mary's friend for only a short time, dying within two months of the birth of her twin sons in 1866. Of the two, one died as an infant and the other eventually married his first cousin, Louise von Noër, the daughter of Mary's stepson.[37] They are the ancestors of Prince Frederick's only descendants. Years later, the widowed Prince Michael Vlangali-Handjeri remarried, in 1875, Ida Ramsay, whose sister, Jessie, married Count Alexandre de Polignac. As Mrs. Lee wrote home to America,

> Prince Handjeri announced to us, by a letter to Mary, his intended marriage to a Scotch lady on the 14th inst., a Miss Ramsay, whose father resides at Brighton. He enclosed her photograph; very pretty, and sweet expression. We were all delighted by the event.... Mary has long been urging him to marry, knowing how lonely he was, and telling him, especially when he was with us at Parkstrasse last autumn, how much happier he would be.[38]

But Mary was not yet finished with her late husband's family, who would play a pivotal role in her future. Queen Victoria's son-in-law, Prince Christian of Schleswig-Holstein, in 1885,

> commenced proceedings in the High Court of Kiel with the object of obtaining possession of the extensive and valuable estates of Grönwald and Noër.... It was contended on behalf of Prince Christian that these domains were only held by Prince Noër for life, and that on his death they should have passed, failing male heirs, to Prince Christian; but the Court has unanimously decreed that, under the settlement of the late King Christian VII of Denmark, the estates were fully at the disposal of Prince Noër, and that he was entitled to bequeath them to whomever he pleased. Prince Christian has appealed against this judgment, but, in the opinion of the best legal authorities, with very little hope of success.[39]

Now Mary was a very wealthy widow and Princess of Noër in her own right (as evidenced in the first section of the all-important *Almanach de Gotha*, where she continued to be listed as "Princess de Noër" even after her remarriage),[40] but she had gained both prizes at great emotional cost. After returning to Paris, she gave in to despair and wrote, "Had not God supported me I could not have borne it."[41] Her mother wrote to her American correspondent, "Oh my dear cousin, what changes since I last wrote to you! Then my darling child was all joyous and bright, enjoying the happiness of having married the man of her choice, who so completely sympathized with her—indeed, her future husband seemed gilded with rainbow tints—now this poor child is stricken-hearted and so sad, constantly mourning over her beloved husband—the Lord in His infinite wisdom has overwhelmed her with sorrow."[42]

After all the stress of the past few weeks, Mary's strength was finally depleted. As her mother wrote to their cousins, "She was taken ill and has been confined to her room and to her bed for the last fortnight—today is much better.... I hope Mary will now regain her strength."[43] Her mother was pleased that her only son, Dave, was soon to arrive from New York.

Everywhere Mary traveled, particularly in royal circles, she was known as the young bride who had inherited a large fortune from her much older husband. Her mother needed to return to America to sell their home and to see her own sister and only son. It was the perfect time for Mary to accompany her and leave all the rumors behind. She wrote of their trip,

> In 1866 she [her mother] and I returned to America for two years to break up her old home, as my father had been dead for many years and she had consented to remain with me. We much enjoyed meeting my brother, whose home is in New York, as well as our visits to our many relatives and friends there, and it has been often a matter of great regret to me that I have so long been prevented by various reasons from revisiting my dear native land.[44]

But Mary remembered her commitment to the Austrian emperor, Franz Joseph, who had been so generous to her. She traveled to Washington specifically to seek assistance for his younger brother, Mexico's Emperor Maximilian. Major General (and former U.S. Senator) John A. Dix was then the United States minister to France, and Mary had met him in Paris. He was in Washington on business at the same time as Mary and introduced her to Hugh McCulloch, the U.S. secretary of the treasury under President Andrew Johnson. McCulloch had been a well-known banker before his federal service, and Mary wrote, "When he learned that I was the daughter of David Lee, of New York, [he] exclaimed, 'I knew your father well, and there was not a merchant in New York more highly esteemed then he.' This was indeed gratifying to me, and I have never forgotten the incident."[45]

Unfortunately, Mary had no success in securing any American assistance for Maximilian. Napoleon III, who had put him on the throne, desperately needed his troops at home and was withdrawing them from Mexico. The United States officially recognized Benito Juarez as president and urged Maximilian to leave Mexico with Marshal Bazaine, commander of the French troops. The emperor's wife, Carlotta, had been born Princess Charlotte of Belgium, only daughter of Queen Victoria's influential uncle, King Leopold, and thus a member of the large royal web of which Mary's late husband, Prince Frederick, had been a member. Carlotta was then in Europe visiting heads of state and the pope in an unsuccessful attempt to solicit financial and military support for her husband.

The best Mary could do was to obtain vague reassurances that the U.S. secretary of state would send a diplomatic message to President Juarez asking for a guarantee of safety for Maximilian. Juarez had already ignored strongly worded papal bulls from the Vatican, so there was little reason to think he would abide by the secretary's communication. At least Mary had tried to honor her commitment to Emperor Franz Joseph. She returned to New York, where she learned in June of 1867 that Maximilian was executed at Queretaro. A courageous gentleman to the end, he gave smelling salts to his priest and gold to his executioners so that his mother would be able to look upon his undamaged face in the coffin. His widow, Carlotta, lost her reason and was declared insane by her brother's doctors. She lived until 1927 and was said to wander her castle calling for her long-dead husband. When the advancing German army occupied Belgium in World War I, her estate was surrounded by the troops who were ordered, because she was the sister-in-law of the Austrian emperor, to leave everything untouched, as Austria was then a key ally of Germany.

Her assignments completed, Mary returned with her mother in the summer of 1868 to a vastly altered Europe. Tired of waiting for treaties and negotiations to take effect, Chancellor Bismarck had gone to war with Austria and taken the duchies of Schleswig and Holstein. A majority of German states took the side of Austria, including Baden, Bavaria, Hanover, Hesse, Saxony, and Baron von Waechter's own Württemberg, while Anhalt, Coburg, and Mecklenberg retained their neutrality. Only Italy sided with Prussia, and its contributions were negligible at best. A Prussian campaign masterminded by Field Marshall von Moltke and led by Crown Prince Frederick, Queen Victoria's son-in-law, fought its way into battle at Sadowa where, on July 3, 1866, the Prussians decisively defeated the Austrians. Now there was no disputing the fact that Prussia was the preeminent force in Europe and would lead the German federation. As Baron Friedrich von Schrötter said even before its full consolidation of power, "Prussia is not a state with an army, but an army with a state."[46]

As Mary made her way back to Paris with her mother, she was only 30 years old, with every expectation of a long life ahead of her. Certainly marriage and children were among the possibilities. She was enormously wealthy and could easily have lived a glamorous and privileged life as a *salonnière* or political hostess. She was already a princess and had married a royal husband. But, as her long-time favored American newspaper wrote of her, "She was continually reported to be engaged to princes and dukes, but she remained single for ten years, devoted to benevolent work, and seeking the improvement and benefit of her fellow creatures, and it was not until she met a congenial soul, a man as truly religious as the late Prince of Schleswig had been"[47] that she could make such a choice again. It had happened once, but was it possible for the second chapter in her life to meet, and perhaps even exceed, her expectations?

Chapter 4

Another Chance at Love

In the summer Mary and her mother departed for America, her late husband's family was the object of much royal attention. For such a relatively minor house, a nephew of Mary's husband achieved in July of 1866 a particularly advantageous marriage. Queen Victoria was intimately involved in the choice of spouses for her children and grandchildren, but her middle daughter, Helena (called "Lenchen" in the family), was proving a particular challenge. The Queen wrote to her eldest daughter, Vicky, "Poor dear Lenchen, though most useful and clever and amiable, does not improve with looks and has great difficulties with her figure and want of calm, quite graceful manners."[1]

The Queen had every intention of keeping Lenchen with her as a companion and secretary and knew that a foreign marriage would take her to a distant home. She wrote again to her daughter, Vicky, on July 1, 1863, "God knows what events may bring about but I must have Lenchen with me for the greater part of the year when she is married, and this she knows and wishes."[2] To her uncle, King Leopold of the Belgians, she wrote, "A married daughter I must have living with me, and must not be left constantly to look about for help.... I intend ... to look out in a year or two ... for a young, sensible Prince for Lenchen to marry, who can during my lifetime make my house his principal home." Fully recognizing what she was asking, she continued, "A sufficient fortune to live independently if I died, and plenty of good sense and high moral worth are only two necessary requisites. He need not belong to a reigning house."[3]

Queen Victoria was well aware of the Schleswig-Holstein-Sonderburg-Augustenburg branch of the Danish royals since one of them, Friedrich, who claimed to be the proper successor to Denmark's King Frederick VII as Duke of Schleswig-Holstein, had married in 1856 Queen

Victoria's niece, Princess Adelheid zu Hohenlohe-Langenburg, whose mother was Victoria's half-sister, Feodora.

The Queen decided that Duke Friedrich's younger brother, Prince Christian, would nicely suit her needs for Lenchen, perhaps because he was penniless and had no other available options. But her family was almost unanimously against the match except Vicky, who seemed to support the choice of Christian if only to oppose Chancellor Bismarck. The father of Alexandra, the Princess of Wales, had been king of Denmark when the groom's family claimed the duchies of Schleswig and Holstein, and she and Bertie, the Prince of Wales, threatened to boycott the ceremony. Both Prince Alfred and Princess Alice opposed the marriage "because Christian was a younger son, had no property, and would become a foreign dependent on the Queen. Victoria appeared nonplussed by her children's reactions to Helena's marriage. It didn't matter at all because she would be able to keep Helena in England—at her side."[4]

The groom was pleasant enough but had few charms to recommend him.

> He was not ambitious to any detectable degree, nor was he any kind of amiable raconteur. Especially troubling was the fact that, notwithstanding the expectations inherent in his caste, Christian possessed nothing remotely approaching a fortune and was, unhappily, near penniless, at least in royal terms. And he was jobless as well, since he had recently left the Prussian Army. A princess of the United Kingdom might reasonably have aimed for something more.[5]

Helena and Prince Christian, who was bald and 15 years older than his bride, were married at Windsor on July 5, 1867. The Queen granted him the style of "Royal Highness," but since it was only valid in Britain, the gift was a cause for derision in Germany, where he was considered far beneath the dignity of "real" royals. Queen Victoria made her son-in-law Ranger of Windsor Park, a sinecure that was well suited to his few talents. Her eldest daughter, Vicky, liked Prince Christian but wrote about him to her mother, "He is almost bald.... Nor is he so distinguished as Fritz [his elder brother, the duke]."[6] Another observer said that Prince Christian "did little but eat, smoke cigars and shoot other people's pheasants."[7] By the time Mary and her mother returned to Europe in 1868, the newlyweds already had one son and would later have another (who would eventually succeed as Duke of Schleswig-Holstein) as well as two daughters.[8] The Augustenburg family was, however, far from ready to exit the royal stage and would reenter Mary's life in a dramatic way.

Mrs. Lee and her widowed daughter returned to their Paris home at Rue de Resberg 6 but much had changed in their absence. While the

Empress Eugénie and her husband, Napoleon III, still held social sway in Paris, the specter of Prussia's rising strength was felt across Europe. Above the Main River, all the small kingdoms except Saxony had been forced into a German confederation headed by Prussia. Whispers of war were rife, but no one was sure when alliances would be formed and with whom.

When the Spanish throne became vacant in 1869 after the revolution that overthrew Queen Isabella II, Chancellor Bismarck put forward the name of a German prince, Leopold of Hohenzollern-Sigmaringen, to assume the throne. Leopold was a Catholic and a member of the Swabian branch of the Hohenzollern family. He was also the elder brother of King Carol I of Romania, who ascended that throne in 1866. (Leopold's son would eventually inherit the Romanian throne in 1914 when the childless Carol I died.) Although there was some vague hope that France might agree to the appointment, since Prince Leopold's grandmother was Stéphanie de Beauharnais, an adopted daughter of Napoleon I, Bismarck fully intended to goad France by threatening to place a German king on the Spanish throne. He could not have envisioned how completely he would succeed.

Although Prince Leopold eventually gave in to French objections and turned down the offer to become Spain's king, Napoleon III sent a diplomatic emissary to visit the elderly Emperor Wilhelm I at Ems, the German spa. He carried a note demanding that the emperor sign a pledge to guarantee that no Hohenzollern would ever accept the Spanish throne. When Wilhelm I refused, the diplomat sent a telegram to Bismarck with the news. Bismarck wanted war and promptly altered the telegram to make it seem far more bellicose than it was. On July 15, 1870, France declared war on Prussia.

Napoleon III was firmly of the opinion that the independent kingdoms in southern Germany would support him against Prussia. He was wrong. Bavaria and Württemberg sided with Prussia, and Mary's brother-in-law presented his papers and left Paris, taking his extended family with him. As Mary later wrote, "After the war of 1870 broke out, my brother-in-law … was named Minister of Foreign Affairs in Württemberg, and in consequence we all spent the winters in Stuttgart, and the summers on his estate in the valley of the Neckar."[9]

The Franco-Prussian War lasted less than a year, culminating not only in the defeat of the Bonapartists and the end of the Second Empire, but also in the unification of Germany under King Wilhelm I of Prussia. The Empress Eugénie, who was so admired by Mary, was able to escape only with the assistance of her American-born dentist, Dr. Thomas W. Evans, of whom Lillie Moulton wrote, "Everyone likes him, and every door as well as every jaw is open to him."¹⁰ Dr. Evans spirited the empress out of France on her way to England. On January 18, 1871, at the Versailles palace, King Wilhelm I of Prussia was declared emperor of a united Germany. His son, Crown Prince Frederick, had been married to Vicky, eldest child of Queen Victoria, since 1858. The latter's son, whom the world would come to know as Kaiser Wilhelm II, was born the following year. The crowning of his idolized grandfather in 1871, just a week before the boy turned 12, had a profound effect upon his self-image as the successor to a heroic lineage.

Mary's brother-in-law returned briefly to Paris to sign the peace treaty on behalf of the king of Württemberg. He was promptly rewarded for his services by being appointed minister of foreign affairs, with his office in Stuttgart. On one occasion when Mary was staying with her sister and brother-in-law in Paris, the following occurred:

> A card was sent in to the American princess, whereon she read a fine-sounding French name. She was puzzled by her inability to recall the name as that of any of her acquaintances. The visitor entered in rustling silks, high heels, startling complexion, and other adornments superfluous to enumerate, none of which aided the Princess in her struggles to recollect where they had met before. Gradually the stranger explained her visit. A French nobleman, unable to obtain an introduction to the Princess de Noër, and anxious to become a possible suitor, had enlisted the services of one of those obliging dames in Paris who make it their business to negotiate matrimonial alliances. Before the nobleman's emissary had half disclosed the object of her errand she was being shown to the door by the indignant young American, who was never able to appreciate the amusement the episode afforded her family.¹¹

Mary and her mother continued to make their home with her brother-in-law's family at Lautenbach, where she encountered many of Prussia's military leaders. "Emerging from the dark cocoon of widowhood, she sallied forth to become a part of the sophisticated life of the international set that patronized Germany's famous spas."¹² As the *New York Tribune* wrote of her at the time, "Her beauty, her wealth, her cleverness, and the touch of romance in her history soon caused her to be surrounded by a crowd of suitors of every nationality."¹³ Her impressive fortune could not have failed to attract even more suitors. "But at none of the spas did she find that particular man who would share her religious and charitable interest as well as her bed, and who could open the right door for her—the door that led to center stage. In other words, she did not find a man as pious, as ambitious, as smart, and as adaptive as she herself was."¹⁴ Wiesbaden was then a socially prominent place to see and be seen. At the time, those who enjoyed its attractions couldn't help but notice "the belle Américaine who, in process of time, acquired so envious a position at the Court of Berlin. Her beauty, her wealth, her title of Princess, and her esprit were the talk of Wiesbaden."[15]

Mary's American compatriots also shared an interest in enriching themselves with her fortune. One ambitious American banker repeatedly tried to make her acquaintance without any success. He finally convinced a mutual friend to give a dinner for Mary to which he was invited. "Before the evening was over he had exerted all his powers of persuasion to obtain the consent of the Princess to an opera party which he desired to give in her honor, but in those days the Princess disapproved *in toto* of all operatic and theatrical performances." He was nothing if not persistent, however, "and eventually won the day by arranging a party to hear Rossini's mass sung at the Grand Opera, and a few evenings later the same party of friends met in his box aux Italiens, where he had the pleasure of sitting beside the object of his adoration, while she listened, with evident enjoyment, to the greatest singers of the day."[16]

Perhaps he had done his homework and correctly guessed that a mass in Rossini's honor composed by Verdi would hold more appeal for Mary than the character of the worldly demimondaine, Violetta, in that composer's *La Traviata*. There was even an intimate supper served in the group's small parlor during intermission. "Alas! All attention, lavish flowers, and unfeigned admiration failed to win the Princess, who smiled and went her way, like a calm Diana."[17] Obviously a life spent in an opera box paid for by her own fortune held no appeal for Mary.

Mary was frequently the subject of press speculation. "She was continually reported to be engaged to princes and dukes, but she remained single for ten years, devoted to benevolent work, and seeking the improvement and benefit of her fellow creatures, and it was not until she met a congenial soul, a man as truly religious as the late Prince of Schleswig had been, that she made a choice from the host of her admirers."[18]

Her sister Josie and her husband the baron had met in 1870 a military attaché at the Prussian embassy, the unmarried Count Alfred von Waldersee. Born August 8, 1832, he was the fourth child of Count Franz von Waldersee (1791–1873), who served as governor of Berlin (1864–1870) and of his wife, Bertha (1799–1859), whose father was Lieutenant General Baron Friedrich von Hünerbein. Bertha had been a lady-in-waiting to the Duchess of Cumberland and died in 1859. Von Waldersee had served during the Franco-Prussian war as a military aide to his kinsman, Emperor Wilhelm I. The Waldersees were a branch of the family of Anhalt-Dessau (a member of the royal house of Ascania that also produced Catherine the

Great, Empress of Russia from 1762 to 1796), who were distantly related to the Hohenzollerns. Count Alfred von Waldersee's grandfather, Count Franz Johann, was an illegitimate son of Prince Leopold III, Duke of Anhalt-Dessau. He married Louise, Countess von Anhalt, who was herself a legitimate great-granddaughter of Prince Johan George I, Duke of Anhalt-Dessau. Thus Count Alfred von Waldersee had two lines of descent from the dukes of Anhalt-Dessau.[19] As an American newspaper pointed out dismissively after he had achieved fame, von Waldersee "is descended left-handedly from a little Prince of Anhalt."[20]

As a fourth son and a member of a family known for military service, Alfred's career was never in question. He attended the Frederick Wilhelm Gymnasium in Berlin before entering the Potsdam Cadet House, then transferred to the Berlin Cadet House, where he graduated in 1849. While serving the emperor as a military aide, he saw battle at Metz and Sedan and eventually commanded the 13th Uhlans, part of the 10th Army at Hanover.[21] Von Waldersee kept a meticulous journal all his adult life that makes it easy now for us to perceive him as vain and self-centered. One observer said von Waldersee was "not a man of genius, though he had energy and intelligence of a very high order. Also, and most unquestionably, he was possessed of charm."[22] Mary's kinsman wrote of him, "He was externally pious, at least sufficiently so to satisfy Mary (a kind of pseudo piety flashes fitfully through his memoirs). But there is considerable evidence that in spite of his several positive virtues and overweening ambition, he was basically a weak man. 'An ambitious nonentity,' the Countess Wedel calls him in her memoirs."[23]

In the fall of 1873, Count Alfred von Waldersee was a guest at a hunting party in Württemberg, not far from the estate of the Waechters. Because they already knew him from their meeting in Paris, Mary's sister and brother-in-law introduced him to Mary then invited him to visit them during his hunting trip. The man she met had "close-cropped fair hair, blue eyes, and a full mustache. He was handsome, a stocky but erect five feet nine inches in height, jackbooted, heel-clickingly polite, and a blood relative of Germany's rulers."[24]

As Mary described their meeting,

> In the autumn of 1873, at the chateau of a neighboring friend, I became acquainted with a very promising Prussian officer, Count Waldersee, who had distinguished himself by his military talents in the wars of 1866 and 1870. He was, at the time of our meeting, commander of a regiment of the lancers in Hannover. His fine character inspired me with perfect confidence and affection, and his remarkable mind, with its unusual capacity for quickly forming correct judgments and acting upon them, was a quality especially to be appreciated by an American woman.[25]

4. Another Chance at Love

Perhaps it was the combination of "promise" and "charm" but Mary made her choice. As she later wrote to her American cousin, "After eight and a quarter years of widowhood the dear Lord, of his great mercy, restored to me again the hope of happiness in causing me to meet, at the house of dear friends, my present loving and devoted husband, Count Waldersee. Our marriage took place 14th April, 1874, and I can never enough thank the Lord for my present happy home."[26]

Count Alfred von Waldersee, Mary's second husband (Wikimedia Commons).

Waldersee's marriage to an American wife is particularly interesting in light of an entry he made in his voluminous journal before he met Mary. While posted at Paris in April of 1870 (where Mary and her mother were living at the time although he never met them), he wrote,

> It is quite the thing for a man, whether married or not, to have a mistress, and for society to know all about it. The women have their lovers, but do not give their favours for nothing, expecting presents in return and being by no means proof against hard cash. It should, however, be added that the numerous foreigners living here try if possible to out-do the French. There are not many Russians here this year, but there are many Englishmen, and above all Americans. The latter are particularly dissipated, and in their case—in contrast with the French—the young girls lead the most easy-going life in the world. American society for this reason is much in favour with the young men.[27]

The couple announced their engagement on December 31, 1873, after the groom received a quick approval from the emperor, whom he considered to be the head of his family since both his own parents were deceased. When von Waldersee went to Berlin to pay his respects to the emperor on New Year's Day, he was informed that he was being promoted to the rank of lieutenant general and would be chief of staff of the 10th Army under the command of Prince Albrecht of Prussia, the emperor's nephew.[28] Evidently his superiors thought he had as much promise as did his future bride, and perhaps they judged her to be just the person to develop his full potential.

As the Princess von Noër in her own right, Mary had to decide whether to adopt instead her new husband's name. Mrs. Lee thought that it would have been "suitable," particularly since Alfred's brother's wife was already "Countess von Waldersee," and thus there would be two of them. As Mrs. Lee later wrote,

> At the time Mary was married, our good friend the Princess de la Tremouille did her best to persuade Mary to keep her title. Mary thought it would not be understood, would seem pretentious and could not listen favorably. The Princesse declared she would never give it up and she never did—to the end of her life every letter—one coming shortly before her death in December '77—she sent to Mary was addressed to "Countesse de Waldersee—Princesse de Noër."[29]

Years later, when her husband was appointed lieutenant general, he was also given the honorific "Excellency," and her mother wrote, "The latter title falling as well on Mary—I think this fact pleases Alfred even more than for himself for he has always felt how high a title Mary gave up to marry him. In our land this would probably go for little or nothing—but on this side it is esteemed the greatest honor."[30]

Mary's mother was delighted with the match, writing to her American family, "Our beloved Mary, finding one who has proved sympathetic in taste and feeling and particularly in her religious aspirations, has decided to marry again and has engaged herself to Count Alfred de Waldersee…. He is Aide-de-Camp to the emperor and Chief of Staff for Prince Albrecht of Prussia…. God has sent him to be a loving companion to my dear child."[31] Mary surrendered her Presbyterian faith and became a Lutheran. They were married on April 14, 1874, at the village church at Kochendorf, next to the Waechter estate. Mary, escorted by her brother, David, wore a white silk dress from Paris and, on her head, "a wreath of white Persian lilacs, white azaleas, silver leaves, and pendants, behind which hung a short tulle veil."[32] The groom (who was forced by his bride before the ceremony to abandon cigar-smoking) "was dressed in his blue, scarlet, and silver colonel's uniform; seventeen medals hung on his chest, and a white feather plume draped the silver decoration on his Prussian helmet."[33] As Mary's cousin later wrote, "It was all very photographic, and just the way Auntie [Mrs. Lee] wanted it—simple, but grandiose in its chic simplicity."[34]

Mary's new husband was dashing in his uniform.

> Still young in years, though high in military rank, Count Waldersee was then, and in fact still is [written in 1892], a singularly handsome man, of elegant figure and clear-cut features, whose ambitious views are tempered by a very clear head and a vast amount of common-sense…. As his wife, the young American was far more likely to be able to enjoy to the fullest extent the advantages of her rank as Princess, than as a single woman and a foreigner.[35]

After a reception at the Lautenbach estate, the couple left for a honeymoon in Italy, including a week in Naples, before returning to Hanover, where Mary had her first opportunity to create a home of her own. They leased a relatively modest house at Parkstrasse 2, where Mrs. Lee lived most of her time with them and the remainder with daughter Josie at Lautenbach. Alfred soon had a bout of ill health, which was successfully countered by his extended visit to a nudist camp on the ocean—all prescribed by his doctor.

Mary now saw her opportunity to come into her own. This was a role for which she had been preparing herself for the last decade. She "wanted to create at Parkstrasse 2 not only a home but a brilliant political salon that would help to advance Alfred's career and bring her closer to the real sources of power in Germany. For this purpose neither the provincial capital of Hannover nor the somewhat limited quarters at Parkstrasse 2 were well suited. However, they constituted a beginning. Berlin was the goal."[36]

Mary gave an elegant dinner party on January 20, 1876, for Martha Bayard Dod Stevens, the wealthy widow of Edwin A. Stevens, an American inventor and engineer whose very generous bequest founded the Stevens Institute of Technology in Hoboken, New Jersey.[37] Mrs. Stevens had been introduced to Mary by a letter from Major General John A. Dix, who had been instrumental when she visited Washington to seek American assistance for Emperor Maximilian in Mexico. Mary's guests that evening included two counts, a countess, a baron, and several high-ranking military officials. Other entertainments followed, and she became adept at serving as a gracious hostess while simultaneously promoting her husband's career. It could not be compared to Mrs. John B. Drexel's comment concerning the amount of entertaining women in Newport undertake, "We society women simply drop down in harness,"[38] but it was good training for Mary's future.

The following February, Mary began a tradition of celebrating American national holidays with a large party for more than 200 guests in recognition of George Washington's birthday. Among those present were Prince and Princess Albrecht. Not only was the prince a nephew of the current emperor, he was also chief of staff of the 10th Army and thus Count Waldersee's direct superior. Within a few years he would become Regent of the Duchy of Brunswick. Prince Albrecht's maternal grandfather was King Willem I of the Netherlands, while the prince's wife was Princess Marie of Saxe-Altenburg, another relative of Count Waldersee's through her mother, Princess Agnes of Anhalt-Dessau. Prince and Princess Albrecht would become the Waldersees' closest friends in Hanover.[39]

Mary was very cleverly laying the groundwork for her husband's career, and those in command in Berlin would have been acutely aware of her success. Count Waldersee wrote to his wife during this period, addressing her as "Dearest," "Should I rise to higher rank, this happiness can never compare to that which I enjoy in possessing you—everything else is vastly secondary to this one great happiness—you are the greatest gift God has bestowed upon me."[40]

Mary also began strengthening her relationship with her former husband's family. Perhaps they thought she would spend her fortune on lavish homes, international travel, and ostentatious display, but they were wrong. The home in which she and her husband lived at Parkstrasse 2 was leased. The only entertaining they did was to further his career. And Mary was quietly generous with her church and several religious charities. When Mary wed Count Waldersee, she received a very gracious note of congratulations from the Dowager Queen of Denmark—sister of Mary's late husband—addressed to "my dearest sister-in-law…. Mary did not know exactly how she would take this change—you can understand how much the letter pleased Mary."[41] There were also warm letters, as Mrs. Lee reported, "from the Duke of Holstein, Prince Handjeri, etc., written in the kindest manner—approving her decision and wishing her much happiness—also warm congratulations from the Princess Henriette—the Duke's sister—and her husband who is a friend of the Count."[42] It marked a public affirmation of the warmth that still existed between Mary and her late husband's family. She would eventually repay many times their kindness by bringing them once more on to center stage.

CHAPTER 5

Mentoring a Future Empress

"Willy," the future kaiser, was still a young, impressionable man when Mary von Waldersee became his friend. There are differing opinions as to when they first met but general agreement that he was immediately taken with her. One account records their first exchange as having occurred when she was seated next to the young prince at a luncheon at the home of Prince Hohenlohe. Although that hardly seems likely considering the strict protocol observed by the German court, Wilhelm was said to have found her "quick-witted, shrewd, and courageous."[1] Whatever the date, the two were certainly warm friends by 1880. Born in 1859 (thus 21 years younger than she), when they met,

> [Wilhelm] was thin and boyish, with a wispy blond mustache quite unlike the one that was later to be his trademark. A nervous tic affected one eye-brow, and he frequently lifted his hand to it in a kind of self-deprecatory gesture. His left arm was withered and almost useless; his shoulder had been wrenched from its socket at birth. He was extremely self-conscious about the arm and clever at concealing it. He talked too much and too loudly in a way clearly recognizable as compulsive. Yet he had a pleasant smile and a boyish charm which he seemed to turn on and off at will…. Mary, a keen appraiser of human nature, could see at once that, in spite of a certain bravado and arrogance of manner and speech, the young Prince was neurotic and unstable, unsuited for and secretly afraid of the great role in which history had cast him…. In her pale blue eyes he could read insight and deep sympathy.[2]

In the first weeks of January 1880, Alfred von Waldersee was occupied by a "lengthy official trip to France." In both February and March, he was in Berlin accompanied by Mary.[3] There, Prince Wilhelm enjoyed getting to know Mary and eventually felt comfortable enough to take her into his confidence concerning the subject of his marriage. He had been deeply in love with his beautiful cousin, Princess Elisabeth "Ella" of Hesse and by

Rhine (their mothers were sisters), whom he often visited when he was a student at Bonn University. When she refused his advances, he gave up his university studies and returned to Berlin. (Ella, arguably the most beautiful of Queen Victoria's granddaughters, would eventually marry Grand Duke Sergei Alexandrovich of Russia, and they were separately assassinated having had no children.) In 1875, Willy wrote to his mother after a visit to Darmstadt, "Ella—who is my special pet—is very much grown & is exeedingly [sic] beautiful; in fact she is the most beautiful girl, I ever saw. She is more quiet than Victoria [her elder sister], but still very intelligent. She & I, we both love each other warmly.... I think that, if God grants that I may live till then I shall make her my bride once if you allow it."[4]

Willy's mother had strongly opposed the match with Ella, using the argument that they were too closely related as first cousins. Of course, her own parents, Victoria and Albert, were first cousins, and there were many other instances of close blood relationships in the family. The real reason was probably because Vicky was well aware Ella's mother, her own sister, was a carrier of hemophilia. Their youngest brother, Prince Leopold, born in 1853, was known to suffer from the dread disease that was obviously passed from their mother, the Queen. Their sister, Ella's mother, Princess Alice, married in 1862 Louis, eventually the Grand Duke of Hesse and by Rhine, and their second son, "Frittie," had died of the disease at the age of three.

> Vicky had herself witnessed the suffering of her Hessian nephew, whom she had breast-fed during the Franco-Prussian War. Thanks to her sister, she was more intimately acquainted than anyone else with the details of the dreadful events of 29 May 1873 in the Neues Palais in Darmstadt. As Alice was playing Chopin's funeral march on the piano, Ernie and Frittie were chasing one another through the bedrooms on the upper floor of the castle. Suddenly she could no longer hear the children. She ran to the window, looked down—and saw Frittie lying below on the stone stairs, unconscious. He bled to death a few hours later.[5]

Thus Willy's well-informed mother knew that his beloved Ella had a good chance of carrying the gene. Not only would another of Alice's daughters, Irene, eventually bring hemophilia into the Prussian royal family, but the youngest daughter to reach maturity, Alix, would tragically do the same with her son, the Russian Tsarevich.

Vicky was instead in favor of a candidate for her son's hand who was a cousin, but not as closely related. She was Princess Augusta Victoria of Schleswig-Holstein, born at Dolzig near Altenburg on October 22, 1858, and called "Dona" within her family. If Dona did not suit, she had

5. Mentoring a Future Empress

a slightly younger sister, Calma, who would be a substitute candidate. They would already have an advantage with Wilhelm's British grandmother since Dona's maternal grandmother, Princess Feodora of Leiningen, was Queen Victoria's half-sister. Dona's mother was first sought as a wife for Napoleon III in an attempt to add legitimacy and luster to the Bonaparte name, but Queen Victoria and her husband quietly nixed that possibility. Vicky had no particular affection for Dona, if she even knew her. It was merely a logistical decision based upon the lack of merit of any other marriageable Protestant princesses at the time. All the other choices would come with too much political or personal entanglement.

By 1878 Vicky was actively discouraging a relationship with the beautiful Ella in favor of her own candidate but was facing active opposition from her son. She wrote to him after another of his visits to Darmstadt that he "had complained bitterly of me, saying I was trying to force you *against your will* to marry Dona, & you had said so—& a great deal more!"⁶ Her sister Alice, Ella's mother, pointedly made sure her siblings knew that Vicky was trying to thwart Willy's choice.

Willy finally gave up his intended bride but preferred to portray it as his own decision. Years later, when his grandson Wilhelm (eldest son of the crown prince) desired to marry an unsuitable bride, his grandfather wrote to him,

Princess Augusta Victoria, "Dona," who was mentored by Mary at Wilhelm's request (Library of Congress).

> You will no doubt well know that only few sovereigns in the world are lucky enough to be able to marry the object of their first love. For example, in my youth exactly the same thing happened to me, when my parents refused to allow me to marry my cousin Ella of Hesse (later Grand Duchess Serge)—a relationship which my grandmother, the Kaiserin Augusta, especially fostered and which I had begged my

parents from the bottom of my heart to permit. My heart bleeding, I obeyed the severe command of duty.[7]

Willy and Dona were together at the Neues Palais in late August 1878 when he suddenly professed to have loved only her from the start, denying his earlier pursuit of Ella. It was vital for his own ego that any decision be viewed as his own, although, as historian John Röhl asserts authoritatively, "It was absolutely Vicky's doing—her last hope of gaining some influence over him."[8] And why would she have selected and championed such an unimpressive wife for her son, the future kaiser? "As for why Vicky chose Dona regardless of her dim wits, one answer is that there was very little choice. The other is that she wanted a daughter-in-law she thought she could control."[9]

Perhaps Wilhelm's mother had taken him into her confidence and explained the tragic consequences should Ella bring hemophilia into their relationship. For whatever reason, Willy openly professed his choice of Dona as his wife and asked for another meeting so the couple could begin to know one another better. It was one of the few times he openly sided with his mother. The two, however, would have a difficult time convincing his grandparents, the kaiser and kaiserin, that they should consent to such a lowly marriage for the heir to their throne. Surely they could have hoped for a more advantageous match. It was left to Vicky and her husband to craft a lengthy and persuasive memorandum to argue the merits of Willy's marriage to Dona. Hoping to enlist the endorsement of Queen Victoria, her daughter was highly disappointed to hear from her mother that "the matter is of such importance for Germany and your family that I cannot give advice on it."[10] She went further, writing that "Willie's extreme youth" was an issue. And what was the reason for Willy's father's support for the marriage, other than his usual deference to his own wife? He wrote to Vicky, "As a couple, the two look quite good alongside each other, & even if he does not exactly tower over her, nevertheless her plumper appearance does not disadvantage him."[11]

The kaiserin was more forgiving on the issue of Dona's royal status but still thought her grandson was too young and unsettled to be married and insisted that the decision belonged to her husband, the old kaiser, who was going to be a difficult sell. Not only had Dona's father opposed him by professing to be the "pretender" to the Schleswig-Holstein duchies,

> With regard to the question of royal birth, the old monarch was incensed at the notion that a member of a house that "has never been sovereign" and "whose mother was a

5. Mentoring a Future Empress 59

countess!" would become the "father-in-law of the future King" of Prussia. The status of the Augustenburgers as princes of royal birth had also "been obscured ... by the numerous irregular marriages in that family," the Kaiser declared, therefore the question was one to which "a great deal of attention would need to be paid if the objective was to try to conjure a Kaiserin-Queen out of such a family."[12]

Vicky met with her difficult father-in-law, who would not commit himself until Dona's father agreed to give up his unsupportable claims to Schleswig and Holstein. "He insisted that the latter [the duke] must publicly renounce his rights of sovereignty to the Duchies before a marriage could be countenanced. The Duke, Vicky warned, would reject the proposed marriage if he so much as caught wind of this precondition. The Crown Prince would therefore speak to Bismarck in the hope that the latter might find a compromise solution."[13] Until then he insisted that any discussions on the subject of the proposed marriage must be kept completely secret. The kaiser had memories of his own great love for Princess Elisa von Radziwill, whom he was not allowed to marry in his youth because she was not considered of equal royal status even though she was a niece of Frederick the Great. Attempts were made to have Emperor Alexander I of Russia, as well as her uncle, Prince Augustus of Prussia, adopt her, but a tribunal ruled that adoption would not make her a princess of the blood. She died of tuberculosis, unmarried, and her intended husband instead married Princess Augusta of Saxe-Weimer; they were Willy's grandparents.[14]

Dona and her next-eldest sister made a secret visit to the kaiser in July of 1879, hoping that they might charm him into agreeing to the marriage. Afterwards he sent his son a "terse" letter, stating, "We have seen certain young ladies and found them both very nice; however, *I* found the 2nd almost prettier. It is naturally hard to guess anything of the inner qualities from such *entrevues*."[15] The kaiser prevaricated even longer, asking for a complete memorandum of the political considerations of the marriage, delaying the issue well into January of 1880. Still, the largest objection remained Bismarck's demand that the duke renounce all his claims to the duchies.[16] And while all these machinations were going on for Willy's benefit, what was he doing? It seems his ardour for his professed love was waning.

On January 1, 1880, Willy's father wrote that several people, including his daughter, Charlotte, had found Willy "remarkably cool" when it came to Dona, "so that they believe he is pretty well indifferent on the matter which tends only to feed his vanity while inclination is no longer present."[17] His mother blamed his military colleagues for putting him off the marriage and expressed concern that his sister, who opposed the marriage, would interpret his new reticence as proof "that her brother is merely being driven & forced into it, & that he himself could not care less about the whole thing."[18]

Dona was, of course, in the untenable position of being made to put her life on hold while her would-be husband vacillated and his mother worked on securing permission for their marriage. She had every reason to wish to escape her home in Primkenau, where her very ill father was being prescribed arsenic for his fatal condition while her mother's rapidly declining mental health was heading toward her eventual commitment to a hydropathic asylum in only a few years.[19]

It was precisely at this crucial time that the young prince impulsively asked Mary for her opinion about his marriage. She knew that Willy had been linked with several women and there were even rumors he had fathered a child. It was thus becoming ever more vital that he choose a wife, even if she might be only marginally qualified.

Mary's own husband had probably given her at least some details of the prince's close encounter with "Miss Love," whose name was actually Emilie Klopp. She was quite possibly his first sexual partner, and their relationship produced a daughter who was eventually reared by her aunts in impoverished conditions. They first knew one another in September of 1879, precisely when Willy's parents were working so hard to obtain permission for him to marry Dona. Not until a decade later would Miss Love's death end her blackmailing of her former lover, and von Waldersee was frequently involved as a go-between in their sad affair.[20]

Those at court who knew of the relationship were not overly concerned. Chancellor Bismarck much later expressed the widely held misogynistic view in writing to his son: "I believe the question of whether a young gentleman has always been sexually moral to be, if not immaterial, then also not disturbing so long as the seduction of honourable girls was not involved."[21] Clearly the woman in question was considered of no importance and was to be left to her own devices.

Sensing a compassion and empathy that he couldn't find in his own mother, Willy told Mary about all the efforts being expended to secure his marriage with Dona and asked her opinion. Since the letter of congratulations sent by her former sister-in-law, the Dowager Queen of Denmark, at her marriage to von Waldersee, Mary and her former in-laws had forgotten (or at least forgiven) their former adversarial positions. Here was the future kaiser asking her opinion about his marriage to her great-niece, and Mary was certainly aware of what such an advantageous marriage could mean for her and her husband.

She and the Augustenburgs were by then "on the most affectionate terms, and, with her large means, she was often able to be of great assistance to them. [They] grew to regard her as their very dear friend, and their children looked on their American aunt as a kind of fairy Princess."[22] Her late husband's nephew, who generously sent a carriage to meet her when she arrived for the funeral, was Dona's father, so Mary could speak firsthand about the family. Should the match take place, the Schleswig-Holsteins, whose prominence had dimmed considerably, might be restored to some degree. That would allow Mary to erase any debt she still felt to the Augustenburgs while also adding a bit of luster to her late husband's family name. And there were decided advantages to having helped choose the future empress. Willy listened to Mary as she extolled the greatniece of her late husband, and responded that he would soon see Dona again.[23]

Ultimately, something happened which allowed the engagement to be taken off the shelf and moved forward. On January 14, 1880, Duke Friedrich of Schleswig-Holstein finally died at an inn near Wiesbaden.[24] The old kaiser decided that "the last impediment was removed"[25] by the duke's death since there was no further need for a renunciation of the duchies since "the pretender" was now dead. But with whom should the marriage negotiations continue since Duchess Adelheid's "increasing oddness"—during the funeral in Primkenau, Willy's father, the crown prince, saw how the Duchess suffered a fit of "hysterics" and disturbed the minister's eulogies with loud shouts—made her unfit to continue negotiations on behalf of her daughter. In fact, everyone agreed that she should remove herself from public view.[26]

Whether because of Mary's encouragement or Willy's reverting to his earlier enthusiasm, once this last impediment was removed the pair became engaged. According to one account, Dona "possessed an appearance of robust fecundity that appealed to a dynastically minded future emperor. Not only was the young woman sturdy, she was wonderfully stupid, a quality of inestimable merit to Willy, given his dislike of being upstaged. Dona for her part was clearly thrilled to have been chosen by Willy and thereby entrusted the destiny to propagate the Continent's most formidable dynasty."[27]

Years later he would write to Lady Mary Montagu, an English woman he so greatly admired that he kept her photo in his cabin on the yacht *Hohenzollern*, women "were to marry, love their husbands, have lots of babies, bring them up well, cook nicely and make their husband's home comfy for them."[28]

In what was to set a precedent, before Willy took his fiancée to visit his own parents, they went instead to see the von Waldersees, "where the grateful and excited girl promptly embraced her 'dear great-aunt' Mary and expressed her gratitude and that of the entire House of Augustenburg for this opportunity to recoup the family prestige. Then Willy took her to England to meet his loved and respected grandmother at Windsor ... and Victoria found her 'gentle and amiable and sweet' and gave the marriage her blessing."29

Queen Victoria had always adored her first-born grandchild. When he was only 5, she wrote to her favorite uncle, King Leopold of the Belgians, "Dear little Willy, Vicky's oldest boy, a sweet, darling, promising child, on whom my own darling [the late prince consort] *doted*, and who has that misfortune with his little left arm, it is he who is come for sea bathing and a change of air ... and this dear child remembers his dear grandpapa!"30

It must have hurt his mother terribly that Willy did not bring his future wife to his own parents before taking her abroad. Vicky wrote to her mother, the Queen,

> He engaged himself to dear Victoria on the 14th, and had to leave again on the next day so as not to attract attention, as it is all yet to be kept a secret. We received the letters yesterday and the news caused us great emotion as you can imagine, but we also feel very thankful and much relieved. You will perhaps see our dear future daughter-in-law before we see her ourselves, as there is a chance of her going to England and we should hardly see her before June.31

Reaction at the Berlin court was not universally favorable. One British historian wrote, "One wonders how Bismarck, then all powerful, could ever have been persuaded to sanction the alliance of the [future] Kaiser with a girl who was not only portionless, but counted for nil as regards influence and position."32 Dona's paternal grandmother was a mere countess from an illegitimate line of the Danish kings. As Willy's mother wrote to her own mother, the Queen, on March 26, "Her smile and her manners and expression must disarm even the bristly, thorny people of Berlin with their sharp tongues, their cutting sarcasms about everybody and everything." She could not resist adding about her son in the same letter,

> I much wish he should see a little of the world before marrying, though all the time he was here it was the same as in Belgium and in Holland and in London—he does not care to look at anything, took no interest whatever in works of art, did not in the least admire beautiful scenery and would not look at a Guide Book, or any other books which give him information about the places to be seen. In this way you will admit that travelling is not of much use, it is decidedly not his turn.33

5. Mentoring a Future Empress   63

Dona's family was, unfortunately, well known to the German court.

> Although a nice gentle-looking girl, Augusta-Victoria was far from shining either by her beauty or her elegance at court which is one of the most cruelly critical and satirical in all Europe. Moreover, she labored under the disadvantage of being the daughter of the Duchess of Augustenburg, who is not credited with a robust intellect, and, in fact has passed the greater part of her life in retirement, and of the Duke of Augustenburg, who was famed thirty years ago for the dullness of his mind. In fact, after Prussia had undertaken in his behalf the conquest of the Duchy of Schleswig-Holstein, to which he was entitled by right of inheritance, and which had been unlawfully seized by Denmark, Prince Bismarck refused to permit the duke to assume the sovereignty thereof, on the publicly expressed ground that it would be an act of the most outrageous tyranny to subject any state to the rule of so intensely stupid a man as the duke.[34]

Still, Willy was to be married and his family was grateful. Mary and her husband were invited to Berlin so that Willy's grandfather and his wife could express their personal gratitude that she had played such an important part by her encouragement at a pivotal moment in settling down their grandson. Of course, they were invited to the wedding on February 27, 1881, at the Königl Schloss, preceded the day before by a magnificent parade. Dona rode from Bellevue Palace in a carriage topped with a huge crown. Mary wrote to her American cousins that it was "the most gorgeous procession I ever witnessed."[35] The guests were made to stand for the next day's entire wedding ceremony, which lasted almost eight hours. Willy's memoirs spoke of the two-day event almost as a military exercise and fail to mention of his bride, "On a freezing day, wearing a bare-shouldered Court gown, there she sat being rocked heavily from side to side in the cold royal carriage drawn by eight fine horses."[36]

The groom's uncle, the Prince of Wales (Britain's future King Edward VII), was there to represent his mother, but he was unaccompanied by his wife, who was still angry that the Schleswig and Holstein duchies had been taken from her father, the king of Denmark. Fifty-four royal relations were seated for a family dinner on the evening of the wedding, and the newly married couple, rather than leaving for a honeymoon, immediately settled down into court life. The groom resumed his military duties and was often away from home, while Dona lived in Potsdam "in the company of her three ladies-in-waiting, known at Court, behind their backs, as the 'Hallelujah Aunts' because of their pious Protestantism."[37]

When Mary and her husband went to Berlin for the customary New Year's Day celebration in 1882, Prince Wilhelm's grateful grandfather informed them that Count von Waldersee would be promoted to a full general, as well as quartermaster general of the Army, and would serve as assistant chief on the staff of Field Marshall Count von Moltke.[38] It was commonly acknowledged at the time that von Waldersee's success was due in part to his wife's quiet expertise and encouragement. As a British historian noted in 1915, the count "played his part so ably and successfully that, when Moltke found himself in need of a capable assistant, he chose the lucky Count. And von Waldersee, somewhat, perhaps, to his surprise, became at a coup Quartermaster-General of the Empire!"[39] For Mary, the most important part of the news was the realization that, finally, Berlin would be their home. There she could realize all the plans she had been formulating for years. She would be an integral part of court life and her husband would be included in every important decision concerning the most powerful army in the world. There, too, she could help guide her new young charge toward the form of popular Protestantism that so interested Mary.

Their departure from Hanover in April was impressive, with all the senior staff of the 10th Army in attendance. Prince and Princess Albrecht were there when the princess "wailed that she was losing 'her truest friend in the world.'"[40] While Mary may have been sad to leave friends who had been helpful to her, she could not have been more pleased with their new accommodations in Berlin. The Generalstabsgebäude (General Staff Building), located at Herwarthstrasse 2, was the headquarters of the general army. The three-storey building on the north side of the Tiergarten was faced with rose-colored bricks. Overlooking the Spree River, the building had an inner courtyard with beautifully maintained gardens blocking the view of the stables and servants' quarters. On the first floor, entered from Königsplatz, was the private apartment of General Count von Moltke. On the second floor the von Waldersees were assigned 12

Dona and Wilhelm, Crown Princess and Crown Prince, future kaiserin and kaiser (Wikimedia Commons).

lavish rooms overlooking Herwarthstrasse and the Spree. Up a grand staircase were three bedrooms for Mary, her husband, and her mother, with a small sitting room that would become Mary's refuge, as well as three guest bedrooms. The servants all came with them from Hanover and were housed in their own nearby quarters.[41] Mary's mother, who lived with the von Waldersees until her death in 1899, was an almost daily correspondent with her relatives and friends in the United States, and her voluminous correspondence (housed at Harvard University's Houghton Library) offers a valuable insight into their lives.

Because von Moltke (who was the same age as Mary's first husband) was widowed, Mary was soon called upon to assume official duties as hostess to the senior military staff. Within a short time, "in addition to the immense demands of society imposed upon her by her husband's station she [found] time for a great deal of charitable and benevolent work, and having no children of her own she [was] called the 'mother of the poor.'"[42]

Mary was treated very well at court as soon as she took up her duties. The Empress Augusta said to Alfred soon after their arrival, "'I'm glad to hear the Countess has arrived and I want much to see her.' This of course was equivalent to a command. Next morning Mary was presented. The Empress received her very graciously—gave her hand which Mary kissed—then leaning over her presented her cheek which Mary kissed also." The Empress even made Mary one of the directors of the "Augusta Hospital," which she had founded.[43]

"Almost at once the salon at Herwarthstrasse 2 gained its principal adornment, and one that insured its political success if not its brilliance—young prince William. No one was happier to see Mary von Waldersee in Berlin than the charming but neurotic young man who had fallen under her spell in Hannover."[44] Mary's salon soon became a safe haven for those who opposed the liberalism of the crown prince and his British wife. Vicky had never been popular since her marriage, and there was a strong—and somewhat justified—perception that she was anti–German. Perhaps it would be truer to say that she constantly compared Britain to Germany and the latter almost always came up short.

It did not take long before Mary's salon came to be viewed as the conservative alternative to that of Wilhelm's mother. "[It] was the rallying place of the Chancellor's party as opposed to that of the anti–Bismarckian Court factions, and the great statesman, who has moulded in so wonderful manner the German Empire and German unity, was never tired of expressing his warm regard for, and high appreciation of, the services rendered to his policy by the American Princess."[45] In fact, "the home of the Waldersees now became the centre of the rising opposition to the Bismarcks. Count Waldersee himself represented the ancient Prussian nobles' traditions of an absolute monarchy and a Hohenzollern unlimited kingly power—traditions that were all at war with this Bismarckian usurpation of authority."[46] As was widely reported at the time, "the bitterest sort of hate has been sown between the Empress-mother and the fair American, whom the former regards as a schemer, an intriguer, and adventuress."[47]

Long before Count von Waldersee met his future wife, he was appointed in the spring of 1865 as aide-de-camp to Prince Karl of Prussia, a younger brother of King Wilhelm I. He was thus in a unique position to observe the growing disappointment with the 1858 marriage of Frederick, the heir presumptive to the throne of Prussia, with the princess royal of Great Britain, who had alienated many of her husband's family members, including Prince Karl. Waldersee wrote in his memoirs:

> It has often been asserted, and the idea has been sedulously put about by her supporters in the newspapers and in pamphlets, that the clever and attractive Princess was received by us in an unfriendly and prejudiced spirit as an Englishwoman and the daughter of the Prince Consort [the German Prince Albert, husband of Queen Victoria], whom we thought of as Liberal; it is maintained that a campaign of opposition against her was organized by the Kreuzzeitung [the newspaper for the Prussian Conservatives] Party and other wicked people. Nothing could be more unjust. She was received by us with open arms.... The Princess of Prussia had favoured her son's marriage and had welcomed her daughter-in-law with open arms, if with the mistaken notion of being able to train her.... Princess Victoria, therefore, came into a world in which she found no rivals, and which she might with ease have entirely conquered. Instead of this she repelled people everywhere; only eighteen years old, she delivered judgment on everything and found everything wrong with us and better in England. She offended and repelled people. And yet, very good-looking as she was, and full of talent and native wit, she could be very fascinating, and she made ample use of her gifts, winning over many men to her side. On further acquaintance, however, most of these changed their opinions of her. With women she never had any success at all.[48]

When Vicky married her Prussian husband at Windsor, his great-uncle was king. The childless Friedrich Wilhelm IV, though a mediocre soldier, opposed both liberalization and unification of Germany, preferring to allow Austria to remain the principal power in the German states. He turned down an offer from the Frankfurt Parliament in 1849 to accept the crown of a unified Germany, saying he would not accept "a crown from the gutter."[49] Although he did grant Prussia a constitution, the military retained most of the power. Left partially paralyzed and mentally incapacitated by a stroke in 1857, his brother Wilhelm served as regent from 1858 until the king's death in 1861, when he acceded to the throne himself as King Wilhelm I. The new king's son, Friedrich, immediately became the crown prince, making the unpopular Vicky crown princess.

As a second son, Wilhelm I was not expected to reign and was thus given little education outside his military training. Although he was less political than his brother, he eventually achieved the unification of Germany and the establishment of the German Empire largely though his appointment of the arch-Conservative Otto von Bismarck as prime minister and chancellor. A devout Lutheran, Bismarck believed strongly in the "Junkers," the land-owning aristocracy of which he was a member. Bismarck was 16 years older than the new king, Wilhelm I, and thus largely ignored his young grandson, Willy (born in 1859) in the belief that he would be dead long before the young man might ever succeed to the throne. That would prove to be a mistake.

Mary's young charge soon had need of her special services. His bride had not been reared at court and had no experience in proper dress, protocol, and conversation. She "seemed a country bumpkin who lacked grace, charm, wit, and all the social artifices and amenities by which royal courts justified their existence. She was so dowdy in appearance that the court ladies immediately snickered."[50] Even her proud husband had to admit "things are always occurring which show that she was not brought up at Windsor but at Primkenau [her family's country home in Silesia]."[51]

He asked if Mary might take her under her wing and instruct her since his wife was

> a total stranger to Berlin court life and Berlin society at the time of her marriage, and at first found it very difficult to adapt herself to the formal etiquette by which royal personages are surrounded at Berlin. It was here that her American aunt, Countess Waldersee, came to her assistance, instructed her, and acted as her mentor, not only in matters of etiquette and manner, but in the attitude to be observed towards the various members of Berlin society as well.[52]

With Mary's vital service to the young bride and, thus, to the future kaiser, "the von Waldersees' power and influence gradually increased. Unquestionably the young lady who ... was changed, in fairy-story fashion, into an Empress was fortunate in having such a friend at Court as the fair Countess her 'aunt,' nee Lée; for, under less favourable circumstances, her life at Berlin—at all events in her earlier years—would have been much duller than it proved to be."[53]

Mary's task was pleasant but not easy. The young bride "was brought up at a very small court, and before her marriage had had few demands upon her socially. She had been taught to cook and sew and attend to domestic duties, because no thought had been entertained by her family that she would be anything other than the spouse of an ordinary prince."[54] Her husband, "seeing that the American woman was singularly qualified to act the part of a mentor to his unsophisticated bride, told her to follow her relative's instructions minutely."[55]

From matters of style it was only a short leap to those of substance. Once Mary had the confidence of the young prince and princess firmly in her hand, it was natural that they should turn to her for advice on other matters. The general impression at court was that Prince Wilhelm's wife was

> neither attractive nor clever, did not meet with much kindness at the hands of either of the Prussian royal family or of the Imperial court. Her mother-in-law ... who is one of the most talented and clever women in Europe, is intensely intolerant of stupid women, and, unfortunately, she made no pretence of hiding the fact that she placed her eldest son's wife in that category. Thoroughly unhappy, disconcerted and friendless, Princess William [Dona] was only too glad to seize the helping hand held out to her by Count Waldersee's wife, and to avail herself of the relationship which existed between them to turn to her for guidance and advice. Few persons were better qualified than Countess Waldersee to act the part of mentor to the young princess among all the pitfalls of the Berlin court and society. Nor was the result long in making itself felt. [Dona] has become completely subject to the will and direction of her clever relative, and Prince William was not long in following his wife's example, and is now almost as subservient as the latter to the talented American.[56]

The resulting makeover was a marked improvement, although Augusta Victoria would never be clever or *soigné*. Courtiers even called her "the Holstein," and her *Dame du Palais* wrote, "The only thing about the house which really interests Her Majesty is the daily menu."[57] Still, the young prince was grateful. As the Baroness von Larisch observed of Mary, "Her Ladyship, extremely wealthy, devout, influential, and above all clever with a cleverness styled 'distinctly American' undertook to steer her niece by marriage through the social Scylla and Charybdis besetting her, and William was delighted."[58] Certainly the young couple was grateful to Mary for the valuable service she gave both of them. "Both Wilhelm and Auguste Viktoria [Dona] were quite taken with Mary Waldersee, who was an American *bourgeoise*, ambitious, clever, and fanatically religious.... Wilhelm frequently dined with the Waldersees and was heavily influenced by them."[59]

Mary's successful efforts were later acknowledged in her own country. One American newspaper reported that she "polished the rough diamond given into her care in a manner which speaks volumes for her wisdom, integrity, good taste, and knowledge of the great world. True, she could not

5. Mentoring a Future Empress

make her a beautiful woman, but she made her the next thing to it, a graceful, worldwise grand-dame, distinguished for tact and thorough appreciation of her position." The same newspaper article also noted that "General Waldersee, meanwhile, profited by his wife's intimacy with the heir to the crown and rose to one position of trust after another."[60]

Willy's parents and siblings did not receive his wife with the deference he thought was her due, and "he strongly resented the attitude of his family towards her, and his friendship with Countess Waldersee owes its origin to the motherly way in which she behaved to his wife, acting as her mentor, as her adviser and guide in the intricate maze of Berlin society, and of court life.... Prince William and his wife ended by becoming very intimate with the Waldersees, and almost daily visitors to their house."[61]

Even Mary's mother was impressed by the young prince, whom she saw often since she lived with Mary, writing to her American cousin that he was "a perfect sunbeam for temper." When the British Ambassador invited the von Waldersees to dinner "to have the honor of meeting Prince and Princess William," Mrs. Lee continued in her letter, "how little he dreamt of the many times Prince William has already conferred the 'honor' of his presence on [Herwarthstrasse] 2!"[62]

Now that his wife was properly mentored, it was time for the young prince.

> He would come unannounced, usually for "second breakfast," which was generally served sometime between ten and eleven in the morning. Then, after Alfred and any other officers who might have come up to the Waldersee quarters for the light meal had gone back to their offices downstairs, the young Prince and Mary would retire to her little sitting room overlooking the Spree, and, as they watched the swans on the river, he would drop his truculent pose and his other neurotic defences and open his heart to her. She listened, she counselled, and she did something that was a rare experience for him—she always told him the truth.[63]

Conversation with his young wife was not interesting; even Count Herbert Bismarck recalled that Wilhelm's marriage to the dull Dona "made him hungry for the society of a clever and audacious woman."[64] Certainly Mary fit both those descriptions. One writer remembered her as having "been so much in the diplomatic coulisses, and had so exceptional a talent for statecraft, that she was regarded as a female Metternich; and those who knew Berlin before the downfall of Bismarck must have heard it said at many a dinner table: 'The present and future rulers of the German Empire are the Kaiser, the Reichskanzler [Chancellor], and the Countess of Waldersee!'"[65]

It did not take long for rumors of Mary's intimate friendship with the prince to become known outside court circles. Diplomats and foreign offices were soon reporting to their superiors that Prussia's balance of power seemed to rest in the hands of this American woman. "Ministers suddenly became very deferential to her.... She was discreet and never abused a confidence."[66] The question that remained on everyone's lips was, "What will she do with her newly won influence?"

CHAPTER 6

Religion and Philanthropy

While Mary and her husband were still living in Hanover, a visitor entered her life who would have a profound effect on her and, through her influence, upon the future kaiser and his empire. Mary had been quietly donating to religious charities much of the fortune she inherited from her first husband. Count von Waldersee was acquainted with someone he thought could guide her in her choices so he invited him one evening to their home.

The Reverend Adolf Stoecker, born in Saxony in 1835, was only two years older than Mary. At the time of their meeting, he was director of the Berlin City Mission as well as editor of the *Ecclesiastical Review*. It is particularly instructive that Stoecker was from Saxony, where Martin Luther successfully campaigned against Jews (as well as in Brandenberg and in Silesia, the home of Mary's fortunate great-niece, Dona). Martin Luther's sovereign, the elector of Saxony, was also head of the Protestant Confederation of Germany and issued, in 1536, a mandate that prohibited Jews from inhabiting, engaging in business in, or passing through his realm. When a rabbi asked Luther to arrange a meeting with the elector of Saxony to intercede on behalf of the Jews, Luther refused.[1] The rabbi later wrote that the condition of the Jews in Saxony was "due to that priest whose name was Martin Luther—may his body and soul be bound up in hell!!— who wrote and issued many heretical books in which he said that whoever would help the Jews was doomed to perdition."[2] Count Friedrich von Beust, a Saxon diplomat who eventually served as the Austrian Foreign Minister, observed, "There are two words that cannot be uttered without causing a Saxon to become greatly agitated: Jesuit and Jew."[3]

Although the Lutheran church has somewhat lately denounced Martin Luther's pronouncements concerning Jews, the Reverend Adolf Stoecker was directly descended from Luther's beliefs and fully subscribed to them. "Historians of anti–Semitism … treat the German anti–Semitic movement as developmental: the German anti–Semitic movement is said to have evolved from cultural or Christian Judeophobia to cultural anti–Semitism and finally to racial, 'volkisch' [ethnic populist] anti–Semitism."[4] It was this middle and last form to which Stoecker subscribed: a Christian social gospel rooted in ultra-nationalism that focused on restoring a Christian and progressive society to its rightful place. Even Stoecker's supporters acknowledged his excessive views, however. Dr. J. F. Dickie, pastor of the American Church in Berlin, wrote of Stoecker, "If his political career was not as successful as he desired, that was due to the imprudence of some of his utterances, due to his excessive antipathy to the Hebrew race and to his own pugnacity."[5] Mary was impressed by this handsome young cleric, however, "and for a number of years Stoecker was to be a kind of Lutheran Rasputin to her."[6] He certainly appealed to her deep sense of faith, since she was "of a deeply religious turn of mind, and with a strong disposition towards evangelism."[7]

Mary initially adopted his premise that the poor workers in Berlin were being crushed by the moneyed classes and, rather than continuing Bismarck's recommended suppression of them, they should be restored to their Christian faith and helped back onto their financial feet. Stoecker did not initially "make it clear to Mary that he identified 'the money power' with the great Jewish banking houses like those of the Bleichroeders and Rothschilds, and that he, himself, while a man who had done much real good for the underprivileged, was almost as violently anti–Semitic as Martin Luther had been."[8]

In 1878, Stoecker founded the Christian Social Party, which originally battled radical Marxism. As Stoecker began openly discussing his theory that a Jewish conspiracy was growing strength in its battle to destroy Christianity, he was surprised to learn that his message struck a responsive chord and began to inspire more followers as his party became more anti–Semitic.[9] It was Stoecker, who served as a member of the Prussian Diet (assembly) from 1879 to 1898 and of the Reichstag from 1881, who eventually proposed draconian legislation that would severely limit the civil rights of Jews, including their exclusion from holding public office or teaching in public schools and universities as well as limiting the number of Jews who could emigrate to his country. Stoecker also asked publicly of the Jewish population, "Where are your missionaries? Perhaps at the stock exchanges of Vienna, Berlin, and Paris?"[10] Stoecker made popular what historian Albert Lindemann called "respectable anti–Semitism."[11]

It would be intriguing to know whether Mary might have met the daughter of another large Jewish banking house with one foot planted firmly in the new world. Heymann Heine, born in Hanover, founded the dynasty in Hamburg and dispatched his sons to various capitals much as the Rothschilds had. One son, Salomon, continued the German branch and became a patron of his nephew, the poet Heinrich Heine. Two of Heymann's other grandsons, brothers Armand and Michael, emigrated to the United States and founded, in cooperation with Rothschild Brothers, their own banking firm in New Orleans and Paris. Michael Heine's beautiful and very wealthy daughter, Alice, was born in New Orleans in 1858. Her family spent a great deal of time at the court of Napoleon III, where Alice became a favorite, perhaps because her father and uncle financed much of France's munitions in the Franco-Prussian War. Alice converted to Catholicism, and, in 1875, a year after Mary's marriage to Count von Waldersee, Alice Heine married the 7th Duc de Richelieu. She was widowed only five years later (having given birth to a daughter and to the last Duc de Richelieu) and, in 1889, married Albert, the sovereign Prince of Monaco (great-grandfather of Grace Kelly's husband, Prince Rainier). Although she enjoyed the style of Her Serene Highness, she was never created a princess in her own right. Mary was 20 years her senior but may well have crossed her path during their earlier years at the court of the Empress Eugénie.[12]

Mary accepted the Reverend Stoecker's invitation to tour the Berlin slums with him and was appalled by what she saw. Germany had lagged behind both Britain and America in efforts to provide better working conditions for the poor. The Social Democrats in Germany were attempting, at the time Mary met the Reverend Stoecker, to limit the working day to ten hours but were met with great resistance. An average weekly salary for a man working in terrible factory conditions who was head of a household was five dollars, while women earned less than half that amount. What little money was left after the bare necessities of life was spent on drink and prostitution in an effort to bring some relief to a wretched existence.

Mary became an immediate supporter of the Reverend Stoecker and provided financial backing for his efforts to found a "Christian Social Workingman's Association." In 1874, a court chaplaincy became available and she used her influence to secure the post for the Reverend Stoecker in order to provide him a reliable income.[13] Prior to Mary's public association with Stoecker, "she had become conspicuous as one of the most influential leaders of the anti–Semite party in Prussia. It was in her salons at Berlin that the great Jew-baiter Stoecker was wont to hold his politico-religious meetings, denouncing the Jews, and it was through her influence, too, that he obtained appointment as court chaplain, in spite of the opposition of the father and mother of Prince William."[14] Once Mary was firmly established at the Court in Berlin, she became Stoecker's most important advocate:

> Every Wednesday evening he [Stoecker] presided at a combination lecture, sermon, and prayer meeting at Herwarthstrasse 2 [Mary's home] where, among his intent listeners, might be found the Prince and Princess William, the Grand Duke and Duchess of Baden (she was Willy's aunt), the Hereditary Prince and Princess of Meiningen, Field Marshall von Moltke, Freiherr von Hammersteint (publisher of the conservative newspaper Kreuzzeitung), and an assortment of General Staff officers and their wives. This group came to be called "the Stoeckerei" by some, although it is more often referred to as "the Waldersee Assembly." It gradually became the nucleus for opposition to the liberal, pro–English views of the Crown Prince Frederick and his wife, Vicky, and was identified in the popular mind with a strange and uniquely German combination of nationalism, Christian socialism, and anti–Semitism.[15]

It was an impressive list of weekly guests. No one could possibly refuse Mary's invitation once it became known that Prince Wilhelm was a regular attendee. And he was not the only member of his family to frequent Mary's salon. In addition to Willy's father's sister, the Grand Duchess of Baden (whose daughter was at the time Crown Princess Viktoria of Sweden), there was another attendee listed above who had an equally difficult time with their mother as did her brother Willy.

Princess Charlotte of Prussia (called "Charlie" or "Ditta" within the family) was the eldest of Prince Wilhelm's sisters and only 19 months younger than he. As the eldest granddaughter of Queen Victoria, Charlotte's relationship with her mother, the future Empress Vicky, was deeply troubled and would transform her into a constant problem for the family. When she was very small her mother wrote of her to her own mother, Queen Victoria, "Alas, she is an unsatisfactory child, poor little thing." Before her fourth birthday, her mother wrote that she was "definitely not very bright." In desperation, her mother continued, "Stupidity is not a sin but it renders education a hard and difficult task." Even the little girl's physical attributes concerned her mother, who wrote that she was "an object for studies in anatomy, nothing but skin and bones." By the time Charlie was 14, her mother wrote of the girl, "Clever she is not—and never will be; she has few or no interests—no taste for learning or reading, for art or for natural history, so it is no use to expect these things of her."[16] She did not escape her grandmother's scorn either. When Queen Victoria heard that Charlotte was biting her fingernails, she wrote, "Tell Charlotte I was appalled to hear of her biting her things. Grandmamma does not like naughty girls."[17] As punishment, the pockets of her dresses were sewn shut and she was made to stand in the corner with her hands tied together behind her back. At 16, perhaps to escape such an oppressive family, Charlotte was pushed into marriage to her second cousin Prince Bernhard, heir to the duchy of Saxe-Meiningen. Her mother's pre-wedding benediction to her own husband, the bride's father, was not hopeful:

> I cannot tell you how it saddens and troubles me to think of Charlotte!—That pretty exterior and the empty inside, those dangerous character traits! Everyone is initially enthralled, & yet those who know her better know how she really is—and can have neither love nor trust nor respect! It is too sad. There is nothing to be done, it is just a fact, & one can only hope that time & life will serve as teachers to her, & that good Bernhard will protect & guide her. Then at least her wicked qualities will not be able to cause any harm.[18]

It would have been a double insult to her mother that Princess Charlotte attended Mary's meetings with Stoecker and brought her husband as well. Charlotte signed her letters to her siblings "Charlotte the Brat," and she would live up to that name in many ways. Known as a great gossip within the family, she may have been the source of scandalous anonymous letters written about the court, and there is little doubt she was sexually promiscuous. Charlotte almost certainly suffered from porphyria, a dreaded disease passed down through Victoria's family with results not quite so devastating as the hemophilia gene, which was also part of their heritage. Porphyria would be inherited by her only child, Feodora, Princess Heinrich XXX Reuss, who eventually took her own life.[19]

As difficult as it is to imagine that it could arise from such worthy intentions as helping the poor, something happened at one of Mary's exclusive gatherings that would prove to be disastrous for relations between the future kaiser and Chancellor Bismarck. The old man had dominated European affairs since he became minister-president of Prussia in 1862. Since designing and creating the German Empire in 1871 and becoming its first chancellor, Bismarck, who was also from Saxony, was the father of "revolutionary conservatism" and believed that power should be concentrated only in the aristocratic land-owning class of which he was a proud member. By the 1860s one-third of Germany's population was Catholic, and Bismarck believed their church had too much power. Thus, in 1871 all Catholic bishops and many priests were imprisoned or exiled and in 1872 the Jesuits were expelled. Bismarck finally ended his personal crusade against Catholics in 1878 only when he needed their Centre Party to secure a majority coalition in his fight against socialism.[20] Clearly he was not a man to cross.

Prince Wilhelm called a meeting at Mary's house of the "Waldersee Assembly" in his own name on November 28, 1887. His intention was to create and fund an assembly of city missions across Germany similar to the ones the Reverend Stoecker was operating in Berlin. His wife, Dona, was particularly supportive of the event, since she was "impressed by the extreme piety of the two Waldersees, and she encouraged them in their efforts to persuade Wilhelm to support the strident, anti–Semitic campaign of Court Chaplain Stoecker."[21]

The fact that the meeting took place at the Waldersee residence was no accident and was further reason for Wilhelm's parents to bemoan the pair's growing influence.

> The Crown Prince and Princess resented Waldersee's influence on their elder son, as did Bismarck, who correctly assumed that Waldersee coveted his job. But Countess von Waldersee was related to Dona, and the young ladies were great admirers of Pastor Stoecker. As was Willy, who described the court chaplain as a "second Luther." Willy and Dona had saved Stoecker from being fired from his post by Wilhelm I a few years earlier and had insisted that the pastor take part in the christenings of their children.[22]

Nor could there be any mistaking who had placed the Reverend Stoecker so intimately inside the young royals' circle. "To these Christian-Socialist views the earliest converts had been the devout Countess Waldersee and her husband, through the Countess her devout niece ... and finally the Prince himself."[23] In fact, "in the salon of the Countess they attend the lectures of Pastor Stoecker, the leader of the furious social war against the Jews, which is a disgrace to German civilization, which displeased the liberal-minded Emperor Frederick [Vicky's husband], and which has on one occasion given Prince Bismarck more than enough to do in smoothing down and explaining away in official notices the forcible phrases of the reigning monarch."[24]

The anti–Semitic Rev. Adolf Stoecker whom Mary helped secure a position as Court Chaplain (Wikimedia Commons).

Although the meeting was successful as far as Mary and Prince Wilhelm were concerned, it met with disastrous results. For

6. Religion and Philanthropy   77

one reason, the prince told the group that Stoecker had the support of both his father and his grandfather, neither of which was true. In fact, his father, the crown prince, wrote a letter of protest afterwards and sent a trusted aide to admonish his son.

> The General [von Waldersee] opened the meeting. He explained the character of this enterprise, which was committed to no party, adding, however, that the "Mission" proposed to propagate the sentiment of fidelity to the King, and the spirit of patriotism. After which Prince William said: "The only way of protecting the throne and the altar against the tendencies of an anarchist and infidel party is to reclaim the masses to Christianity and the church, and by that means to respect for authority and love of the monarchy." Pastor Stoecker thanked the Prince and Princess for having "boldly worked for the kingdom of God," expressing himself in terms of considerable familiarity towards both the Almighty and the Prince. This little incident widened yet further the breach between Prince William and his parents.[25]

Public reaction to the meeting was decidedly negative since there were certainly political underpinnings to Stoecker's activities. Young Wilhelm was surprised and hurt, defending Stoecker "by claiming that the public outcry was purely the result of Jewish control of the papers. 'When I have the say, I will not allow Jews to operate in the press!' he announced. Advised that such a decree would violate the constitution, Willy responded, 'Then we shall repeal it.'"[26] In 1891, when he was informed that an agent was in St. Petersburg to negotiate the emigration of Russian Jews to Argentina, Willy responded, "If only we could send ours there too."[27]

Still, Willy was proud of the evening's accomplishments and informed Chancellor Bismarck of their plans. Bismarck was as anti–Semitic as his colleagues, although he tried not to have it known openly. A dispatch from Berlin to London, quoted in the *New York Times* seven years before the meeting at Mary's salon, reported,

> A pretty general feeling prevails, which is founded on the utterances of the Conservative semi-official press, that the authorities are inclined to wink at, if not openly encourage, the movement for stemming the rising tide of Jewish power and influence in the Empire. At the beginning of his career, Prince Bismarck made no secret of his opinions on the subject, declaring in Parliament that he was opposed to the admission of Jews into office, and, though subsequent events have shown that he has somewhat modified his theories, there is nothing to show that he does not regard the more moderate phases of the present agitation with a certain degree of sympathy. In the last session of Parliament Prince Bismarck's son introduced and got passed a bill against usury, but everyone knew the real author of the bill. The court has not yet given any distinct opinion on the matter, though it is thought exceedingly strange that one of the Emperor's chaplains—the Rev. Stoecker—should still have the courage to pursue his anti–Semitic course with undiminished virulence.[28]

Prince Wilhelm was thus surprised and extremely displeased to receive a negative reply to his report from Bismarck. The prince wrote to the chancellor on December 21, 1887, "I regret that Your Highness is not in sympathy with a task which I have undertaken in the interests of the poorer classes of people." Assuring Bismarck that the Reverend Stoecker would not be sole director of the project, he listed among those who would serve on its committee Count Stolberg, Count Hochberg, and Mary's husband, and concluded, "I am inspired only by the desire which His Majesty has so often expressed that the wandering masses of the people may be won back for the Fatherland by the joint labor of all the good elements of every class and party in the sphere of Christian activity." Finally, he assured him that his plan would offer "the most effective means for a lasting campaign against Social Democracy and anarchy."[29] The Chancellor waited two weeks to reply with only one sentence, "The old saying of 1848 is still true: 'Only soldiers avail against democrats.'"[30] It was the beginning of a breach between Bismarck and the future kaiser that would not be healed; Mary also suffered to some degree from guilt by association since the plans had been formulated at her home. It was the first opportunity for criticism of her mounting influence.

The Reverend Stoecker made a public statement that directly insulted Willy's father, the crown prince, and made it clear he looked forward to his impending death. Only five weeks after the meeting, "as if still further to demonstrate their sympathy and favor towards their father's assailant, Prince and Princess William actually took the trouble on New Year's day to drive to Pastor Stoecker's house and to convey to him in person their good wishes—an unheard-of compliment, and entirely in contradiction of the traditional Court etiquette. This will suffice to show how great is the influence [of] Countess Waldersee."[31] And how did the crown prince, the object of Stoecker's ire, react? He "went so far as to be present with his wife at the solemn inauguration of a Jewish synagogue, in order to show how thoroughly he disapproved of the persecution of the Jews."[32] The liberal politician and journalist Eugen Richter, who opposed anti–Semitism, declared in a speech on the floor of the Prussian Diet, "One day, it will not be the smallest leaf of laurel in the wreath of our Crown Prince [Frederick] that already at the first stirrings of this movement … he declared to the president of the Jewish corporation of Berlin that this movement is a disgrace for the German nation!" His remarks were met with sustained applause.[33]

The next year Stoecker would repay his dangerous enemy. On June 11, 1888, Stoecker publicly attacked Bismarck's personal banker, the Jewish Gerson von Bleichröder, as a capitalist "with more money than all the clergymen taken together."[34] Bismarck was certainly not pro–Jewish. He had inveighed against "the Jewish proletariat" in both the press and in Parliament and once said it was sometimes necessary that "the German stallion mate with the Jewish mare. Money must be freely circulated."³⁵ Still, he could not afford to alienate their financial and political power. He couched his letter of protest to Stoecker's comments in broader terms, writing, "His speeches address themselves to the envy and greed of the havenots against those who possess."³⁶

"William and Dona treated Stoecker as a god and worshipped him. Most Bismarckians were also followers of Stoecker, but Bismarck himself was shrewd enough to guess that to admire the man openly would harm his relation-

The 99-day Emperor, Fritz, and his too-English wife, Vicky, who failed at leading their son toward a more liberal constitutional monarchy (Arturo Beéche collection).

ship with the German people, who loathed and feared the chaplain."³⁷ Time did not diminish Stoecker's hatred of Jews. He later proclaimed in the Prussian House of Deputies that

> the Jews were "leeches" and "parasites," "an alien drop in our blood." The struggle against them was a struggle of "race against race," for the Jews were not part of the German nation but "a nation unto themselves," linked to all other Jews in the world to form "one mass of exploiters." The "war" against the Jews was a fight for the very existence of the German nation, cried Stoecker in 1882. "We offer the Jews a fight until complete victory and we will not rest until they have been thrown down from the high pedestal on which they have placed themselves here in Berlin into the dust where they belong."³⁸

Wilhelm's mother, Vicky, was highly offended by such public statements by Stoecker and his followers, whom she thought should open a

Crown Prince Frederick and his wife, Vicky, with their two eldest sons (*The Illustrated London News*, August 17, 1901).

lunatic asylum in Berlin with themselves as the inmates, writing that they "behave so hatefully towards people of a different faith and another race who have become an integral part (and by no means the worst) of our nation!"[39] Mary's husband's diaries were heavily expurgated and edited before they were published, but there is no doubt of von Waldersee's virulent prejudice. Historian John C. G. Röhl, "the foremost authority on Wilhelmian Germany and an unsurpassed historical detective,"[40] examined the original unpublished diaries, noting "Waldersee's dreadful anti–Semitism."[41] He refers to the count as "the reactionary anti–Semite and war fanatic," although he confirms that Waldersee "was a kind of surrogate father for Wilhelm, and had a decisive influence on him during the 1880s."[42]

Mary's mother's correspondence also contains frequent anti–Catholic and anti–Semitic language. Writing from Berlin on March 8, 1889, to former U.S. Congressman John A. Kasson, who had been head of the U.S. legation at Berlin but was then serving as a special diplomatic envoy, Mrs. Lee wrote, "I am grieved to know such bad reports of the Emperor are rife in America. Still I thank you for telling me, as it gives oppor'y [opportunity] to let you know the truth. A malicious set of Jews are here, who thinking it unlikely the Emperor wd [would] befriend them, have put their heads together to injure him in every possible way they can both on this and our side of the water." Later in the same letter, mentioning that her son had been visiting during the emperor's birthday, she assured Kasson that the emperor was "very popular, whatever lies Jews may tell you to the contrary. I hope dear Mr. Kasson you will improve upon every oppor'y [opportunity] to let yr [your] friends know the base origin of the bad reports."[43]

Bismarck was concerned about the increasing anti–Semitism of the Reverend Stoecker and may well have thought these new missions would be a means by which his beliefs would be spread across Germany. Even though Bismarck was not pro–Jewish he must have thought the monarchy would be damaged by such an undertaking that would appear to be officially sanctioned. Not long before the meeting took place, the Reverend Stoecker preached in one of his sermons (which was reprinted in newspapers), "The Jews are such an intolerable nuisance that they should be rooted out as Joshua rooted out the Canaanites; yea, they should be destroyed as one would destroy vermin from an old, worm-eaten bedstead!"[44] The next week Berlin's Chief Rabbi read this passage during his sermon, "Then, with a significant wave of his hand, said, 'Truly, brethren, a *most* Christian sentiment!'"[45]

While young Prince Wilhelm simmered in his antipathy over Bismarck's negative reaction to his plans, Mary continued her own good works in the quiet manner she had developed since inheriting such a large fortune. She founded and endowed a home in Berlin for homeless or single working girls, and also a Magdalen Mission both for the care and rehabilitation of prostitutes as well as the care of single mothers and their babies. She even helped fund a mission house for Berlin cab drivers. Her most lasting impact, however, was the establishment of a German YMCA. For the remainder of her life Mary was so generous to the care of the working class that she became known as "the little mother of the poor."[46] "That the working classes enjoy Sunday rest nowadays in Germany is due to the Countess von Waldersee."[47]

If, in fact, Wilhelm's mother considered Mary's religion "violently low church,"[48] at least it was not quite as regressive as that of Wilhelm's wife, Dona. "She disliked all rationalists, found all atheists repugnant, and sensed a malicious enemy in each Catholic. She believed in the literal truth of every sentence in the Bible, insisting, for example, that her children be taught that the Prophet Jonah had spent several days in the belly of a whale."[49] Bernhard von Bülow, who would eventually serve as Germany's chancellor, thought that Dona would have been the perfect wife for a Provincial Governor or Commanding General or Minister of State as she was too petty, and narrow-minded to be the German Kaiserin. "She disliked foreigners. She thought Russians were barbarous and light-minded, Frenchmen immoral, the Mediterranean races untrustworthy; the British, in her eyes, were a race of selfish and unscrupulous hypocrites, for whom she felt even less affection than the rest."[50]

If the Reverend Stoecker's influence upon Mary and Prince Wilhelm was largely negative, at least he must be given credit for opening her eyes to the plight of the poor and the working class. Not only did she give generously to open the first YMCA at Wilhelmstrasse 34, she also solicited contributions from her wealthy and influential friends. Nor was she merely a contributor to these institutions, but also visited them frequently and kept informed of individual cases who were being helped through her munificence.[51] As her cousin wrote, "The salon which Mary created at Herwarthstrasse 2 was the most brilliant, the most politically powerful, the most influential in Europe. From its vibrant nucleus—Mary, Prince William, Stoecker—there spread an aura of rich, cultured conservatism and energetic German nationalism, the strong rays of which were tinctured by Protestant piety and tempered by an active Christian charity."[52]

CHAPTER 7

A Clear Path to the Throne

Wilhelm I, king of Prussia and first emperor of a unified Germany, died on March 9, 1888, only days short of his 91st birthday (his widow outlived him by almost two years). His last words were an affirmation of what he knew lay ahead for his very ill son, "Fritz, dear Fritz."[1] The king had survived two assassination attempts and been injured in the second, although the latter would-be assassin lingered three months before succumbing to his own self-inflicted gunshot wound. An accomplished soldier, Wilhelm I chose to allow Chancellor Bismarck to make the most of the diplomatic decisions and foreign negotiations for his empire. No one can argue with their results although some would question the methods.

As the old king sleepwalked toward the end of his long reign but still held on to life, Bismarck and the other conservative members of his government were visibly concerned about the prospect of the coming new regime. "The Crown Prince and Princess shared the outlook of the Progressive Party, and Bismarck was haunted by the fear that should the old Emperor die ... they would call on one of the Progressive leaders to become Chancellor. He sought to guard against such a turn by keeping the Crown Prince from a position of any influence and by using foul means as well as fair to make him unpopular."[2]

Immediately young Prince Wilhelm's father ascended to his father's throne as Friedrich III. Fritz, as he was informally known, was already gravely ill from cancer of the larynx, although almost no one outside a small circle knew it at the time, and, of those few, none would tell him. Perhaps even worse, his wife refused to believe it. He had been crown prince for 27 years, and his wife, Vicky, formerly Great Britain's princess royal, had waited 30 years to become queen and empress, two titles she could finally share with her mother (since 1876 Queen Victoria had been empress of India). She and her husband planned to reign as equal consorts, replacing the position of chancellor with a cabinet style of government much like the British.

At his father's death, the new emperor was summoned from his sick bed at the Villa Zirio in San Remo in the Italian Alps. When he was handed a telegram, "He took it up with languid interest, but when he read the address, 'His Imperial Majesty the Emperor Frederick William,' there was no need to open the envelope, and it is said that his habitual self-control deserted him, and he burst into tears."³ His son, Prince Wilhelm, now automatically became the new Crown Prince. Count von Waldersee had been keeping a vigil at the bed of the dying man who had been so kind and generous to him. Mary, "in robe and slippers, and with her long, gray hair cascading about her shoulders ... repaired to her little sitting room and sat there in the dark, gazing pensively out through the cold, moonlit night.... She had much to think about, for the death of William I would bring almost to fruition all her hopes and plans for Willy, for Alfred [her husband], for her friends of the General Staff."⁴

As soon as the official news reached San Remo, the new emperor walked to the drawing room of his villa and wrote out an announcement (he could not speak after a failed tracheotomy) that he would succeed as Friedrich III although he angered Bismarck by flirting with the idea of reigning as Friedrich IV of the defunct Holy Roman Empire. His first act was to award his wife the ribbon of the Black Eagle, the highest honor in his power to grant. He turned to his British doctor, Morell Mackenzie, and wrote out these words: "I thank you for having made me live long enough to recompense the valiant courage of my wife."⁵ Before leaving for Berlin, the new empress wrote to her mother, Queen Victoria, "To think of my poor Fritz succeeding his father as a sick and stricken man is so hard!! How much good he might have done! Will time be given him? I pray that it may and he may be spared to be a blessing to his people and to Europe."⁶

Count von Waldersee had the advantage of years in observing the development of young Prince Wilhelm who was now the new heir. In one of his early journal observations (December 6, 1883), he wrote, "I have now seen the Prince a good many times and have begun to make up my mind about him. He is more than ordinarily vigorous, and he goes into everything he takes up thoroughly and conscientiously. He seems to have a good deal of his grandfather about him. If his parents have aimed at training him to be a Constitutional Monarch ready to bow to the rule of a parliamentary majority they have failed. The very opposite would seem to be the result."⁷

Only six months later, Mary and her husband had dinner with Prince

Wilhelm's parents at their palace on June 10, 1884, when the count wrote that the

> atmosphere of depression prevails there, which was noticed even by Marie [his name for Mary], who knows little about the internal feud. The [then] Crown Prince is naturally disappointed at having to wait so long for the Throne.... Under the influence of his ambitious wife he began busying himself much with plans for the future, with his mind full of Liberal ideas; now we have gradually become so Liberal without his help that there remains scarcely anything for him to do, so that he himself often becomes anxious lest he may not have to tackle the task of working the machine backward again. The Chancellor, who can't bear the Crown Princess, and whom, therefore, the Crown Prince no doubt cannot bear in return, continues to rise in the esteem of the world.... This makes it difficult for the Crown Prince to establish a position for himself.[8]

As far as von Waldersee was concerned, the entire blame lay with the British Princess Vicky, since "the mental ascendancy of his wife has come to be a great misfortune. Out of a simple, brave and honourable Prince of a good Prussian disposition she has made a weak man who has no confidence in himself, who is no longer outspoken and honourable; who no longer thinks like a Prussian. She has taken from him even his faith. The Prince, in fact, no longer has any opinions of his own; he listens to everyone and agrees always with the latest comer."[9]

Young Prince Wilhelm of Prussia, the future Kaiser Wilhelm II (Wikimedia Commons).

The effect on their eldest son and heir, wrote von Waldersee,

> results in very arduous conditions for Prince William. To his grief he is able to see quite clearly that his mother has not become a Prussian Princess but has remained an Englishwoman—not merely as regards habits of life but in her heart, especially in relation to political matters. He knows that she is consciously in favour of English interests as against Prussian and German. With his own out-and-out Prussian feeling this hurts him deeply, and he often finds it difficult to curb his fiery temperament.[10]

Clearly the man who entrusted those opinions to his private diary could not be looking forward to the imminent arrival of a liberal English-inspired court.

Mary and her husband had continued to be drawn closer into the family as events moved toward the old king's death. On January 26, 1885, the two had dinner at the home of the then-Crown Prince where, "it was quite a family gathering, only the three youngest daughters being present, in addition to the Crown Prince and Princess. The pair were extraordinarily friendly." The woman he had come to despise queried him on the care of the war-wounded and ended by giving him a list of questions for further discussion. "Whether she had any ulterior motives, I cannot yet say."[11]

Only a few days later the count recorded that "relations between Prince William and his parents are becoming more and more accentuated," and noted that the Prince's father had gone out of his way to represent his son "as being immature and lacking in judgment." Waldersee believed that the son "behaved very sensibly and that the Crown Prince was incredibly at fault. I have advised Prince William to keep as calm as he possibly can in such situations, but I doubt to what extent he can, especially as I am convinced that his parents are out to make a scandal and want to bring things to the point of a breach."[12]

Shortly afterwards, Mrs. Lee joined Mary for a walk through the Tiergarten,

> where it was quiet and we could better talk—had not gone far when who should we meet but Crown Prince and Princess [Vicky] and their daughter Princess Victoria—probably taking same path for same reason—they stopped at once and all shook hands with us in the pleasantest manner. Crown Princess took my hand and smilingly said she was so glad to see me able to be out again. After a few minutes of same kind of talk, they all shook hands with us in the most friendly way and we parted. On that evening they gave grand ball. Mary told me Crown Princess talked to her of me—how pleased she was to see me well—with other pleasant saying.[13]

A few months later Mary and Alfred enjoyed a long-anticipated holiday to Copenhagen, where she kept her mother abreast of their activities. It must have been strange for her to visit the family home of her late husband, as she described to her mother,

> The Castle of Fredericksborg, where the Kings and Queens of Denmark formerly lived—about an hour from Copenhagen—are really most magnificent. In it are the dining hall and the Queen's tribune in the Chapel, of which I possess two small oil paintings—hanging in a corner of yellow salon and formerly belonging to Fritz. In this castle the Queen Caroline Matilda and her husband, the King Christian VII, lived and there are several portraits of them and also of Fritz's sister, Queen Caroline Amelie and her husband, King Christian VIII.[14]

By November of that year the situation between Prince William and his parents had deteriorated even further. Count von Waldersee recorded in his diary on November 17, 1885, "The relations between Prince William and his parents, especially his mother, threaten to take on a serious character.... Without any doubt the parents are chiefly to blame, but on the other hand the Prince has been very inconsiderate and above all very indiscreet in his utterances regarding his mother."[15] The count thought it best that the young man be sent away to lead a regiment rather than being allowed to go pleasure-shooting so often, ending with the observation that "the Prince's development has not been satisfactory during the last half year." If von Waldersee is to be believed, it was he who began advising the young prince from this point forward. Even the old kaiser seemed to be displeased with his grandson at one point, when von Waldersee recorded in his diary, "Once again has a difference broken out between Prince William and his parents, or, more accurately, between them and the Kaiser over the Prince."[16]

Mary and Alfred, 1900 (*Von Klarheit zu Klarheit*).

By 1887, it seems that the count had persuaded Prince William that his nation should be more bellicose. On February 15, he recorded, "Prince William is very keen on the idea of war and regrets that things seem now to look more pacific. He was pleased when I expressed to him my opinion that the enlargement of our army will soon set the stone rolling. He wants me to give my advice to the Chancellor; should the latter consult me, I shall not fail to do so."[17] Indeed, by May the count noted (in an entry that first included mention of the crown prince's serious illness), "People are telling me that I am regarded by the Chancellor (and indeed in wider circles) as the leader of the so-called War Party, and by no means favourably, as the Chancellor is most anxious to avoid war. I shall soon begin myself to believe that I am a thoroughly bad man! What will be brought up against me next?"[18]

One month later the count was recording in his diary multiple disagreements over Prince William's official visit to England for the celebrations marking his grandmother's Jubilee. Queen Victoria, with her eldest daughter's agreement, wanted him to bring only a small retinue and to make his visit low-key but Prince William and his Prussian grandfather, the kaiser, had other ideas. Von Waldersee wrote, "It is now proposed in view of the suffering condition of the Crown Prince that Prince William shall represent the Kaiser, the Crown Prince, however, also proceeding to England in order to go through the cure of Dr. Mackenzie.... The refrain from all sides continues to be to the effect that Prince William is being treated unkindly by his parents, and that naturally he is becoming more and more alienated from them."[19]

There was general agreement that he might not be ready to succeed should his ailing father die before the kaiser. "Princess William is a sincere, excellent woman; she was certainly giving me her real feeling when she said that she wished from her heart that the Kaiser might continue to live, and that Prince William is still too young to wear the crown. I remarked to her that the Prince might often err in his youthful impetuosity but that he would be a success in essential matters, thanks to his many good qualities." He could not resist a self-congratulatory line about spending hours in the inner sanctum of the court, noting, "One felt that one was in a family circle in which there was no trace of stiff etiquette or of courtier-like insincerity or of enmity."[20]

The health of the crown prince had so deteriorated by November of 1887 that von Waldersee met with Prince William, who

> told me that the news of the Crown Prince was really bad and that by the Kaiser's command he was off to San Remo today in order to find out the truth as to his father's condition. The Crown Prince is deeply to be felt for. All the hopes which he has cherished for some time past are destroyed at once. It does not seem to me right that Prince William should go to San Remo. He can't help, and should he try to get rid of the English physician against his mother's will he must fail in the effort; he will only give occasion for excited scenes and cause more distress to his father, already an object for so much pity.[21]

Evidently the chancellor, in anticipation of the death of the old king, conspired to have Prince William represent his very ill father in what would amount to a regency. Court chaplain Stoecker certainly supported the plan for a regency, "not because he loved Prince William more, but because he hated and feared Frederick's liberalism."[22] On November 26, 1887, von

7. A Clear Path to the Throne

Waldersee committed to his diary a conversation he had that day when the Prince related the contents of a letter he sent to his father on the subject.

> The Crown Prince on reading it broke into tears, and eventually it transpired that the Crown Princess had suppressed the letter from the Chancellor in which news of the arrangement made for the representation was officially communicated to the Crown Prince. From all one has heard, the most incredible state of affairs exists at San Remo, brought about by the Crown Princess who seems to be nearly off her head. It is even believed that she has been intriguing with the Orleans family [France's royals] against us.[23]

An operation was performed on February 9 that brought about no improvement in the patient's prognosis. Von Waldersee wrote, "Judging by his general condition they give him only a few months to live. What must be the feelings of the Crown Princess!"[24] Prince William decided that he must go to San Remo to see for himself the true condition of his father, but his mother was adamantly against the decision. Because she would not tell him so directly, she deputed a staff member to forbid the journey. As usual, he disobeyed his mother's instructions and, at the beginning of March, made the trip anyway. Von Waldersee noted in his journal that the prince "has come into sharp collision with the Crown Princess. She seems to be scarcely responsible for her actions any more, so fanatical she has become in her notion that her husband is not seriously ill. She is coming in for severe blame on all sides." She concocted a bizarre scheme to pretend the crown prince was perfectly healthy. By her plan, Prince William would proceed directly from the funeral of his grandfather, which all knew was imminent, "to go on a visit to Rome and there allow himself to be fêted, no thought being given to the difficulties which, through the King and the Pope, confront every visitor to Rome, to say nothing of a future German Emperor."[25] Of course the wild scheme was immediately cancelled.

Finally, after long anticipation, the old kaiser was ready to draw his last few breaths. Not only were Prince William and his wife there, but also von Waldersee, who recounted, "We were permitted to go forward so that I came quite close to the bed.... We began to feel the Kaiser was breathing his last. One heard only weeping, interrupted by short prayers." There was a brief rally so several attendants, including von Waldersee, left the room. The kaiser spoke of war and of his treaty with Russia. After a few hours they all assembled again and death finally settled on the old man. "After a time the Kaiserin [his wife] was wheeled out on her chair. While Prince William, the tears running down his cheeks, remained standing by the bedside, the other members of the family stooped down, one by one, to kiss the hand of the deceased Sovereign; then the Prince motioned to us, and

I was able to kneel down and imprint a last kiss on the hand already growing cold. My loss is great, infinitely great."[26]

It was expected that the new emperor, even though mortally ill, would immediately come to Berlin. Until then, however, he sent word that his son, now the crown prince, as recorded by von Waldersee,

> was not to act as his deputy; an action which gives us the best measure of his disregard and dislike for his son. To the latter, who had announced to him the Kaiser William's death, there came back a telegram in the afternoon which went beyond all bounds in its frigidity; it was couched in some such words as follows: "In deep grief over the death of my father, at which it was not granted to me, though it was to you, to be present. I express my confidence, on coming to the throne, that you will be an example to all of fidelity and obedience!"[27]

In other words, don't even attempt to speak for me; I will not allow you to instigate a regency on my behalf. But the new emperor did not yet realize how strongly affairs were stacked against him. As von Waldersee continued, "The veto on his son's acting as his deputy had to be referred to the Ministry, which decided, very correctly, that it was unconstitutional."[28]

Willy's eagerness to assume the throne was palpable and, at the very least, distasteful. Even Bismarck made it clear that he disapproved of the young prince's actions. "Anticipating the deaths of both his grandfather and his father, Willy had already drawn up exact plans for the transition of power to himself.... He was currently drafting his accession proclamation, which Bismarck advised him to burn."[29]

Of course Count von Waldersee's immediate concern was for his own future. At the invitation of the new crown princess, Mary's own great-niece, he visited Prince William to offer advice. In a long discussion,

> I spoke with the greatest frankness and to the following effect: The view which we had all held that it would be a misfortune if the Kaiser William died before the Crown Prince had been quite mistaken; the new Imperial couple would do so many foolish things that the ground would be prepared for him (Prince William) in the best way. Therefore it was merely a question of remaining quiet; after a short interval the Emperor would have to invite him to represent him [at Queen Victoria's Jubilee]. The less conspicuous he made himself, the less he demanded in the meantime, the better his position would be. He admitted all this fully, and left me in the friendliest fashion, expressing the hope that we should have much to do with each other.[30]

Von Waldersee obviously had no loyalty whatsoever to his new sovereign, and only thought of himself.

> If the new Emperor were well, I should, of course, have to go, but as things stand, he will scarcely find time, I think, to trouble himself about me. It would be another matter if Bismarck, perhaps in order to make himself agreeable to the new Emperor, were to decide on my removal. But Bismarck also will say to himself that the new regime can

7. A Clear Path to the Throne 91

only be of a short duration.... The Chancellor will, doubtless, be willing to remain on, but in view of the Empress's animosity no man can say whether this will be possible.[31]

With such a nest of vipers scheming against the new imperial couple,

> it was essential that the new Emperor and Empress should at once proceed to Berlin. The decision to go was made by the Emperor, and within twenty-four hours they were en route. Much criticism was leveled at the new Empress for bringing back the Emperor to Berlin, but the decision was his. Always he had put duty before comfort, and he was not the man to abdicate or fall short even on the brink of the grave.[32]

The Emperor slept most of his first day home after such a harrowing trip, then wrote a very long and surprising letter to Bismarck asking him to remain as chancellor for the sake of continuity. Bismarck later said that he assumed the reason for his being retained was that he "shared with him (the Emperor) the conviction that in the interests of the dynasty it was necessary that I should be maintained in office at the change of reign."[33] The emperor's letter, signed, "Yours very affectionately, Frederick III," laid out an elaborate system of beliefs on which his reign would have been based had he enjoyed the opportunity of life. He ended by writing to Bismarck, "Not caring for the splendor of great deeds, nor striving for glory, I shall be satisfied if it be one day said of my rule that it was beneficial to my people, useful to my country and a blessing to Europe."[34]

A national day of mourning was held on March 16, 1888, when the Berlin funeral was held for the man who had been king of Prussia since 1861 and emperor of Germany since 1871. The new empress's brother, Edward, Prince of Wales, had arrived to represent their mother, and he did much to see that his sister was treated with the respect she deserved. The bitter cold prevented the emperor's attendance. "I thought [the service] rather conventional, stiff and cold.... One can hardly talk of service in the German Church, as it is only an address and an extempore prayer," the new empress wrote to her mother, the Queen. As she continued in her letter recording her husband's thoughts of the day,

> When the hearse passed close under his window he quite broke down and was overwhelmed by his feelings, as you may well imagine! Directly afterwards we went to him and he was calm again and is now resting a little in his bed.... I think people in general consider us a mere passing shadow, soon to be replaced by reality in the shape of William. I may be wrong, but it seems to me as if the party that opposed and ill-treated us so long, hardly think it worthwhile to change their attitude, except very slightly—as they count on a different future! ... Yes, we are our own masters now, but shall we not have to leave all the work undone which we have so long and so carefully been preparing? Will there be any chance of doing the right thing, any time to carry out useful measures, needful reforms?[35]

Although she would not admit it, the Empress Frederick (as she was now) already knew the answer to that question.

As a contemporary wrote of that funereal day,

> There have been few scenes in the history of Prussian royalty more touching than that which occurred in the Palace of Charlottenburg, when this illustrious sovereign, prevented by ill health from following his father's body to the grave, stood at the window and watched the funeral procession of old Kaiser William wind through the park to the imperial mausoleum. He must have known then that the hour of his own departure could not be far distant; and solemn, indeed, must have been his thoughts, as he stood speechless and alone, in royal isolation, gazing upon a funeral pageant in which all other members of the royal household, including even his own wife and children, were participating, but from which he, the reigning sovereign and son of the dead Emperor, was excluded.[36]

Chapter 8

Ensconced in Power

Willy always blamed his father's death on a British physician who has been judged harshly by history. Dr. Morrell Mackenzie was a pioneering English laryngologist sent to Germany at the personal direction of Queen Victoria to care for her son-in-law. The then Crown Prince Frederick's German doctors had already diagnosed his throat cancer and urged an immediate operation. Dr. Mackenzie, however, insisted the vocal-cord polyp was nonmalignant and treatable. For that mistake he would eventually be excoriated. Under Mackenzie's care, Frederick traveled to London for Queen Victoria's Jubilee celebrations in June of 1887 marking her 50th year on the throne. The Queen knighted Mackenzie just four months later, and his patient's uncle awarded him the Grand Cross of the Hohenzollern Order.

Because young Prince Wilhelm's withered arm occurred during his birth, administered by a German physician, his mother harbored a deep distrust of any doctor except an English one. Dr. Morrell Mackenzie had been sent after Vicky appealed to her mother for medical help for her husband. What was not nearly as widely known as Mackenzie's missed diagnosis of cancer was the fact that he relied upon the expert medical advice of Dr. Rudolph Virchow, who examined the biopsies, taken by Mackenzie, and adjudged them to be nonmalignant. Not only was Virchow an eminently respected German pathologist, he was also a friend of the patient's and shared his liberal political leanings. Virchow openly opposed Bismarck's militarism and so angered the older man that Bismarck challenged him to a duel. According to one account, Virchow was allowed the choice of dueling weapons and chose sausages, one normal and the other loaded with Trichinella larvae.[1] Supposedly Bismarck then declined the duel since he thought it was too risky.[2] The one area in which the two adversaries were united, however, was in Virchow's support of Bismarck's *Kulturkampf*, an anticlerical campaign against the Catholic Church.³ Now remembered as "the father of modern pathology," Virchow's misreading of the cancerous polyps is rarely mentioned, while no reference to Sir Morrell Mackenzie fails to omit his role in the Emperor Frederick's death.

Mrs. Lee, Mary's mother, wrote to her friend, diplomat John A. Kasson, about Dr. Mackenzie's having been called in by Vicky to attend to her husband's medical needs.

> Grand Duchess of Baden [Willy's aunt, Emperor Fritz's sister] then staying with her father told Mary the English Dr. made light of her brother's trouble, was using iodine, had cured hundreds of throats of a similar kind and believed he wd [would] cure the Prince…. A Gen'l [general] who was much with them dined with us one day, said consultation of six German Drs [doctors] had decided the case was cancer, but Dr. Mac had gained the perfect confidence of the Princess [Vicky] by assuring her it was no cancer and her husband wd [would] be well in a short time.⁴

One possible, though weak, explanation for Mackenzie's misdiagnosis is that he did not want to disabuse his patient's wife of her firm belief that her husband was rapidly improving. She constantly wrote to her mother, the Queen, "Our Fritz is so much stronger this week than last," and he "continues to show improvement."⁵ Prince Hohenlohe visited Vicky during the new emperor's illness and "was so shaken by what she said to him that he recorded her words in his diary, 'It is perhaps possible that the illness will be of long duration. The expectation of a speedy end has not yet been confirmed.'"⁶ She even wrote to her daughter, Charlotte, "In a week everything will be all right again. We are going to Potsdam, and there the emperor will recover quickly."⁷

There is another possible reason for Mackenzie's misdiagnosis, however, that is more plausible; perhaps it was deliberate. Had the new emperor been suffering from an incapacitating illness, he might have been skipped over and his son would rule as regent for his father, much as the Prince of Wales (later King George IV) did for his father, Britain's King George III, who suffered from mental illness. In fact, the British Regency was an elegant time of unprecedented excess for the English nobility and aristocracy.

Many in Wilhelm's coterie would have been delighted had his very ill father abdicated in his son's favor. Failing that action, they would have favored Wilhelm's ruling in his father's name until his rapidly imminent death. Surprisingly to the entire court who knew of Bismarck's open feuds with Vicky, he was asked to remain in his position by the new emperor. As he wrote of the decision in his memoirs, "Her influence on her husband was at all times great, and it increased with years, to culminate at the time when he was Emperor. She also, however, shared with him the conviction that in the interests of the dynasty it was necessary that I should be maintained in office at the change of reign." Bismarck also contradicted the rumor that Frederick had earlier signed a document abdicating in his son's favor should death come to him before his own father, writing, "I will state that there is not a shadow of truth in the story."[8] Bismarck's opinion of the new empress was that "she is in general a very clever person, and really agreeable in her way, but she should not interfere in politics."[9]

There is no surprise at Count von Waldersee's opinion on the subject in his diary: "My conviction is that only two courses stand open to the Emperor: either he lays aside the Crown, which would be the simplest and most correct thing to do; or else he says, 'I am temporarily disqualified from ruling.' For the moment the second way is barred, for the desire to use his son ill is obvious; perhaps the first way will be taken as soon as the Empress has ensured her future, which she will soon be able to do."[10]

Only a few days later he wrote, "The Emperor is convinced of his incapacity to rule and would willingly authorize the Crown Prince to act as his deputy, but the Empress will not permit this."[11]

By March 23, his entry recorded, "The Crown Prince has become deputy for his father; the Order is indistinctly worded, but in practice the fact will soon be made clear."[12]

An interesting comment about the subject was later written by Mary's mother to her diplomat friend, John Kasson. "I have read somewhere that by a law of Prussia if the heir to the throne had an incurable malady, it (the throne) must pass to next heir. I don't know if its [sic] true, but if it is I've never heard of the Emperor even hinting such a thing. As far as I know he has always treated his mother Empress Frederic with greatest respect."[13] Either she was particularly obtuse or, far more likely, merely following the family line about her "perfect sunbeam for temper."[14]

Wishing to dispel public rumors of her husband's impending death, Vicky arranged for him to be driven in a closed carriage in Berlin's Tiergarten. Upon arrival at the palace, he appeared twice at the window, where he was cheered before returning home to bed, exhausted. As von Waldersee wrote, "Every intelligent doctor says that in his present condition the only kind thing one could do for the patient would be to prevent him from being in any way disturbed. The unfortunate gentleman, however, owing to this kind of inconsiderateness, has to bear the burden of Government business besides putting up with his intriguing, emotional wife, with whom there are excited scenes every day."[15]

The emperor harbored no illusions about the lack of days left to him. His finance minister visited to ask for a photograph to imprint on newly

The Moltke bridge leading to the Military Staff Building on the right where Alfred, Mary, and her mother lived overlooking the Spree. The cupola of the Reichstag can be seen behind to the left (Wikipedia).

minted coins. When the minister admitted that the process might take several months, Frederick answered, "I shan't survive that long."[16] Among his first orders was awarding the Black Eagle to justice minister Heinrich von Friedberg. Although von Waldersee approved, he sniffed of the recipient, "He is of Jewish origin; I believe indeed he has remained a Jew. The bestowal therefore suggests a programme; it is an open attempt to win favor with the Liberals and the Jews."[17]

Recalling his extreme anti–Semitic views, the new emperor "agreed to sack Stoecker as a court preacher, but final decision was left in the hands of the church authorities who did nothing."[18] Rather than attempt to make his father's last weeks peaceful ones, Wilhelm, in celebrating Bismarck's 73rd birthday, gave a speech which caused both pain and embarrassment by comparing "the Reich to a regiment where the general had been killed, the second-in-command badly wounded, and where it was vital that a junior officer take command."[19]

As if more excitement were needed, Queen Victoria arrived in Charlottenburg on April 24 for what von Waldersee termed "a very inopportune visit"[20] on her return home from Florence. Her daughter, Vicky, had been attempting for several years to arrange for the marriage of her second daughter, Victoria (one of many in the larger family, she was called "Moretta" to distinguish her from her mother and cousins of the same name), to the very handsome Prince Alexander of Battenberg, called "Sandro" by friends and family. He had in 1879 been appointed the first prince of modern Bulgaria with the active support of his uncle, Tsar Alexander II of Russia, who expected him to act as little more than a puppet for Russian interests.

Moretta's grandfather, the old Emperor William, and his powerful chancellor Bismarck strongly opposed the marriage, as did Sandro's cousin, who had succeeded to the Russian throne as Tsar Alexander III and was highly offended at his young cousin's estrangement from the powers who placed him on the Bulgarian throne. Sandro was finally forced from power and abdicated in 1886. His youngest brother, Henry, had married in 1885 Queen Victoria's youngest daughter, Princess Beatrice, despite his being the product of a morganatic marriage and thus not a royal highness.

Vicky had never given up on the idea of her daughter's marriage to Sandro, however, and perhaps thought that this union would further strengthen her sister's royal standing since Queen Victoria's gift to the groom of the style of "Royal Highness" was only valid in the United Kingdom. Vicky was so much in favor of the wedding of Moretta and Sandro that Bismarck even accused her of a "bottomless sensuality" with her own "incestuous thoughts" about the handsome young man.[21] Her son, Wilhelm, was violently opposed to the marriage and made it clear that his sister would be banished from the family should she go forward with her plans. It was into this complicated web of matrimony and diplomacy that Queen Victoria made her visit.

An earlier visit by the Queen to the Prussian court had not gone well. In recounting the current visit, Mrs. Lee wrote of the past one,

> 32 years ago she came with Prince Consort [Albert, her husband]. Frederic Wm. then reigning King gave the Queen a grand dinner. Count S. [Schlippenbach, who related the story to her] I think was present. Coming to the table, she found the Prince put far below. The Germans are such sticklers for etiquette they thought as Consort was only Prince of little Saxe Coburg—the many of much higher rank must be placed before him. But this did not prove to be of the Queen's mind. She ordered a chair brought, and had the Prince seat himself on it—then by much pushing and squeezing he managed to reach the table. The Queen was greatly displeased and full of indignation declared it should be the last time she would ever come to Berlin. She has kept her word up to this time.[22]

Queen Victoria's extended family in Coburg for the 1894 wedding of two of her grandchildren. She is seated between her grandson, Kaiser Wilhelm II, and her eldest daughter, Empress Friedrich (Vicky). Directly behind the kaiser are the tsar and tsarina of Russia. The man in the lighter overcoat behind the tsar is the Prince of Wales, later King Edward VII. All the others are royal relations (Wikimedia Commons).

8. Ensconced in Power

This later visit was to be the first and only time she faced in person the formidable Bismarck, who was reported to have said of her during the visit, "You can do business with that woman."[23] When the Queen told Bismarck she feared that, given the precarious health of his father, her grandson might not be ready to rule, he told her, "If thrown in the water, he would be able to swim, as he was certainly clever."[24]

Queen Victoria met privately with Bismarck concerning Vicky's insistence on the proposed marriage of Moretta to Battenberg, and, as he later reported, she "behaved quite sensibly ... and urged her daughter to change her ways."[25] In reporting on the Queen's visit, her ambassador to Germany, Sir Edward Malet, wrote to his superior, Lord Salisbury, "There is no doubt that the Queen's visit to Berlin has been a political success.... The breach, such as it was, has been closed, not widened.... Prince Bismarck ... has said that if the action of England should correspond with the sound sense and practical character of the views held by Her Majesty, the danger of a European war would be minimized."[26]

Upon Victoria's arrival back in England, her grateful daughter wrote to her, "It all seems like a dream! Your dear visit so ardently wished for and hoped for has come and gone like lightning! ... I am indeed thankful that you were able to come and that the pleasure and emotion did dearest Fritz no harm!"[27] Sir Edward Malet wrote to Lord Salisbury that Prince Wilhelm spoke with him about his grandmother's visit, "in warm terms and seemed to be delighted at having had an opportunity of conversing with Her Majesty."[28]

Although the visit was deemed a success in diplomacy, the same could not be said for Vicky's hoped-for marriage of her daughter, Moretta. Finally admitting defeat when even her mother, the Queen, opposed the marriage, Vicky agreed "to sacrifice her daughter's happiness on the altar of the Fatherland."[29] For the would-be groom's part, by that time young Prince Alexander of Battenberg had already lost his ardor for the princess and become enchanted with an Austrian actress and opera singer, Johanna Loisinger. The two would marry the next year when he assumed the title "Count von Hartenau" and they had two children.

Poor Moretta was then pressed into an engagement with the handsome but dull Adolph, Prince of Schaumburg-Lippe, who was almost seven years older than she. While plans for the wedding were being developed, Moretta fell in love with a British naval officer, Maurice Bourke, who was a younger son of the 6th Earl of Mayo. He commanded the royal yacht of Moretta's uncle, Prince Alfred, Duke of Saxe-Coburg & Gotha. Moretta's first cousin, Marie, later Queen of Romania, wrote of Bourke, "But the greatest of all our friends—so to say, our hero—was Maurice Bourke, at that time commander of our father's yacht, H.M.S. Surprise. How we loved him! He had every quality needed to make him the ideal of three little girls with high spirits and a desire for hero worship."[30]

Of course, Bourke was not considered sufficiently royal as the husband of Queen Victoria's granddaughter even if she had not been engaged at the time. When Vicky and Dona traveled with Charlotte and Moretta to Athens for the 1889 wedding of their sister, Sophie, to the future King Constantine I, they sailed on a ship on which Maurice Bourke was serving. The ever-pious Dona wrote to her husband, Wilhelm,

> God preserve us from further scandals, but somehow I do not feel reassurance yet, that Moretta will really marry that nice Adolph, so good looking, I think, and with such charming honest fine eyes ... you can give Grandmama a good talking-to, for this is really going too far, when a girl, particularly a princess, is engaged, that her own mother is probably trying to break it off! You must also make it clear to Grandmama that Vicky [Moretta] must not travel back in the Surprise, for the constant contact with the man, when someone is like Vicky if she gets very worked up, she might well do something quite frightful and then will tell you that there were reasons which compelled her to marry the fellow. With Victoria anything is possible in my opinion.[31]

Moretta was reported to be deeply depressed as her wedding to Adolph approached but then seemed to become somewhat better as the date drew near.[32] Empress Frederick wrote to Queen Victoria that she was "satisfied with her fate."[33] Perhaps "resigned" might have been the more correct term.

Moretta was married in 1890 to Adolph, Prince of Schaumburg-Lippe. They remained childless and he died in 1916. In 1927, despite strong objections from her siblings and friends, she married a Russian ne'er-do-well named Alexander Zoubkoff, who was 35 years younger than she. Moretta told the press that she wanted "to exchange the title of 'princess' for that of a happy woman."[34] Zoubkoff spent her remaining fortune and borrowed heavily in her name. She was eventually forced to sell the contents of Schaumburg Palace even though the proceeds covered only a third of her debts. Moretta moved into a single furnished room and was finally divorcing her husband when she died in poverty in 1929.

The Bulgarian throne that had been held by Alexander of Battenberg was given in 1887 to Prince Ferdinand of Saxe-Coburg & Gotha, whose father was a first cousin of both Queen Victoria and her consort, Prince Albert. When she learned of plans to appoint her bisexual cousin Ferdinand to the Bulgarian throne, Victoria telegraphed to her prime minister, "He is totally unfit ... delicate, eccentric and effeminate.... Should be stopped at once."[35] In the end, however, he performed masterfully, later became tsar, and was the grandfather of Bulgaria's last king, Simeon, who was eventually elected prime minister of the country over which he had previously reigned as a boy.

Bismarck was to recall how divisive the question of Moretta's marriage had been for him and his empress. "She never ceased to regard England as her country.... This difference of opinion, which rested on the difference of nationality, caused many a discussion between Her Royal Highness and me on ... the Battenberg question."[36]

Count von Waldersee had earlier noted that the new empress would "ensure her future"[37] well in advance of her husband's death. He was almost certainly referring to her realization that once her son came to power, she would be cut off from all authority as well as funds. Baron Kohn, the old Emperor William's private banker, had ensured that the sum of 54 million marks, as a personal Hohenzollern fortune, would be bequeathed to his son, Frederick, upon his succession. This very substantial amount, however, was found after Fritz's death to have been invested abroad in the name of his widow, Vicky. Her uncle, the Duke of Saxe-Coburg & Gotha, and her cousin, King Leopold of the Belgians, were named as trustees. It was claimed that Prince Stolberg, minister of the imperial household, resigned from his position when he learned of the transaction. Later, however, the bequest was reportedly discovered to be devised in such a way that most of the funds were only available to her during her lifetime and would be passed to her younger children at her death.[38]

During her limited days as empress, Vicky held only one formal court, remembered by an attendee. "The Empress was dressed in the deepest mourning, indeed wrapped in black from head to foot, her face hidden by a crape veil, while a long procession of women likewise veiled in crape filed past the throne, their black gowns high in the neck and skirts banded with crape a quarter of a yard wide, while long folds of double crape fell upon the floor in guise of Court trains."[39]

There was to be one happy event in the emperor's last days. His second son, Henry, who became an accomplished Navy officer, gave his father as much pride as his eldest son caused him grief. He was married on May 24 in the chapel of Charlottenburg Castle to his first cousin, Princess Irene of Hesse and By Rhine. Count von Waldersee and Mary attended, and he recounted of the frail Emperor's appearance at the wedding, "holding himself erect he moved forward to his place with three big strides, which were not natural but obviously the outcome of a great effort, and at once sat down.... He presented the appearance of a man severely stricken, his difficulty in breathing being especially noticeable, for his breast kept moving as when a man is deliberately taking a deep breath."[40]

Once the ceremony had concluded, the emperor was changed from his uniform to civilian dress and pushed in a wheelchair through the group where, as von Waldersee said, "We now saw him as he really was—a harrowing sight."[41]

Henry's bride, Princess Irene, was a sister of the beautiful Ella, whom Wilhelm wanted to marry in his youth, and thus another grandchild of Queen Victoria's. His mother, however, had prevented Wilhelm's union, knowing that Ella would probably bring hemophilia into their family. Perhaps she allowed this marriage to her second son because she had already ensured that her eldest son's progeny would not be afflicted by his marriage to the dull Dona. Tragically, her first instincts were correct, and Princess Irene was to do precisely what Vicky feared to her children by Henry. Their eldest son, Waldemar, was a hemophiliac. Although he married, there were no children born of the union. He and his wife fled their home in Bavaria as the Russians approached, and the couple reached the town of Tutzing, where a German doctor was able to give him an urgently needed blood transfusion. The American army overran the area the next day and diverted all medical attention to skeletal victims in concentration camps. Without an additional transfusion, Prince Waldemar died the next day. Even more tragically, Irene and Waldemar's youngest son, Henry, was also a hemophiliac. When he was four, his mother left him unsupervised for a few moments and he climbed onto a chair and table. As he heard his mother reenter the room, he jumped down quickly but slipped and hit his head. He died from a brain hemorrhage only a few hours later.

After helping resolve her granddaughter's marriage issue before her departure, Queen Victoria monitored her son-in-law's rapid decline by daily letters. Less than a week after her return home, von Waldersee wrote in his diary, "The Empress now rules the land…. The Chancellor and the Head of the Cabinet are finding themselves in a very uncomfortable position; their sense of duty tells them that the voiceless Emperor, very weak and quite incapable of work, no longer able to hold Councils even of the briefest duration, is simply not qualified to rule." He could not help adding in a self-congratulatory tone, "I must admit that I did not think she could be so unwise. What a terrible misfortune it would have been if we now had a healthy Kaiser Frederick over us! Under his wife's leading he would put the whole German Empire out of joint. How wonderfully everything is working out! All are looking with high hopes to the Crown Prince. Who would have believed it a year ago?"[42]

Finally, on June 14, at 11:15 a.m., Frederick's 99 days as emperor came to an end. But "scarcely had the Emperor's eyes closed in that last long sleep than there broke out a virulent campaign of vituperation against the Empress such as few have had to endure. The Empress was much pained to find that her son could scarcely bring himself to express sorrow for his father's death, and that he gave the impression that he held his memory in small esteem."[43] Both Bismarcks, father and son, followed their new emperor's lead, and the son even called his dead leader an "incubus" and "an ineffectual visionary."[44]

Wilhelm II had long looked forward to exacting revenge upon his mother, but few thought he would be as ruthless as he was.

> As soon as it was known that the Emperor Frederick was dying, a cordon of soldiers was secretly drawn round Friedrichskron, so that no documents might be removed without the knowledge of the new Emperor. The Master of the Household hastened to promulgate the order that, "No one in the Palace, including the doctors, is to carry on any correspondence with the outside.... If any of the doctors attempt to leave the Palace, they will be arrested." The Empress and her suite were practically under arrest.

As one of Wilhelm's early biographers pointed out, "It was as though a monarch had been murdered, and his hostile successor, long prepared, had seized upon the newly acquired authority."[45] The new widow's first message after her husband's death was to his aged mother: "She whose one pride and happiness it was to be the wife of your son grieves with you, afflicted mother. No mother ever had so good a son. Be proud and strong in your sorrow."[46] To her own mother, she wrote in despair, "I am his widow, no more his wife! How am I to bear it! You did, and I will too. You had your nation, your great duties to live for! I have my three sweet girls—he loved so much—that are my consolation.... Those who really loved him will be kind to me for his sake!"[47] She certainly knew that her first-born son was not in that number.

The younger Bismarck disclosed that Wilhelm II had once said to him about his mother, "I see that everything I can do will be in vain: we stand on different ground, my mother will always remain an Englishwoman and I am a Prussian; so how can we ever be in harmony with one another?"[48]

Wilhelm made his first official speech on July 25, only six weeks into his reign, and its words cast a dagger into his mother's heart. "He did not mention his father's name, but spoke of his late grandfather, whose policy he said he was determined to follow. Vicky read every word of this deceptively humble speech and it showed her, with a fresh stab, that she and Fritz had been nothing. A generation had been skipped."[49] Even worse, he asked her to move out of her home, the Neue Palais, which she and her late husband had spent so much time and effort to restore. He directed her to remove all of her personal belongings as well as those of her late father.

His uncle, the Prince of Wales, had relayed to Queen Victoria his nephew's answer to his question as to where Vicky would live: she was to have the Villa Liegnitz (where Wilhelm's sixth son would eventually commit suicide), "a poky little place and she had to tell William firmly that it 'would not do for your mother who is the first after you and who is the first Princess after Aunt Alix in Great Britain.'"[50]

The more his British relatives heard of the new emperor's actions to humiliate his mother publicly, the more their long-held disdain for him grew. For their part, his British relations never approved of their bombastic and ill-mannered German nephew and cousin. "None of his English relatives ever really liked this Imperial quick-change artist, who in the first years of his reign was completely under the thumbs of Count and Countess von Waldersee."[51] The question now, of course, was whether Mary and her husband's influence on their younger friend could be beneficial or, in fact, even sustained.

Wilhelm II's long-awaited accession, of course, had an immediate benefit for the von Waldersees.

> In August 1888 the old Field Marshal Count von Moltke stepped down from his post as chief of the Great General Staff and was succeeded by Wilhelm's fatherly friend Count Alfred von Waldersee, whose influence now became so apparent that he was regarded everywhere—even abroad—as the future Reich chancellor. Immediately after Wilhelm II's accession Waldersee noted in his diary that he had reason to be "almost too proud," for he was "definitely greatly in favour with the Kaiser, which the whole world knows, and plenty of people run after me in consequence. The Kaiser thinks a great deal of me, likes to hear my opinion on many things and in fact has friendly feelings towards me."[52]

CHAPTER 9

Father Figure

Without a father and with a mother whom he distrusted, the new emperor was a perfect candidate for Count von Waldersee to step into a role as trusted advisor. "Waldersee was a kind of surrogate father for Wilhelm, and had a decisive influence on him during the 1880s. The Quartermaster-General had good reason to hope that he might one day become Reich Chancellor under Wilhelm. Waldersee was also Wilhelm's *confidant* in the latter's extra-marital affairs."[1] It certainly seems logical that Mary's husband would have shared with her at least some of the details of these sexual peccadilloes. As distasteful as she would have found them, that knowledge would prove valuable when Wilhelm came to her with a very delicate mission.

> With much stammering and many excuses he eventually asked her to help him to defeat the machinations of a certain Bavarian beauty with whom he had been on very intimate terms…. This woman was in Berlin and was threatening to publish letters which she declared the emperor had written to her when they were lovers. Wilhelm swore that the letters were barefaced forgeries, but, nevertheless, he was anxious to have them destroyed.[2]

It seems a daring request to ask of such a pious woman, yet "he had called in Mary Lee's help because the task required cleverness, discretion, and diplomacy, all of which he and his countrymen lacked."[3] Her ample purse would also have been a decided advantage. Although there is a possibility that the woman in question was Emilie Klopp, the "Miss Love" of Wilhelm's probable first sexual encounter, it is far more likely it was a woman who would cause great consternation to him and his court.

Countess Elisabeth Wedel-Bérard was born Elisabeth Bérard somewhere in Germany on December 27, 1848 (therefore more than ten years Willy's senior and only eight years younger than his mother), perhaps of an American mother. Much later in her life she would claim to be a daughter of Kaiser Wilhelm I, Willy's grandfather, as well as a great-granddaughter of the louche King Frederick William II of Prussia, who had so many illegitimate children his subjects called him "the much-loved."[4] There is no reason to believe her claims. What is certain is that she was a great beauty and for more than two decades was the talk of the court.

Elisabeth was discovered at the Berlin racetrack at its opening in May of 1869 by Chamberlain Louis von Prillwitz, son of a royal father, Prince August of Prussia, and his beautiful Jewish mistress, Auguste Arend, who was ennobled as a baroness in 1825. As a young man, Wilhelm I, Willy's grandfather, had an affair with a Berlin actress, Edwine Viereck, by whom a son was born. In order to shield his royal master, von Prillwitz acknowledged the child as his own, thus proving his loyalty as an illegitimate member of the Hohenzollern family. At the racetrack, von Prillwitz took great interest in young Elisabeth among the wealthy and socially prominent attendees and made certain she met several of his choice.[5]

It did not take long for Elisabeth to become the mistress of Prince Friedrich "Fritz" of Hohenzollern-Sigmaringen, from the Swabian/Catholic branch of the German relations. Fritz's sister, Stephanie, had briefly been Queen of Portugal, and his brother, Karl, became King Carol I of Romania, while their youngest sister would become the mother of Belgium's King Albert I. French opposition to the candidacy of their eldest brother, Prince Leopold, for the throne of Spain triggered the Franco-Prussian War, which led to the founding of the German Empire in January 1871. Elisabeth was in a particularly fortunate position among her lover's family, although she was always aware that he would not be allowed to marry her even if he wanted to do so.

Elisabeth had twin sons, Eugéne and Fréderic, who were widely acknowledged to be Fritz's children. In 1879, it became necessary for her lover to take a royal wife. He married on June 21, 1879, Luise, Princess von Thurn und Taxis. Her mother was a duchess of Bavaria and her father was the family's crown prince but died before his own father. Her sister was the ancestor of the current claimant to the Portuguese throne. Although Luise was 16 years younger than Fritz, the marriage remained childless.

A husband had to be found for Elisabeth who could give a noble title to her already-born sons. He was Count Hermann von Wedel, brother of the German military attaché in Vienna who, under Wilhelm II's reign, would become ambassador to Vienna as well as viceroy of Alsace-Lorraine. They were married on November 24, 1879, but when Elisabeth learned on their wedding night that he already had a mistress in Düsseldorf who had given birth to their child, she denied him conjugal rights and locked him

9. Father Figure

Kaiser Wilhelm, left, with his sons in birth order, Crown Prince Wilhelm, Eitel, Adalbert, August, Oscar, Joachim (Library of Congress).

out of her bedroom. This, of course, was from a woman who had already given birth to illegitimate twins. They formally divorced in 1884 but were seen together during the intervening years, as each needed the other, but she supposedly never relented to let him into her bed.

Elisabeth had learned a great deal during her time with Fritz, including how lucrative contracts with governments were awarded based on personal contacts. On one of her trips with her husband to Baden, they met Archduke Carl Salvator of Austria, brother of Tuscany's Grand Duke Ferdinand IV. "The ingenious Carl Salvator had developed a novel repeating rifle that could fire off more rounds than the gun then being used by the Prussian army."[6] He applied for a patent for the rifle in the fall of 1884.[7]

Wilhelm went to Austria in October of 1884 for a hunting trip with the Grand Duke of Tuscany (Carl Salvator's brother) and the king of Saxony. It was almost certainly on this trip that he met the beautiful Elisabeth von Wedel (or Countess von Wedel-Bérard, as she had begun calling herself in preparation for her divorce). It did not take long for Elisabeth to lure the young prince into her bed, although years later she would insist they had never consummated the relationship. "In Potsdam she stayed at the Palasthotel opposite the Stadtschloss. Here William presented her with a diamond necklace. She was evidently a cut above the usual whores whose bills he tried to wriggle out of honouring. The necklace was not enough.

Waldersee had to find the odd 1,000 marks too. Eventually Gräfin Wedel moved into a flat in Charlottenburg where she continued to receive the prince until the end of the year."[8]

Wilhelm fell hard for this beguiling woman. When he learned that she had blocked her bedroom door from her husband on their wedding night, he wrote to her, "Chère comtesse, you have indeed a difficult life behind you. Oh ma chère adorée, how great you are in my estimation! You sacrificed your love out of patriotism! That is magnificent! You refused your former husband everything, would you refuse me, adorée, everything too, if we should one day be together? If I knelt before you and begged?"[9]

By the end of the year, however, Wilhelm was seeking Count von Waldersee's assistance in dealing with the young woman whom he had come to know only too well. On Christmas Day of 1884 the prince sent a note asking to see him on "a secret matter." Waldersee then records in his diary that they spent a "long time" together.[10] Within days there were several more private meetings between the two. They used Archduke Carl Salvator's repeating rifle as a pretext for their meetings, and there is no question that the Countess von Wedel-Bérard was part of those negotiations. Waldersee was particularly pleased with the faith being placed in him by his young charge, confiding to his diary,

> I do believe he is beginning to trust me somewhat; he discusses numerous delicate family matters, and I almost fear that he is not circumspect vis-à-vis others. In a certain matter which is occupying him greatly at present, he assures me I am his only confidant. I have advised him on several occasions not to trust anyone completely so as not to forfeit his independence. He is a very idiosyncratic young man.... Perhaps he is not overly endowed with heart, but I believe that this is something which will stand him in good stead in the future.[11]

The meetings between the two continued as acquiring the repeating rifle was coming closer to fruition. "Since December 1884, Wilhelm had been secretly negotiating by mail with Countess Elisabeth Wedel in Vienna on equipping the Prussian army with the repeating rifle invented by Carl Salvator."[12] Wilhelm sent to Waldersee on the evening of February 19, 1885, a letter directing him to join him and Elisabeth in Potsdam the next day along with several other generals. "Countess Wedel arrived with the weapon in Potsdam on 19 February 1885, had an 'entrevue' with Wilhelm, and on the following morning the new weapon was tested in her presence by the Prince" as well as several of his generals.[13]

In the countess's memoirs, she states that she enjoyed a long visit from the prince after the weapon was tested. "We had very serious matters to discuss, and our conversation lasted for several hours." It was on this day that he gave her the diamond necklace engraved with "the Imperial W."[14]

Things started going slightly downhill, however, when she began asking Wilhelm for money. He wrote in a note to Waldersee,

> Dear Count. Was with Countess W. yesterday. She is in an embarrassing situation, as Archduke C. S. gave Dormes [the agent sent by the Archduke] too little money for the journey, despite his assurance that he had provided plenty. She must now pay for Dormes as well, although she had not planned for this. Please send me a 1000-mark note or give it to me this afternoon when I come to visit you. She intends to pay it back as soon as she reaches Vienna; and once again refused to accept payment for the trip. Details in person. Yours, Wilhelm Pr. of Pr.[15]

Wilhelm's notes to Waldersee became even more frantic over the next few days. In one, he spoke of "old Goltz" having had tea with "their majesties" on the day before,

> and also related that "a mistress!" of the Archduke was here, who was also very involved in the purchase! I was thunderstruck! ... It had been explicitly agreed that no one was to mention the Countess! ... Please investigate the matter and give the gentleman or gentlemen a piece of your mind! ... I naturally told Goltz straight off that it was nothing more than a fairy tale and nonsense, and that ladies had nothing to do with rifles.... It sounds like him: "mistress of the Archduke"—to make her position impossible from the start. The poor Countess, if she only knew, she would have Bronsart challenged to a duel on the spot.[16]

Wilhelm also made it clear that the woman's husband, although a military attaché, was to know nothing of the matter. The ordeal brought the young prince even closer to his would-be mentor. "Thus, it was the support that Wilhelm needed both for the procurement of the repeating rifle and in his relations with Countess Wedel that brought about the deeper friendship between the Prince and Waldersee which we can observe from early 1885 onwards."[17]

The letters continued between Wilhelm and the countess, and they make clear not only that he was besotted with her but also that she was deeply involved in financial and military matters concerning the repeating rifle. She asked to have the privilege of addressing him with the intimate "du" as opposed to the more formal "Sie," and he responded,

> You wish to address me as "Du"! Oh, how wonderful, that makes me very glad and I am grateful to you! Yesterday we had a court ball, which was brilliant, and to which people thronged. But I thought of you constantly, and although many tried to tempt me, I did not ask a single lady to dance, did not dance a single step. At present my heart is not light enough to dance; my thoughts always return to you.[18]

By this point the countess was his principal contact with Archduke Carl Salvator, as Wilhelm ended his letter, "Keep C. S. in a good mood, and amenable to our interests! Promise him everything!" She soon left the archduke and moved into an apartment in Wilmersdorfer Strasse 1 in the Charlottenburg district of Berlin, where she continued to host Prince Wilhelm.[19]

Shortly after her return to Vienna, the countess began to blackmail Wilhelm using his many letters to her. He turned to Waldersee as his intermediary, writing to him on April 4, 1885,

> My dear Count. Please forgive the pencil. Many thanks for your letter and package. The "matter of urgency" is that the Countess is suddenly in need of money because of the malice of a Jew, who managed her affairs following her divorce. The rascal wanted to marry her and, after she threw him out on his ear, the beast bought all of her debts from her creditors and is putting so much pressure on her that she is quite at a loss. She asked for an extension, as in the autumn of this year she will receive 150,000 francs from Victorien Sardou for pieces she made for him. But the man refuses! Now I am to procure advice and money, without telling you! Because she is ashamed in front of you! I have racked my brains for a solution, but to no avail! That is why I am asking you to handle the matter! Tell her that until I asked for your help I was unable to achieve anything and that is why I haven't yet answered, as I did not know what to advise.[20]

Waldersee's attempts to placate the young woman only made her angry. She noted in her memoirs that he evoked "shame and rage" in her. "I pack all the letters together and send them back to the Prince in Potsdam. I terminate my friendship with the Prince!"[21] However, it is clear she did not return all of the letters. When Wilhelm sent his adjutant to retrieve the additional letters, she gave him only one. She then wrote imploring letters to the prince, even asking that he adopt her two children if she did not survive her current ailment (a supposed "haemorrhage from the mouth"[22]).

Evidently it was at this point that the prince decided to approach his friend Mary. She was only ten years older than Elisabeth, and perhaps Wilhelm thought she was more likely to invoke sympathy from the younger woman. Of course, it is also true that Mary's ample fortune might be very fortunately applied to the situation. Whether Mary depended chiefly upon her tact or her checkbook is not certain, but "the countess accepted the commission promptly, and two days later she brought the packet of letters," which were burned before her eyes.[23]

But Mary's success did not bring an end to Wilhelm's troubles with the beautiful young woman. She became a "lady of honour" and moved into the home of the Persian envoy, Field Marshal Mirza Reza Khan Muayid-es-Sultane, who was his country's diplomatic representative to Berlin from April of 1886 until 1901. While she was in that position, five of her letters from Wilhelm in his own hand somehow found their way into the safe and were not discovered until 1956 and were later published in a German magazine. Although she had been vilified over the years and her memoirs completely discounted by historians, the letters confirm much of what she related. They also make it clear why both Wilhelm and the German police were eager to recover them.[24]

Late in 1886 Elisabeth met a Silesian military officer, Lieutenant Alexander Schlarbaum, and became engaged to him. Wilhelm wrote a note to Waldersee suggesting that her "happy mood" might entice her to return the letters from him still in her possession. Waldersee wrote her a cloying letter asking for the return of other letters and the result was another demand for money.

Mary and Alfred on the cover of *Bilder vom Tage* ("Images of the Day") 33 (1901): 1433.

After Wilhelm became kaiser, Elisabeth asked him for a loan of 50,000 marks, supposedly because her husband had incurred heavy gambling debts. She wrote that a notary named Weiss (perhaps the "Jew" mentioned in Wilhelm's letter to Waldersee) told her she should demand millions of dollars for the letters in her possession. Instead she received 600 marks from a court official then went to Potsdam in August of 1888 to turn over what she said were the last of the letters. (Obviously that was not the case since at least five were discovered years later.) Elisabeth asked in return that her husband be appointed director of the Royal Demesnes and that her surviving son be accepted into the cadet corps, as Wilhelm had promised her long before. The new kaiser agreed instead to an annual payment of 2,400 marks for five years to pay for her son's education. When she admitted to having even more letters in her possession, she was offered an annual pension of 4,800 marks, paid quarterly, if they were all returned immediately.

In 1892, Elisabeth took her children to the United States but returned to Germany within a few months. Her memoirs, *Meine Beziehungen zu S. M. Kaiser Wilhelm II* (*My Relations with H. M. Kaiser Wilhelm II*), were published in July of 1900 by Caesar Schmidt, in Zurich, with a sequel, *Aus den Katakomben* (*From the Catacombs*), added from Florence in 1901. One syndicated newspaper column about the book that was widely reprinted at the time was headlined "The Kaiser's Secrets Betrayed by a Woman." Elisabeth claimed "it was she who prevailed upon the Emperor to forbid gambling in the army, who originated the policy of expansion, who suggested to the Empress to take under her patronage institutes for the cure of tuberculosis, and who initiated the Muravieff circular proposing the [Hague] peace conference." The countess took advantage of the opportunity to attack Count von Waldersee, who "is singled out for rough handling. Countess Wedel alleges among other accusations that he attempted to blacken the German Empress' character and that he intrigued against the Emperor."[25]

Elisabeth then moved to Paris and sent many letters to the German ambassador, the king of England, the Grand Duke of Baden (Wilhelm's uncle), and several other authorities, insisting that she had vital evidence that held "the balance between war and peace in her hands. She asserted that she had divorced her husband Schlarbaum at the Kaiser's insistence, had gone to prison for the Kaiser's sake, and now demanded revenge—an eye for an eye and a tooth for a tooth unless her daughter [by Schlarbaum] were provided with a house."[26] She followed up with a letter to the governor of Berlin demanding that he and the kaiser meet with her within 48 hours if they wished to avoid worldwide bloodshed. She also insisted that she would publish Wilhelm's letters to her containing valuable state secrets. At the time, her book of memoirs, published in 1900, was suppressed in Germany, but it was being sold surreptitiously by mail order under other titles. A Berlin court ruled in January of 1901 that the book was to be confiscated "and the plates destroyed. The whereabouts of the Countess is unknown."[27] As one historian wrote of Elisabeth's literary effort, "When she found herself abandoned by her titled lover, who, by the way, did not exclusively enjoy her favours, she revealed their secret relations and thereby laid bare the heart of an adventuress. In the course of five hundred pages of a *livres à scandales*, she expatiates upon the detached and coarse society which surrounded her changing life."[28]

While authorities were still trying to decide what to do, Elisabeth appeared with her daughter at the German consulate in Basel with the expectation that the kaiser would soon be there to retrieve her. The official consul, after their first meeting, reported that the "rather weathered former 'beauté' did not really give one the impression she was insane."[29]

Within weeks, Elisabeth was taken by police to the closest lunatic asylum, Friedmatt, after her loud protestations while running in the streets that the kaiser was in Basel and was about to be assassinated. Because she had been medically adjudged "dangerously insane" but had no money, officials tried to have her sent to Silesia, where she was officially domiciled under her ex-husband's residency. While the kaiser's civil cabinet debated whether he should pay for her treatment at the asylum, her young son came forward and offered to pay from his small military income. Obviously something more permanent had to be arranged when the son was informed that his mother was dangerously "deranged and agitated."[30]

Meanwhile, Elisabeth was convinced that the kaiser had married her, making her the kaiserin, and she was demanding royal treatment. In mid–1904 the kaiser's advisors agreed that he would pay for her treatment in a Swiss lunatic asylum. A month later, when she demanded a private room and first-class meals, the kaiser agreed to the additional costs. The Swiss officials kept requesting that she be repatriated to a German institution since she was a difficult and expensive patient. Finally, on September 18, 1905, Elisabeth was locked away in a railroad compartment with two female guards, driven across the border, and delivered to German officials in Lörrach. As the German consul in Basel reported, "Neither the police here, nor I myself, have been able to discover where she was taken from there." The cost charged to the kaiser for having hospitalized her then deported her to Germany was 789 Swiss francs.[31] By one account headlined "German Countess Has Bar Sinister," she was taken to a psychiatric clinic at the University of Freiburg in a case of "administrative removal for the good of the state," where she was deemed to be dangerously ill.[32] In 1907, the *New York Times* reported that she had recently attempted to escape from a lunatic asylum near Basel "where she has been incarcerated for many years," although the same article ends, "The Countess, by means of a trick employed by her family, was enticed on German territory, arrested, and confined as a dangerous lunatic."[33] Whatever the truth, at that point, she disappeared from history.[34]

Although the court did everything in its power to discredit Elisabeth's memoirs, the letters that were eventually found in a Teheran safe, as well as specific details contained in her account, in large part vindicate much of her story. It is obvious the kaiser did, in fact, discuss highly confidential matters with her. He was the last person who could have allowed that fact to become public. The kaiser's closest friend, Philip, Prince zu Eulenburg (of whom more later), said that Carl Wedel, whose brother had been married off to Elisabeth, "could never have made such a meteoric career without the ability 'to terrorise' the Kaiser over 'certain profligate actions' in Vienna in the 1880s."[35]

The kaiser's memories of the unfortunate episode seemed to dim over the years although those of von Waldersee did not. The count was offended when Wilhelm recommended a promotion for Elisabeth's former brother-in-law, Prince Fritz of Hohenzollern-Sigmaringen, "whom Wilhelm, under the influence of Countess Elisabeth Wedel, had formerly abhorred as a dangerous intriguer, was promoted to commanding general of the III Army Corps in the autumn of 1893. Waldersee strongly condemned the preferential treatment shown to this 'indolent' Prince, for he was 'a very insignificant man, without a trace of passion for his career, without ambition—not even of smart appearance, and very poorly trained as a soldier.'"[36]

Clearly von Waldersee's disillusion with the kaiser was growing stronger. Within a few months he confided to his diary, "I wish to God I were in a position to record something good about the Kaiser! I often ask myself whether I do not judge him unfairly and in a prejudiced fashion, but I always come back to the conviction that he is quite vague as to his aims and consequently weak-willed and not to be relied upon."[37]

CHAPTER 10

"The Empress' American Rival"

Count Alfred von Waldersee was becoming well known to the world not only as an accomplished military advisor but also as a proponent of war. The *New York Herald*, referring to him as "the personal confidant of Kaiser Wilhelm and the successor of Marshal von Moltke in the management of the great German General Staff," thought him sufficient to warrant a full-length interview that was quickly reprinted in a French newspaper. Describing his office building as "a Moorish edifice constructed of dark red stone," his visitor appraised him as

> a man of average size, a little older than 50. The hair is very thick, but with the whiteness of snow. His eyes are clear and placid, but his look is of an unusual fixedness. When the Count speaks, it is slow, and each word is pronounced clearly and vigorously. The attitude of the man, the manners, the voice and the gestures, or rather the complete absence of gestures, give an impression of cold determination that nothing would disturb…. The Count, in full uniform, but without his sword, wears braids of gold and silver which indicate his rank of General of Cavalry, and the red bands on his trousers of an officer of the General Staff. [1]

His interviewer informed the count that he was said to believe war was inevitable and that it was "better for it to break out." Von Waldersee contemplated for a short while before responding, "To say I desire war is absurd. I only wish one thing: that our enemies renounce completely the idea of attacking us. I know too well what war is and am convinced that it is my duty as an honest man to wish that it be used only as a last resort, as much in the interests of the Fatherland as in the interests of the entire world." He professed his duty to avoid a war and his hope that he could be successful. However, he was adamant in declaring, "I am familiar with Germany's spirit of sacrifice. I know with such confidence they will march behind their young emperor. I am familiar also with our army and I am

Mary and Alfred on the cover of *The Sphere*, vol. 11, no. 32 (Sept. 1, 1900).

certain of its superiority. The other nations can adopt our tactical formations and our weapons, but what they cannot imitate is the moral force which is the principal element of the strength of the German army."[2]

Meanwhile Mary was being drawn closer into the web of what Queen Victoria called "the Royal Mob."[3] Princess Helena, the Queen's third daughter, liked to visit her eldest sister, the future Empress Vicky. Since Helena's husband, Prince Christian, was a member of the same extended family as Mary von Waldersee's first husband, there was a natural bond between them. In February of 1884, Mrs. Lee recorded,

> Prince and Princess Christian are in Berlin. Soon after their arrival the Prince called to see Mary, and the Princess set a day and hour for Mary to come to her, had Mary brought up to her room, and received her with affection- kissing her cheek on coming in and on leaving. This, you know, is extra for Royalty! They had a long talk. After this, on Sunday morning came a note from the Princess to Mary saying she would come to see her next day. On the same afternoon the Grand Chamberlain of the Crown Princess [Vicky] arrived to say to Alfred that the Princess instructed him to say she had been long wishing to come here, and finding her sister was to come the next day, if agreeable, she would join her. Of course word was sent back how greatly the honor would be appreciated, etc., etc.[4]

The royal visitors arrived the next day in "an elegant state carriage, with servants in grand livery," and stayed for more than an hour. Mrs. Lee, who did not speak German and suffered from increasing deafness, stayed in her room but was particularly pleased to write to her cousin, "Directly on the two Royalties reaching here, they enquired about me, and on leaving the Crown Princess said she had been disappointed in not seeing me." Mrs. Lee then quickly added to her cousin, "I don't relish blowing my own trumpet—hope the sound may die out before it gets over the water!"[5] During Princess Helena's visit she asked Mary to arrange to invite a few people in to meet her. As Mrs. Lee recorded the conversation, "'Certainly,' said Mary, 'But who would your Royal Highness like to meet?' 'Oh, well, dear, just invite whom you like.'" So Mary set plans in motion for a "soiree" on the evening of March seventh.[6] Royal visits became so commonplace that Mrs. Lee merely mentioned rather than described them. Her correspondence boasts many instances of royals "dropping by" unannounced, in addition to young Wilhelm, as well as several written "summons" for Mary to visit the crown prince's palace. At one point Mrs. Lee wrote home, "The last royalty that found himself in Alfred's bedroom was the Duke of Connaught [Prince Arthur, Queen Victoria's third son]—he asked to see Mary, told her he had heard his sister Princess Christian speak so often of her, that he wished to make her acquaintance himself."[7] The only day on which Mary turned down any invitation was for Sunday, which she declared should be spent in prayer. She broke her own rule on only very limited occasions and could rarely be persuaded to do so even by a royal summons. As her mother wrote of Mary's invitation to a "grand dinner" hosted by the emperor, "Being Sunday Mary could not think of going—Alfred respected her feelings and said he would have her excused, which he did— no easy matter, as an invitation from Royalty amounts to a command. Mary has taken pains to have it understood here, she cannot enter into visiting on Sunday. I must confess from the Empress down, her motive is appreciated."[8] Even when Mary was awarded in 1884 the Order of Louise, an order of chivalry limited to 100 women, she asked to be excused as the ceremony was to be held on a Sunday; the emperor agreed to award hers separately on a weekday.[9]

Only a few months after Princess Helena's visit, much of the Royal Mob was to be in Darmstadt for the marriage of the eldest daughter of Princess Alice, Queen Victoria's second daughter. In 1861, when the Queen's beloved consort (and first cousin), Prince Albert, contracted typhoid fever, it was their young daughter, Princess Alice, who nursed him back to health earning eternal gratitude from both her parents. The next year she married a relatively minor royal, Prince Louis, heir to the Grand Duchy of Hesse. Tragically, in 1878, when Alice's children contracted diphtheria, she caught the disease and became the first of Queen Victoria's children to die (on the anniversary of her father's death). The Queen took a vital interest in her grandchildren by Alice and felt it was her right and duty to meddle in their lives.[10] In fact, the Queen wrote to her eldest daughter, "These poor children have been like my own since their darling mother's death and I feel like an old hen when her ducklings go on the water."[11] Among those children, most of whom married well, would be Alix, the last tsarina of Russia.

Alice's husband had wisely remained a widower, as his mother-in-law would certainly have expected him to do in memory of dear Alice. In 1884, however, the Queen and most of her family traveled to Darmstadt for the marriage of Alice's eldest child, yet another Princess Victoria, who had been born at Windsor Castle with the Queen present. The family gathered to witness her marriage to a handsome if penniless minor royal, Prince Louis of Battenberg, her father's first cousin. He enjoyed a distinguished naval career, eventually becoming Admiral of the Fleet, and he and Victoria would become the grandparents of Prince Philip, Duke of Edinburgh, consort of Queen Elizabeth II.

The old Queen had her eye set on her widowed son-in-law, father of the bride, as a prospective husband for her youngest daughter, the shy

Beatrice (who did not bear any romantic interest in her brother-in-law). She was enraged, then, when, on the same day his daughter was married, he secretly married his mistress, the somewhat dissolute Alexandra Kolemine, the divorced wife of a diplomat.

Mrs. Lee faithfully reported on the event, relating how moved the Queen had been to visit the tomb of her late daughter, then continuing (with her own punctuation),

> The Grand Duke [of Hesse] witnessed the marriage of his daughter Victoria and entered into the festivities permitted on that occasion. "Hereby hangs a tale" which I only heard yesterday. On evening of that day, about 10 o'clock—the guests separated each going to their own rooms and it was supposed the Grand Duke went to his. He probably did—but when all was still he slipped out, went to the Mayor's and married a Russian woman—born a Countess but a "very disreputable character"—who after ceremony started for St. Petersburg and he, dropping his *grandeur*, slipped back to the Palace—thinking no mortal would know it. *But*—somehow next morning bag got open and out jumped the cat—Crown Princess [Vicky] happening to catch it. She said to her brother-in-law, "So you went and got married"—oh, no, he replied. But I know to the contrary—you certainly did. Oh, well, it was nothing but a civil marriage." [*sic*] Now I leave to your imagination how this great shock fell upon assembled Royalty—especially the Queen—who lost no time in leaving for England![12]

It took several weeks for the grand duke's marital knot to be untied. The bride "had been bought off for 500,000 marks (then £25,000). Who furnished the money is unknown, but it may well have been [Queen] Victoria."[13] At the time, Hermann Sahl, retired German secretary to the Queen, wrote to Sir Henry Ponsonby, the Queen's private secretary, "In the last few days, I have heard some remarkable details of the way the Queen of England alarmed and tyrannized over her family in Darmstadt. A quarter of an hour before dinner ... she would say which of the royal personages was to dine with her. The rest of them ate elsewhere. She completely ignored the attendants of the various princes and princesses." Even when her daughter, Vicky, the crown princess, presented her ladies-in-waiting, "the Queen did not even raise her eyes, and there was no question of her addressing even a single word to them."[14]

As if it weren't bad enough that the Queen lost the marital prospect for her daughter, Beatrice (there could be no question now that the grand duke had betrayed the family and been divorced), Beatrice found her own husband at the wedding ceremony. He was the groom's younger brother, the handsome Prince Henry of Battenberg. While a morganatic marriage might be acceptable for Queen Victoria's granddaughter, it was highly inadvisable for her daughter. The mother of Prince Louis and Prince Henry was a mere countess, Julia Hauke, perhaps partly of Jewish heritage, and her sons were not in any line of succession. The Queen finally gave her long-withheld consent only on the condition that the couple live with her so that Beatrice could remain serving as her secretary. Among their children was Victoria Eugenie, "Ena," Queen of Spain.

Hermann Sahl confided to his own diary the tyrannical Queen Victoria was "an undersized creature, almost as broad as she was long, who looked like a cook, had a bluish-red face and was more or less mentally deranged." He conceded that she was "very rich" and thought she would enjoy the wealth "for many years to come, unless the effects of alcohol prevent it."[15]

The next year Mrs. Lee wrote again,

> Princess Christian [Helena] is in town at her sister's Crown Princess. I have told you she is always very friendly for Mary—last Friday she sent for M. to come and see her—kept her a long time and on M.'s leaving told her she wanted to pass an evening here this week. Of course M. responded. After consultation with Alfred, M. wrote same evening to "Her Royal Highness" to ask what time would be agreeable, who she wished to meet, etc. Next day Princess went to Potsdam and could only reply to Mary on her return. She wrote Wednesday evening would suit her. It left but little time to secure all wished for, however M. and A. set to work, wrote out 70 cards and dispatched them by coachman Monday morning. Crown Prince and Princess, Prince and Princess William are invited, hence the busy time—very grand to be sure—but for myself I think friends coming with less ceremony are more enjoyable.[16]

As Mrs. Lee was writing the letter, Mary came up to her room and informed her that she had been downstairs with Prince William, who, of course, would attend.

Not only was Mary increasingly more intimate with the extended royal family, but her mounting influence was also becoming better known, although it is highly doubtful the disclosure would have pleased her. In 1888, the *New-York Daily Tribune* referred to her as "The Empress' American Rival," calling her "for many years one of the leaders of aristocratic society in Berlin." The story continued,

> When the present Crown Princess [Dona] was received with coolness by her royal mother-in-law [Vicky], and Prince William was lectured and snubbed by his father, the Countess [Mary] took compassion on them and made them the central figures in her set, thereby incurring the enmity of all the Anglo-Germans. Her influence over the Prince is strengthened by ties of relationship, since by her first marriage she is the grandaunt of the Crown Princess. But the real secret of her power in society and politics is inherent energy of character directed by ambition.[17]

Their verdict was that "the Countess' salon has been one of the gathering-places of rank and fashion, and has been frequented especially by German statesmen, generals and nobles who look with disfavor upon the present Empress and her English circle of admirers and partisans."[18] Another

10. "The Empress' American Rival"

American newspaper called her "the Chief of the Anti-Empress Victoria faction."[19] It was not the kind of publicity that would have endeared Mary to the empress, who referred to her in a letter to Queen Victoria as "a thoroughly good woman but violently low church ... and a great friend of Dona's."[20]

Those rumors of Mary's influence certainly reached inside the royal court. Mrs. Lee wrote to report that the king of Württemberg sent his personal representative, "a General in full uniform," to present to Mary the "Order of Olga," which the king had previously awarded to her sister, Josie. In the same letter, she reported on a grand dinner for 40 given by the ambassador of Prussia honoring the emperor and empress.

> Herbert Bismarck led Mary in to dinner and placed her at Emperor's left and Ambassador sat at his right. Emperor asked Mary if she was still "Commander in Chief"—you'll recall what paper said—it always amused his Majesty—he told Bismarck all about it and both declared it had been stated in English papers that "Countess Waldersee was the most dangerous woman at the Prussian Court." I told Pussy [her mother's pet name for her] she should have retorted as they were *warned* she couldn't be blamed if they were harmed! All this pleasantry made a smile for all it could reach.

Three nights later there was a dinner given by the French Ambassador at which "Duke Günther [the Duke of Schleswig Holstein], Empress' brother, led in Mary and she was 3rd from Emperor. I'm glad to say touching Royalty don't 'harm' her."[21]

Only a month later, Mrs. Lee wrote again of the same subject. "Notices in papers again—one in Paris paper—headed 'from Berlin'—speaking absurdly of Mary's 'great influence even in Europe'—and not finding cleverness enough in Princess William [Dona] to please her and lot more of same *I* say *stuff*—utterly false."[22] She referred again to a reference to Mary in the *London Truth* as "the commander in chief" of the Crown Princess's household. As Mrs. Lee wrote,

> You will be pleased to hear it has had contrary effect—sometimes when Alfred is leaving Crown Prince he will say Remember me to Commander-in-Chief! Soon after article in "Truth" Prince and Princess William invited Mary and Alfred to dine—among the guests was Crown Princess of Sweden and Prince Heinrich—after dinner Prince William laughingly announced—Countess Waldersee is our commander-in-chief!! When they returned in evening I was in Alfred's room below—he said to me, "Pussy is Commander-in-Chief!"[23]

Of course, Mary's access and influence, no matter how trivial or substantive, would have been increasingly resented by those who did not share it. There also would have been understandable gossip about the occasions the crown prince spent privately with Mary. As Mrs. Lee related one instance which underscored his ease with her,

> June 11th Alfred gave dinner to 12 officers—among them was Crown Prince William. Mary had strained sinew of her foot and could not go down—in evening Prince came up to her room to see her on the couch, Alfred and Count George [his brother] with him. He brought 2 beautiful bouquets—one from Princess and the other from himself to Mary. He chatted very pleasantly—moving his hand back and forth, light from lamp struck a splendid diamond on his finger.[24]

Mary's supposed power became such a topic of conversation that, soon after Wilhelm became emperor, Mrs. Lee wrote of "a long letter from Paris—written seriously—as though believed—urging Mary to use her influence with the Emperor in promoting peace!" Not only did Mary not attempt to keep it from him, she "took French letter along and showed it to the Emperor and Empress—it amused them very much and caused a general laugh."[25] Mrs. Lee tried to assure her cousins that Mary desired and held no power at court. She wrote just after a French paper alleged Mary was "the intermediary between Emperor and Bismarck—'it was very desirable to know whether Countess Waldersee was for peace or war'— these nothings go the round of papers—it is a marvel *why*? for Mary never interferes in affairs of State. Well it answers to laugh about!"[26] Evidently not everyone was laughing about the influence held by the von Waldersees.

In 1889, on the kaiser's birthday, Alfred wrote in his diary,

> I received the Grand Cross of the Order of the Red Eagle and in addition was made a Life Member of the *Herrenhaus* [the Prussian Upper House of Lords]. The Kaiser wants me to keep my eyes open regarding matters outside the purely military sphere, and is to reckon on me as a counselor occasionally in regard to Home and Foreign policy ... the Chancellor in consequence has looked on me more than once as a rival.[27]

Just a year later, he wrote, "I feel certain that I am an object of undiminished hate to the Chancellor—I imagine his wrath is particularly fierce now because there is no ground on which an attack can be made against me."[28]

As relations between the kaiser and Chancellor Bismarck further deteriorated, von Waldersee urged that he be forced to resign, to which the kaiser answered "he would rather the Chancellor resigned of his own accord, as it would look better before the world."[29] When Bismarck finally capitulated and tendered his resignation on March 18, 1890, he was given as recompense a new title of Duke of Lauenburg, which he joked would be useful when traveling incognito. Convinced that he would be recalled to service when the kaiser realized the error of his ways, Bismarck retired in resentment to his estate, proclaiming a year before his death with accurate prescience that the great European War "will come out of some damned foolish thing in the Balkans."[30] Mrs. Lee wrote home, "Berlin papers tell you is full of changes—the greatest is—resignation of Bismarck and his

10. "The Empress' American Rival"

Wilhelm's manipulation of von Waldersee as portrayed in *Puck*, vol. L, no. 1280 (Sept. 11, 1901) (Library of Congress).

son Herbert—which startled every one. The shock fell on me Monday. The capital is full of rumors and one must wait to know the truth."[31]

With Bismarck finally out of the way, many court observers believed that Alfred von Waldersee would be made chancellor. The *Boston Transcript* reported, "That General Waldersee is to be the next chancellor is settled, the denials of the official press notwithstanding."[32] Instead, the position was given to General Count Leo von Caprivi. Among the policies he was to pursue was opposition to von Waldersee's advocacy for a preventive war against Russia. "Caprivi will have a very difficult position and will scarcely manage to get on with the Kaiser,"[33] a jealous von Waldersee confided to his diary. Yet within two days von Caprivi visited Alfred to ask his counsel in how best to deal with the kaiser. His flattery did the job and von Waldersee wrote in his dairy, "Caprivi is an absolutely trustworthy man and he shall not be disappointed in me."[34]

In October of 1890, the von Waldersees' good friend and neighbor, Field Marshal von Moltke, celebrated his 90th birthday. They gave a "tête-à-tête lunch" with a serving tray engraved with von Moltke's initials and coronet in the center.[35] That afternoon Mrs. Lee went downstairs with Mary to return the visit and to marvel at the birthday gifts on display. Mrs. Lee, who was only three years younger than he, could not resist writing, "Moltke's dress was Military. But for the stubborn fact—his body was so erect and his step so firm no one could imagine his age."[36] Her hearing was almost nonexistent by this point and she carried a small writing book so her friends could write notes to her. As she recalled of von Moltke, "He wrote on my book nearly covering one page with pen and ink—how pleased he was that I came, etc., and gave me an Alpine lily." She would keep the page with his notes as a cherished memento of their friendship. That evening they all watched the "torch light procession" together.[37]

Evidently von Waldersee remained in the kaiser's good graces if frequent references to private conversations with him are to be believed. But his entries also began to include more complaints about his sovereign. "It has concerned me most of all to observe that the Kaiser has no fixed opinions. Luckily this has not been widely noticed. How often have I seen him waver to and fro between Austria and Russia! How many different opinions I have heard him express on persons! A man may be an excellent fellow today and count for nothing tomorrow."[38] The last statement should have been a warning to von Waldersee, who began to voice his doubts to a few confidantes.

In the fall of 1890, as events were conspiring against the count, the kaiser's sister, Princess Viktoria, wed in Berlin, on November 19, 1890, her lackluster fiancé, Adolph, Prince zu Schaumburg-Lippe. Called "Moretta" or "Young Vicky" in a family of too many Victorias, she was the one whose star-crossed engagement to the handsome Prince Sandro of Battenberg was thwarted. Of course, the kaiser and his wife, as well as his mother, the Dowager Empress Victoria, all attended her wedding, as did the von Waldersees.

Mrs. Lee took great care to write of Mary's preparations for the wedding, whom she affectionately addressed by the pet name "Pussy."

> My Pussy got new dress and made by man I *call* the great *bow wow* for dresses—under skirt white satin, waist and long court trains of silver brocade satin—also white—very elegant and such as I had never seen the like before—hair dressed with diamond broaches and white tips of ostrich feathers—all Pussy's diamonds sent out brightness here and there—necklace of three rows of pearls made expressly for her by our dear Prince [Noër]—the sizable diamond Anchor of hope from him and also the souvenir so valued, in shape of locket owned and worn by his grandmother the famed Caroline Matilda [Queen of Denmark, sister of Great Britain's King George III]. I must not forget the splendid diamond broach Alfred gave—from back of head fell tulle veil—the rest I leave to your imagination.[39]

Fortunately, she also included her son-in-law in her compliments, finding him "in gala attire—his brilliant stars, cordon and all—well, I said to him, 'I don't think you'll see any one you like better than my Pussy'—he and I agreed!"[40]

In the fall of 1890, the kaiser made a decision that surprised his senior staff and had momentous effect upon the count. He would personally participate in planned two-day military maneuvers.

> On September 19, 1890, during the army's maneuvers in Silesia, the Kaiser took command of an army corps, which, unknown to him, would most likely fail according to the plans Waldersee crafted. Receiving many thanks for letting the Kaiser face failure for once, Waldersee replied that he was only doing his duty, but he knew he would have to pay dearly for it. After Wilhelm's inevitable defeat, the Chief of Staff had to provide an assessment of the military exercises. In the presence of Prussian officers and generals, the Emperor of Austria, the King and Crown Prince of Saxony, and the Crown Prince of Bavaria, he [Waldersee] tactfully critiqued the Kaiser for his poor performance.[41]

The count did not employ tact in his own diary, however, when he insisted, "He has had no war experience, hence come his exaggerated notions as to the extent to which cavalry can be used.... He is always determined to win, and therefore takes in ill part any decisions given by the umpire against him."[42] There is no surprise that the kaiser was furious at his public humiliation. Making excuses and deluding himself that there would be no consequences, von Waldersee wrote in his diary, "If he bears me a grudge because of his poor command of troops he shows that he lacks greatness of spirit and deserves to be treated as a little man. But if he has allowed himself to reflect calmly and to examine himself a little, he cannot but be grateful to me and tell himself that I acted without fear and did my duty. Then one could say: there is nobility in him after all."[43]

Only four months later, the kaiser "sent for the Count, decorated him with the Grand Commander of the Hohenzollern Order, and told him he had an important new appointment for him—command of an army corps. The fall from chief of the German staff to a corps commander was so great, Waldersee could find no words in reply."[44] After fuming overnight, the count decided to retire but the kaiser refused to consider it. "He took my hand and said: 'You will accept, won't you? Your Kaiser asks you.' I remained adamant, however, and I thank God that he gave me the strength to do so."[45] Finally realizing that his only hope was to regain the confidence of his sovereign, however, von Waldersee then accepted the appointment as corps commander at Altona, a post that would take him and Mary far from the court life in which they had flourished. He was particularly appalled that the kaiser employed Mary's name as an argument for accepting the new appointment, as the count recorded the conversation in his dairy, "'Your wife, I am sure, will rejoice at returning to her native place' (she never lived there!). 'She has made so exceptionally a distinguished a position for herself here in Berlin that she will soon be able to do the same there, moreover, she will be able to exercise an admirable influence on Hamburg.' (So Marie is to associate with the anti–Church, Social-Democratic women! A nice mission!)"[46]

Mrs. Lee took great care to let her American cousins know of their heartbreak in a lengthy letter in which she wrote of "the great surprise that has roused Berlin" and underscored the words "Resignation of Alfred."

> Alfred is directed—Emperor would not accept his resignation—to take command of 9th Army Corps at Altona in Holstein—close to Hamburg. Alfred and faithful Heinrich [his servant] left this morning to go there.... When Emperor first spoke to Alfred of the appointment he "assured A. he was very much attached to him"—this deepens the "mystery" as it is called. Last evening Mary had telegram from Alfred that he had been on saddle 4 hours riding in all directions to find out what his duties were. On the 4th Emperor gave to Alfred a long audience and quite alone they had interesting talk with each other—three times the Emperor embraced Alfred in most affectionate manner. Well, we must wait patiently to learn what the Lord means by it. You will be pleased that the circumstances have caused all to praise Alfred and their opinion has gone up as high as it possibly can go—they "call Count Waldersee a chief prop and column of the State and express for him the strongest hope." I must say what is true of Alfred—He has not a bit of envy but seemingly to me a most conscientious man and always ready to serve in best way he could his King and Country.[47]

10. "The Empress' American Rival"

If anyone expected Alfred to denigrate the kaiser he would have been mistaken.

> He made a beautiful speech on taking leave of his companions for years—the General Staff—everyone was greatly moved and felt it deeply—he said a true solder must obey without asking the why? Emperor maintains he is much attached to Alfred and makes the change for his benefit—what that may be is difficult for us to see. But by no means difficult for Mary and myself to see it is *not* for our benefit to empty this great apartment which must be accomplished in *March*! Sorrow prevails—Mary has constant notes of sadness. Duchess of Baden [the kaiser's aunt] sent Telegram of her sorrow—how hard it will be for her to come to Berlin and not see Mary.[48]

And yet on that same day the news was delivered, "Last evening Mary had to make extra dress—white satin—long train embroidered in gold—diamonds and pearls—tips of white ostrich feathers—tulle veil back of head—all very elegant and go to Castle to what is called the cour. You must think of us and pray for us—it is only by the Lord's help we can bear up."[49] Knowing that it might be dangerous to commit full details in a letter, Mrs. Lee added, "I could tell you much if face to face."[50]

She did add some details in a subsequent letter, explaining,

> On evening of "Birthday" Alfred was with the Emperor who spoke to him of "9th Army Corps." Alfred was surprised—told the Emperor his feelings were much wounded and frankly his opinion. He hurried home wrote his resignation and sent it in—in doing that he meant to leave the service. But the Emperor would not accept it—they had a long and private audience. Emperor assured Alfred he was as much attached to him as ever and embraced him 3 times—that he wanted Alfred to take command of 9th Army Corps and fit it for war in case war should come—so Alfred still full of health and vigor and ready to serve his Country accepted.[51]

The clever Mrs. Lee did not see it in the same light, adding, "Emperor affirms he made change also for Alfred's benefit. I confess Alfred don't see exactly in that light! Certain it is—that emptying this great apartment—where things have accumulated for years is no *benefit* to Pussy and myself—there seems no end to them and makes me often think—'blessed be nothing!'"[52]

Just the week before, Alfred and Mary had been invited to the royal family's private christening of the kaiser's sixth son, Prince Joachim (the kaiser himself came down to tell the von Waldersees of his birth), and the next night they gave a "dinner in library here of 65 covers in honor of the Emperor."[53] Mrs. Lee could not resist writing, "I was only sorry it was not a daughter—5 sons I think are heirs enough for the throne."[54] Also within the week, the "Grand Mistress of Empress called here—but Mary was out—last evening she sent a letter telling of her sorrow to miss Mary on 7th, also that the Empress wished Mary to come today at 3 o'clock for private audience—begged Mary to come earlier so she could first come in to see her the Grand Mistress. I'm particular to tell detail so you may know how high and low sympathize in this sad going away." When Mary's meeting with the Empress took place, she "tried to comfort Mary and told her to write to her."[55] While the Empress was deeply sorry to lose her friend and mentor, she certainly knew better than to intervene in her husband's decision.

Mrs. Lee kept her cousin informed, writing from Altona on March 17,

> Here we are, dearest Mary—leaving Berlin as expected on 5th. My darling Pussy's eyes filled with tears as we stepped for the last time from the home that so long had been a happy one—friends were coming all the days to see her. Y.M.C.A. were determined to honor her in a special way—they made it known and crowds came to their building—in the large hall they garlanded with flowers an arm chair for her seat.[56]

While there was consternation by some on Count von Waldersee's demotion, there was universal sadness at Mary's departure. A Baden newspaper published the following extract from a conservative Berlin press:

> With the Chief of the general staff, Count Waldersee, his wife will likewise quit Berlin soon. All the friends of God's kingdom must deeply regret this loss, as it cannot be replaced. What has this faithful noble and true Christian woman been to the city of Berlin, to the evangelical Christians therein! We do not wish to laud man in any way, for here likewise we may say: "By grace I am *what* I am," and: "To whom much is given, from him will much be required." Still many hearts desire it to be made known here, with what sorrow we see her depart. The Y.M.C.A., the Berlin City mission, the Oberlinverein, the Magdalene mission, the mission amongst cab-drivers and many others, down to the Sunday schools, know what they had in her. She was the prima [first] and ultima ratio [last resort] of the inner mission, and no Christian undertaking ever sought her in vain. That she has been a personal angel of comfort to many sufferers we will only hint at. "Let not the left hand know what the right hand doeth." We feel and know it well, that with her own meek and humble spirit, she will not like the foregoing to be publicly said, still gratitude has also a right to speak a word, and all the more, as the Countess does not look to thanks from mankind, but acts and performs her charities in looking up to Him who has said: "What ye have done unto one of these little ones, ye have done it unto me!"[57]

Chapter 11

Distaff Diplomacy

Mary was almost completely surrounded by men other than her one constant female companion and assistant, Maria. She had no children and, of course, all the military officers surrounding her were male. She certainly had female friends in her active charitable work, but they could not be considered part of the society into which Mary was expected to be somewhat active. In 1890, a New York magazine mentioned "an intimate friend" of hers whose life was almost as interesting as Mary's. The magazine referred to the friend as "one of the handsomest women in Europe. She is one of the most brilliant amateur musicians in Germany."[1]

Romaine Madeleine Goddard was a wealthy American born in Ohio in July of 1847, making her nine years younger than Mary. Her mother, Sarah Madeleine Vinton, was the daughter of Samuel Finley Vinton (1792–1862), a Congressman from Ohio and leading figure in the national Whig party as well as an extremely rich coal mine owner. In the 30th Congress he declined the speakership but accepted the chairmanship of the Ways and Means Committee. He rejected President Fillmore's offer to become secretary of the Interior and became a railroad president instead, retiring to Washington, D.C., with his wealth in 1854.

Samuel Vinton's daughter, Sarah, married in 1846 her first husband, Daniel Convers Goddard, an attorney who became deputy secretary of the Interior. Their wedding was attended by his classmate, future president Rutherford B. Hayes. Goddard died in 1852 leaving her with a daughter, Romaine, who was to become Mary von Waldersee's friend, and a son, Vinton, born in 1850. The widowed Sarah retreated with her little family to her father's home in Washington, D.C., and became a prolific writer as well as an anti-suffragist.

In 1865, Sarah married Admiral John A. Dahlgren (1809–1870), a famous naval officer and inventor of the Dahlgren gun, a cast-iron muzzle-loading cannon. He helped General William T. Sherman secure Savannah, Georgia (which must have been particularly distressing to Dahlgren's brother, Charles, who was a brigadier general in the Confederate states army). By this second marriage to Dahlgren, Sarah had two sons, John and Eric, who married very wealthy Drexel sisters from Philadelphia,[2] and a daughter, Ulrica (Eric and Ulrica were twins). She would become the grandmother of Romaine Dahlgren Pierce, wife of David Mountbatten, 3rd Marquess of Milford Haven, who served as best man to his first cousin, Prince Philip, when he married in 1947 Princess Elizabeth, later Queen Elizabeth II.[3] The royal and noble marriages did not end there, as Romaine's Goddard cousin, Maud Ely-Goddard, married in Paris in 1884 Charles, Prince Poniatowski.[4]

Mary's friend, Romaine Madeleine Goddard, was married in a high-profile wedding at her mother's home in Washington, D.C., on March 16, 1870 (four years before Mary's marriage to von Waldersee), to diplomat Gustav von Overbeck of Austria (1830–1894), in a ceremony attended by President and Mrs. Ulysses S. Grant, Chief Justice Salmon P. Chase, several cabinet members, and many ambassadors.[5] She was escorted down the aisle by her brother, Vinton, and her stepfather recorded of the day, "It would be difficult to conceive a more wild, wintry morning than this. A white snow whitens every object, and is driven with violence through the air by a strong N.W. gale that howls around the corners of the house, down the chimneys, and moans at every crevice of door and window."[6]

The groom had a life that would not be believed if written as fiction. Born in Lemgo, Lippe-Detmold (in North Rhine-Westphalia), on March 4, 1830, von Overbeck was knighted by the emperor of Austria on March 24, 1867, and created a baron on October 27, 1873. He came to America in 1850 then went to Hong Kong in 1854 to accept a job with the British trading house of Dent and Company. There, he was appointed Prussian vice-consul in 1856, and in 1864 became the imperial and royal Austrian consul, resigning in 1866 because of the Prussian-Austrian War. While in Hong Kong he had four children by a native woman, Lam Tsat Tai. In 1869, the year before he married Romaine Goddard, von Overbeck transferred two lots of property in Hong Kong to Lam "to provide for her and her children." She later sold those lots in 1875 to a Chinese trader for $6,500, and then came under "the protection" of an American, Edward Constant Ray, by whom she had additional children.[7] One of von Overbeck's Chinese daughters, Oi Moon Chan, married Chan Kai Ming (also known as George B. Tyson), head of the Hong Kong opium monopoly and eventually one of the richest men in Hong Kong.

As noted, von Overbeck was elevated to the Austrian nobility before his marriage and met his wife while serving in Washington. Whether she knew about his other family is unrecorded, but it seems unlikely he could have kept that secret indefinitely. He and Romaine lived for a while in Stuttgart, where their youngest son, Alfred, was born in 1877, but the baron soon returned to Hong Kong, leaving Romaine to her own devices. She was an accomplished pianist and returned to her family's home in the U.S. capitol while her husband pursued his business interests in Asia. Between his frequent trips abroad, the couple had two sons, Convers in 1871 and Oscar in 1873. Another brother, Alfred, would eventually join them in 1877.

As the Baroness von Overbeck, Romaine was befriended by Kurd von Schlözer, German ambassador to the United States from 1871 to 1882. In 1875, he introduced her to Hans von Bülow (1830–1894), a German conductor, virtuoso pianist, and composer. As a child, von Bülow was a student of Clara Schumann's father, but his parents, wishing him to be an attorney instead of a musician, sent him to Leipzig to study. There he met Franz Liszt and heard the premiere of Richard Wagner's *Lohengrin* in 1850. The law was forgotten, and, on Wagner's recommendation, he was given his first conducting job in Zurich. In 1851, he began studying with Liszt, marrying his daughter, Cosima, in 1857. They had two daughters as his career continued to excel, and, in the year he married Cosima, he premiered in Berlin her father's Piano Concerto in B minor.

Conducting the premiere of two of Wagner's operas, *Tristan und Isolde* and *Die Meistersinger von Nürnberg* in 1865 and 1868, his professional career continued its dramatic rise even while his personal life was shattering. His wife, Cosima, began an affair with Richard Wagner and had two daughters by him while her husband refused to grant her a divorce. Finally, after she gave birth to Wagner's son, von Bülow relented and they divorced in 1870.

During von Bülow's 1875 American tour, while in Washington, Ambassador von Schlözer, who thought Romaine was talented enough as a pianist to have become a professional, introduced von Bülow to the talented and attractive Baroness Overbeck on December 9 at a post-concert reception at the German embassy. Still distressed over his divorce and his former wife's treatment of him, von Bülow immediately was smitten with Romaine, as he "was quickly swept away by her charms, and appears to have built up some false hopes of a permanent liaison."[8]

Von Bülow's letters to Baroness Overbeck quickly became fervent. Five days after their meeting, just before leaving Washington, he wrote to her, "If I don't see you again in two weeks in New York, I'll kill myself."[9] She did see him twice more in New York City, and he then wrote to his mother to enlist her help in having his diplomat brother-in-law intercede to prevent Romaine's husband from being called back to Washington from his official duties in Hong Kong. Von Bülow wrote to the ambassador who had introduced them, "Oh, the Romaine question! To be or not to be! ... I'm half out of my mind—and all because you introduced me to paradise!— and at the age of 45, too!—But age is no guarantee against the ravages of youth."[10]

While it is unclear whether the relationship was physically consummated, the baroness knew she had too much to risk by accepting his offer. She finally agreed to meet him in Baltimore but did not appear, her absence making it clear to von Bülow that she was not going to leave her husband and sons for him. He wrote to her, "I imagine that as a child you amused yourself by tormenting flies and butterflies, considering that you excel with virtuosity in making me suffer, me who loves you, me who adores you so—superlatively!"[11]

Von Bülow would continue his distinguished career, serving as the soloist in the world premiere of the Tchaikovsky Piano Concerto No. 1 in B-flat minor in Boston in 1875. He was also the first to perform the complete cycle of Beethoven's piano sonatas, which he played entirely by memory. From 1878 to 1880 he served as Hofkapellmeister in Hanover but a public disagreement with his star tenor forced his resignation. The tenor was singing the "Knight of the Swan" role in *Lohengrin*, but von Bülow, upon hearing him sing, called him the "Knight of the Swine [Schwan/Schwein]." After moving to Meiningen he became a great champion of Richard Strauss's, giving him his first job as a conductor. In 1882, von Bülow married the actress Marie Schanzer and died in Cairo in 1890.

And what of the Baron and Baroness von Overbeck? In early 1876 he paid $15,000 for the soon-to-be-expiring commission rights of the American Trading Company to certain territories of North Borneo, conditioned upon his securing an extension of those rights from Brunei's ruler. The next year he formed a joint partnership with his former employer, Dent and Company, then sailed to Borneo in charge of the steamer *America* as the Austrian consul in Hong Kong. In a meeting with the Sultan of Brunei at the Brunei Palace on December 29, 1877, von Overbeck was successful in securing the concession. The sultan's signature created von Overbeck "Maharajah of Sabah, Rajah of Gaya and Sandakan." Three weeks later he received a further concession from the Sultan of Sulu, who also held some of the rights, creating von Overbeck "Dato Bendahara and Rajah of Sandakan" on January 22, 1878.[12] The *Washington Post* reported at the time, "This cession is one of the greatest secured by a commercial company since the days of the famous East India Company."[13] Von Overbeck even had the power to coin money, raise an army, and impose customs.

Much like the British Brooke family who ruled as the Rajahs of Sarawak, also on Borneo, from 1841 to 1946, von Overbeck's commission gave him "the power of life and death over the inhabitants with all the absolute property rights invested in us over the soil and the country."[14] Sarawak remained a separate crown colony until 1963 when it joined Malaysia.

At the point of the sultan's signature, the American-born Romaine Goddard, Baroness von Overbeck, became the Maharani of Sabah along with several subsidiary titles. She was the first American woman to become a maharani, a dignity that was not conferred again on an American woman until 1928, when Nancy Miller married the Maharaja of Indore.[15] Romaine's husband, having failed to enlist Austria's assistance in developing Sabah, eventually transferred his rights to his former partner, Alfred Dent, who in 1882 formed the British North Borneo Company. "Although it became a protectorate, control remained in the hands of the Company until the Japanese invasion. In 1946 it became a separate Crown Colony.... In 1963 colonial rule ended and it joined Malaysia as the state of Sabah."[16]

Romaine moved to Germany when her husband was given a diplomatic post and she lived in Baden-Baden and in Berlin. They separated but, of course, never divorced, as his diplomatic career would have been as badly affected as her position in society. She could easily thrive on the substantial income she enjoyed from her family's coal-mining interests in Ohio. In fact, a legal dispute among the Dahlgren and Overbeck descendants concerning their share of a still-large estate began in 1862 and continued until 1928, two years after Romaine's death.[17] Her youngest son, Alfred, had married in 1923 Theodora van Bueren, and Romaine lived to see the 1925 birth of her grandson, Alfred E. von Overbeck, a highly respected Swiss legal scholar and the principal draftsman of the Hague Convention on Trusts. Romaine's husband died in London on May 8, 1894, at the age of 63.[18] Even today, there is still a legal dispute between Malaysia and the Philippines over the ownership of Sabah.

Romaine became very attached to Mary and to her mother, who wrote home about "our intimate friend, Baroness von Overbeck ... [who] has become much attached to me, calls me and constantly writes me as 'dearest Second Mother.' I think it strange as she is still young—about 30—is now at Baden-Baden—her husband is in London."[19] Mary had earlier written to her mother from Copenhagen that Romaine's mother was "a fashionable woman, absorbed by earthly things—this daughter is just the reverse—

otherwise we should not take to her as we do."[20] Mrs. Lee had an opportunity to judge for herself the merits of Romaine's husband when he brought "a small chest of extra fine tea that came to him direct from China—where you know they lived for many years." She found the baron "a perfect man of the world—has had a very eventful life and can tell much that interests one and we passed a pleasant evening."[21]

Romaine wrote to Mrs. Lee on her birthday, addressing her as "my precious 2nd Mother," sending a blanket she had made, adding, "I only hope you will not think it unworthy of a modest place in your room, perhaps on the dear red sofa where we had so many nice talks together, alas, now long ago. If you will use it to throw over your feet when you are resting, and then think of the absent, loving little friend who made it, I shall be content."[22]

Like Mary, Romaine had left her native country as a young woman and only returned as a visitor. Mary understood the sacrifices necessary for a wife of a German diplomat or military officer, and Romaine's friendship and advice would be put to great use in later years when Mary needed it most.

Mary's charitable work often brought her into direct contact with the beneficiaries of her generosity. A boy named William Boetcker, born in Altona near Hamburg, was only eight years old when his father was beaten by striking workers at the factory where he was employed. The boy's interest in labor relations was sparked by the incident, and, when he was only 17, he published a book about puzzles and riddles. Mary heard about him and, impressed with the young man's intellect, offered to pay his $65 steamship passage to America, where she thought he would have a much better chance to thrive.

Boetcker arrived in Chicago in 1891 and enrolled in the Chicago Theological Seminary. Since he spoke no English and his professors knew no German, they conversed in Latin. After two years he transferred to the German Theological School in Newark, New Jersey, where he graduated in 1897. Boetcker was ordained as a minister by the Reformed Church of America and eventually became a successful Presbyterian leader and public speaker. He remained in contact with Mary von Waldersee and credited her with having placed such a high level of trust in him and his prospects.[23]

In 1896, Mary received a public recognition of her many services to the kaiser and his family. In January of that year, he instituted a new order named for his grandfather, Wilhelm I ("the Great"). The Wilhelm Order was created to celebrate the 25th anniversary of the proclamation of the Prussian Empire. The first recipients were the emperor and empress, the

Dowager Empress Friedrich (Vicky), the Grand Duchess of Baden (the emperor's aunt), and the king of Saxony. The next awardee and first non-royal to receive the award was Mary von Waldersee.[24] Although she had been given several awards by the kaiser as well as by other sovereigns, this one meant enough to her that she arranged for a formal studio portrait to be taken of her wearing it around her neck. Later that year she wrote from Josie's estate at Lautenbach that the emperor and empress invited Alfred and Mary to "dine with them on their splendid Hohenzollern 'lying in the bay.' Their Majesties were very gracious and both looked very well. I wore my new Wilhelm Order and profited by the occasion to express my thanks in person to His Majesty for his gracious gift which I had already done in writing."[25]

Older Mary (*Von Klarheit zu Klarheit*).

Of course, her husband had been given many orders, including the Order of the Black Eagle, the highest order of chivalry in the kingdom of Prussia, as well as the "plaque and grand cordon of the Prussian Order of the Red Eagle" and the Pour le Mérite (with oak leaves),[26] given when he returned from his post in China, and Württemberg's Military Merit Order. His foreign decorations included the Honorary Knight Grand Cross (Military) of the Order of the Bath from Great Britain,[27] the Order of St. Andrew (with brilliants and sword), personally conferred by Russia's Tsar Nicholas II, and two he was given in Italy, the Grand Cross of the Military Order of Savoy and the Order of Pius XI, as well as the Polish Order of the White Eagle, given to him while the tsar was visiting Berlin. Alfred also was given the prized order of the Legion of Honor, and, knowing how anti–French he was, Mrs. Lee wrote, "When telling us of it he laughingly said he had not expected to wear a *French* Order!"[28]

When the emperor of Austria gave him the Order of Leopold, Mrs. Lee wrote home that he had been given "the high Order of Leopold set in diamonds. Alfred had the Order already, but not in diamonds. Well, I said to Pussy, if all trades fail—Alfred can open a show of Diamonds!"[29] The next year, when Alfred and Mary were invited to an elegant dinner including the king of Saxony, Mrs. Lee wrote that Alfred was "in full uniform with his grand Orders—broad blue cordon and great Star of Russia, composed entirely of diamonds, making a most brilliant show." Mary was equally dressed: "On her head was a hat—a beautiful white ostrich feather encircled and quite over-powered the so called hat—her dress was dark purple satin—lilac brocade trimming—over this she wore the richly embroidered white crepe shawl long ago mine. I was pleased it should go into the presence of Royalty—certainly the last place I ever thought it would appear in!"[30]

Mary with her mother, Ann D. Lee (*Harvard Alumni Bulletin* 38, no. 15 (Jan. 17, 1936) (photograph of original photograph [undated] by a staff photographer of *The Christian Science Monitor*, reproduced courtesy *The Christian Science Monitor*).

Chapter 12

Command in the Boxer Rebellion

As Count von Waldersee continued to seethe over being passed over once again for the chancellorship that had been promised him, events in Asia unexpectedly changed his fortunes. Surprisingly there was another American bride involved as well. On February 24, 1897, in Detroit's Saints Peter and Paul Jesuit Church, Matilda Cass Ledyard married Baron August von Ketteler, then the German minister to Mexico. Detroit's bishop performed the ceremony, and a special dispensation was granted by the archbishop since the bride was not Catholic. The groom, whose uncle was the influential Catholic Bishop of Mainz, was born in 1853 at Münsterland in North Rhine–Westphalia and had served in the Prussian army before being appointed to the diplomatic corps in 1882. He spoke Chinese fluently and first served as an interpreter at the German consulates in Guangzhou and Tientsin. The baron was then posted to Washington, D.C., between 1892 and 1896, where he met his wife, before being assigned to Mexico in 1896.

The bride, born in 1871, was called "Maud" by her friends and family and was a descendant of the distinguished Livingston and Schuyler families, having included among her ancestors U.S. Supreme Court Justice Henry Brockholst Livingston and New Jersey Governor William Livingston. Maud's father, Henry Brockholst Ledyard, was born in the American embassy in Paris while his grandfather, General Lewis Cass (long-time governor of the Michigan territory and U.S. Secretary of State), was serving as United States minister to France, and his father, Henry Ledyard, was serving as secretary of the legation in Paris.

Ledyard was president of the Michigan Central Railroad and of the Union Trust Company, and married, in 1867, Mary L'Hommedieu, whose father, Stephen L'Hommedieu of Cincinnati, was president of the Cincinnati,

Hamilton & Dayton Railroad. Henry B. Ledyard's brother, Lewis Cass Ledyard, was personal counsel to J. P. Morgan and commodore of the New York Yacht Club. Maud was therefore not only wealthy but of very distinguished lineage.

She met her future husband while visiting in Washington her close friend Amy McMillan, whose wealthy father was Michigan's senator, James McMillan. (Amy would eventually become Lady Harrington, wife of Sir John Harrington, British ambassador to Ethiopia; after her husband's death she would renounce her title and regain U.S. citizenship.)[1] Maud was described by contemporaries as "a tall and handsome girl, with her delicate rose-tinted complexion, large blue eyes, and soft-blonde hair."[2] The baron proposed rather quickly, which one can hope was more attributable to her charms than to her considerable fortune. The kaiser, however, was not fond of his diplomats marrying foreign brides (particularly one who was 18 years younger than the groom) but negotiations were finally successful.[3] At their wedding, Amy McMillan, who had originally introduced the pair, acted as Maud's only attendant while the groom was assisted by the second secretary at the German legation in Washington, Baron Adolf von Brüning (who would two years later marry his own wealthy American wife, divorcée Marion Treat McKay, after receiving the kaiser's approval only with great difficulty and delay). The German ambassador in Washington, Baron Max von Thielman, attended the ceremony, which attached an imprimatur of official sanction.[4] The groom wore his diplomatic uniform and the church was decorated in green and white, the colors of Mexico.

The couple returned to his post in Mexico where they remained for two years before von Ketteler was named the German ambassador to China in 1899. Their appointment to Peking could not have come at a worse time. The Boxer Rebellion, a violent struggle against foreigners and Christians, began within weeks of their arrival, and, immediately sensing the impending danger, von Ketteler warned fellow Europeans not to travel to the country.

American missionaries who wished to convert the "yellow hordes" to Christ first named the athletic young men who made up the rebellion "boxers" because they were active proponents of martial arts and boxing. The Boxers practiced spirit possession, which consisted of "the whirling of swords, violent prostrations, and chanting incantations to Taoist and Buddhist spirits."[5] They believed that, with proper training and sufficient prayer, they could actually fly and would summon to their side great warriors from the sky. They also believed themselves to be impervious to bullets and cannon fire.

12. Command in the Boxer Rebellion 139

A great drought followed by floods in one province led to widespread food shortages throughout China. Foreign missionaries had been given the legal right to seek converts anywhere and to purchase land to build Christian churches.[6] When two German missionaries were murdered in 1897, Kaiser Wilhelm II took advantage of the opportunity to order the occupation of a bay on the Shandong peninsula and to press for concessions. In October of the next year the Boxers attacked a Catholic church that had been built on the site of a shrine to the Jade Emperor. Relations became even more strained when the French minister in Beijing secured official status for every order within the Catholic hierarchy. As one Chinese official proclaimed, "Take away your missionaries and your opium and you will be welcome."[7] As part of the great powers' efforts to subjugate China, they forced their acceptance of importing opium, which resulted in widespread addiction.[8] On May 31, 400 soldiers from eight different countries arrived by boat at the port of Tianjin and immediately boarded trains for Beijing. In retaliation, Boxers destroyed the rail lines into Tianjin on June 5 to prevent reinforcements from arriving.

On June 12, 1900, the Boxers invaded the inner city of Beijing, burning down churches in their path. Ambassador von Ketteler's reaction was to order his embassy guards to hunt down the criminals by any means necessary. Two days later German soldiers protected their embassy from Boxers who were attempting to storm the building, killing more than a dozen. An already explosive situation became even worse when, on June 18, German soldiers captured a Chinese civilian who was suspected of being a Boxer and took him to their legation. A gathering crowd demanding his release was fired upon by Austrian guards and many were wounded.

Although a high-ranking British officer warned von Ketteler against drastic action, he ignored the advice and had his soldiers shoot at Chinese Muslims who were throwing stones at the German embassy. Von Ketteler brutally attacked a Chinese civilian then beat a boy after taking him back to the legation. In full view of the protestors, von Ketteler shot the boy in the head.[9]

Not surprisingly, thousands of Boxers and Chinese Muslims immediately began wanton killing of westerners and Chinese Christians, even roasting alive a few who had been assisting the Germans. Several Catholic priests were killed, and the Japanese chancellor was torn limb from limb.[10]

On the morning of June 20, von Ketteler's party, accompanied by armed guards, was ambushed only one block from their destination, the Ministry of Foreign Affairs, where they were to participate in a meeting with Chinese officials. The ambassador was specifically targeted for murder in retaliation for having killed the boy days earlier (his killer proudly turned himself in after attempting to sell von Ketteler's watch and refused to express regret before his own execution). A Muslim commander then ripped the skin off von Ketteler's body and ate his heart.[11] His head was paraded through the streets stuck on a spear while his mutilated body was quickly placed in a freshly dug unmarked grave. Much later the kaiser ordered that it be disinterred and brought back to Germany for burial.[12]

It took quite some time before news of the murder could reach the United States, and it was feared that Maud, the Baroness von Ketteler, might have suffered the same fate as her husband. In fact, a prominent American newspaper reported, "There is a woman in China for whom the greatest concern is felt in this city. Indeed, there are those who have almost become satisfied that the worst has occurred." The article recounted of her family, "The Ledyard family appears to be pursued by some fatality. A couple of years ago Mrs. Ledyard [Maud's mother], who had always been well … dropped dead in the street; and within a year a son, Cass Ledyard, was killed in the Philippines where he had gone with the army. The body reached Detroit only a few weeks ago at just about the time that news of the Chinese disturbance came."[13]

Maud's American family still heard no news of her. In fact, her father "spent a small fortune in cable tolls endeavoring to obtain information regarding his daughter, and has all but lost his health owing to her danger and the loss of his son, Lieutenant Ledyard, who was killed in the Philippines."[14]

And what actually happened to Maud during those anxious weeks after her husband's murder? Sarah Conger, wife of the U.S. Minister to China, Edwin H. Conger, (whom American newspapers immediately reported as "undoubtedly dead" along with all the Americans then living in Beijing), was deputed to break the news of Maud's husband's death. As she later recalled, "It fell upon me to state to the wife of the German Minister what had happened. She is a young, sweet American woman. How my heart ached for her. I did so wish that I could blot the whole thing out of her life."[15]

Maud refused to believe what she was being told and it took three hours for Mrs. Conger to convince her that she would never see her husband again. With the Japanese and German ministers dead, the remaining diplomatic representatives and their guests had every reason to fear for their safety. It was decided that because the British legation was the largest (approximately seven acres) as well as the easiest to defend, all the foreign diplomats and their families would immediately move there. Thus Sarah

Conger had to convince the new widow to pack up immediately and move out of her home only hours after learning of her husband's death.

There, virtually cut off from the outside world, Maud had little privacy to grieve. Mary Gamewell, wife of a Methodist missionary in China, wrote of watching a grief-stricken Maud standing at the window just as morning light broke through. "One day she caught her black robes about her and stepped toward me. We clasped hands…. She looked only a girl." She reported that Maud was sitting with Polly Condit Smith, a Boston girl whose supposed death had also been mistakenly reported by the *San Francisco Call*.

> One day a bullet whistled past her [Maud's] ear as she and Polly were sitting on a bench on the tennis court. Polly immediately dropped to the ground and tried to pull the baroness under her but she refused. Polly was forced to find a young student to help her and between them they dragged the despairing widow back to the British Legation. Polly believed that "in her agony of mind … a bullet to end her suffering would have been truly welcomed."[16]

What the outside world had no way of knowing at the time was that as many as 900 soldiers, marines, and civilians from Europe, Japan, and the United States, as well as about 2,800 Chinese Christians, took refuge in the Beijing Legation Quarter for 55 days as they held out against the violence directed at them by Boxers and Chinese Muslims. The area allotted to foreign diplomats was approximately two miles long by one mile wide, housing 11 legations as well as some foreign banks and businesses. Knowing that they would all face certain death if captured, the British, American, French, German, Japanese, and Russian military guards each in turn took responsibility for the defense of their legations while the Austrians and Italians abandoned theirs, allying themselves respectively with the French and the Japanese, as the two were outside the larger area and thus very difficult to defend. Food and water became rather scarce and the missionaries shared theirs with Christian converts although not with starving Chinese Catholics.

Both the American and the British ministers wired home asking for immediate military support to defend the besieged legations. The National Library of China, located near the British legation, was burned in an attempt to destroy the Legation Quarter, and all its books were lost. There were also repeated efforts to dig tunnels into the quarter. The Chinese lit firecrackers all night in an effort to prevent sleep within the quarter. Learning that an allied force of 20,000 soldiers had landed at Tianjin, the Chinese agreed to an armistice, although they almost certainly would not have done so had they known that more than one-third of the besieged legation guards were dead or wounded.[17]

The first word from outside the quarter came on July 28, when a Chinese boy was able to sneak inside the gates with news of coming reinforcements. Finally, on August 14, almost six weeks after von Ketteler's murder, the British, American, Japanese, Russian and French troops advanced on the quarter's wall, each with a specific gate as its objective. Chinese resistance delayed the Japanese and Russians while the small French contingent lost its way. Rather than forcing their way through a fortified gate as instructed, the Americans successfully scaled the walls. The British forces, however, arrived first and were given credit for relieving the siege when they entered the city through an unguarded gate with almost no opposition.[18]

Mary and her husband were staying with his family at Neverstorff on their way to Berchtesgaden when he received a telegram from the kaiser on August 7, one week after the legations in Beijing had been reached by their liberators. As von Waldersee wrote in a rather offhand way in his diary, "I had been appointed Commander-in-Chief in China." He would lead the troops from Japan, Russia, the British Empire, France, the United States, Germany, Italy, and Austria-Hungary (a task that would prove akin to herding cats). Both Russia and England considered themselves entitled to it, but neither would concede it to the other. Therefore Russia's tsar had already expressed his confidence in von Waldersee as commander, and that seemed to settle the question.

Even then the fate of the diplomats and their families was still unknown. "It was believed that the Legations in Peking [Beijing] were completely cut off from the outer world. The general impression was that the catastrophe must have already taken place and that probably the entire foreign colony must have fallen victims to Chinese fanaticism,"[19] von Waldersee wrote. He could not escape a self-congratulatory note: "It was very right, and of great advantage to me, that he placed the German sea forces under me; the gentlemen of the Navy were a bit annoyed over it, foreseeing all kinds of friction. It seemed, indeed, to be the first time that land and sea forces were placed under the same Supreme Command."[20] Russia's Tsar Nicholas II wired his approval to the kaiser, saying of von Waldersee, "I know him well; he is certainly one of your most able and experienced generals and his name stands high in the Russian Army."[21]

While permissions from the other nations were still being received, the kaiser sent from Hamburg to U.S. President William McKinley a telegram thanking him for his approval. As the kaiser proclaimed, "Field Marshall Count von Waldersee, who will have the honor of leading your forces, is not a stranger to America. His wife is an American by birth. I

12. Command in the Boxer Rebellion

Von Waldersee inspecting French troops upon his arrival in Shanghai (*The Graphic*, Nov. 17, 1900).

beg your Excellency to accept my heartfelt thanks for the confidence of the United States placed in the leadership of Count von Waldersee." The president quickly cabled his response, assuring the kaiser, "I see in our common effort to discharge a common duty of humanity an additional recognition of the kindly ties and mutual interests that exists between this country and Germany."[22]

The *New York Times*, in reporting von Waldersee's appointment, pointed out that it met

> with general approval.... The wife of the Field Marshall von Waldersee is an American.... She was then [at the time of her first marriage] considered the handsomest and most accomplished woman in Paris.... Afterward the Emperor of Austria created the young widow a princess in her own right under the title Princess von Noër.... During the short reign of Emperor Frederick, Countess von Waldersee acquired great influence at the German court, and has since retained very high standing in Berlin.[23]

Within days of von Waldersee's appointment, both the Emperor Francis Joseph and King Victor Emmanuel III telegraphed to congratulate him.[24] He first announced that he would travel to China via San Francisco and that Mary would accompany him to the United States. The plan was not, however, for her to join him in China. It would be the first time in their marriage they had been apart for more than a few days and would eventually lead to heartache on at least one side.

Plans changed, however, and his departure would not include the United States nor would Mary accompany him on his initial journey. He also decided not to take his long-time servant, Heinrich, as he "was not strong enough to rough it—and so, younger men were taken."[25] Heinrich and his wife, Frieda, would remain with Mary. After getting fitted out in Berlin, he met with the Ministry of War, the Naval Office, and the Foreign Office. On the 18th, von Waldersee met with the kaiser and his senior staff at Cassel. He recorded in his diary, "It became obvious to me that, apart from punishing the Chinese, our policy had no definite aims. The kaiser had merely some vague ideas about the 'Partition of China.' The great thing for him was the necessity of playing a role in world politics—he lacked any clear conception as to the consequences of such an attitude."[26]

Armed with the field marshal's baton personally presented to him by the kaiser on May 27, 1900, von Waldersee looked forward to being the liberator of China. Imagine his surprise when

> on the previous evening the news had reached Wilhelmshöhe that the allies had entered Peking and that the Imperial Court had fled. Naturally, this was at first a great disappointment for the Kaiser. He had got it fixed firmly in his head that the Ministers and their personnel had been murdered long ago, and it was only after my arrival that the combined march on Peking—which had been regarded as impracticable during the rainy season—was to begin under my Supreme Command, thus winning for me the fame of having taken Peking. This dream was now demolished, the Ministers were still alive … and Peking had been occupied without any great sacrifice.[27]

Von Waldersee and the kaiser were obviously disappointed that mass murders had not taken place since their earlier liberation would now greatly diminish joint fame. "After a little reflection, however, it was felt that much still remained to do, and I urged that the Expeditionary Force should be considerably strengthened, which was at once decided on."[28] After determining that he "would trouble nobody with questions" and "find my way for myself," von Waldersee took his leave and could not resist recording that "the Kaiser, indeed, was touchingly solicitous for me. He gave me two men of his bodyguard and told them they would be held personally responsible for my life and that they must never let me out of their sight."[29]

On August 16, von Waldersee, accompanied by Mary and by his brother, Vice Admiral von Waldersee, visited the United States Embassy in Berlin and asked the secretary of the Embassy to "present his best compliments to President McKinley." He said of the American forces, "It is a great honor to have such gallant soldiers under my command."[30] American

12. Command in the Boxer Rebellion 145

newspapers reported daily on his preparations for departure, and the *New York Times* could not help wondering, "If the commander of the allied forces in China does not hurry up he is going to be left out of the procession. His title is most imposing, and it is said that he has even started for the scene of action. But he is still a long way from the front."[31]

Just prior to von Waldersee's departure, the kaiser gave an unfortunately bellicose speech to the assembled expeditionary forces of 30,000 men at Bremerhaven. It included these words: "There will be no quarter; no prisoners will be taken! As a thousand years ago the Huns, under King Attila, gained for themselves a name which still stands for terror in tradition and story, so may the name of Germany be impressed by you for a thousand years on China so thoroughly that never again shall a Chinese dare so much as to look askance at a German!"[32] The word "Hun," often accompanied by the adjective "dirty," would follow German soldiers into the next two world wars, depicting them as ruthless savages. Winston Churchill would even refer in a broadcast address in 1941 to "70,000,000 malignant Huns, some of whom are curable and others killable."[33]

Traveling on the *Sachsen* via Naples, von Waldersee kept up a steady stream of telegrams to the kaiser, always informing him of the great pomp and respect shown him on his journey ("I was accorded the most courteous reception, with all the honors appertaining to my position."[34]). He met with King Victor Emmanuel on his stop in Italy and was informed of developments in China by lengthy telegrams from the kaiser. Speaking of the various troop nationalities he encountered, von Waldersee assured the kaiser, "It was everywhere a matter for special pride that a German General should have been entrusted with the Supreme Command in China."[35]

Upon his arrival in Tient-sin (now Tianjin), von Waldersee, not surprisingly, found the German soldiers to be "on good terms with all, and their bearing is universally admired. The Japanese are conspicuous for their remarkably good military organization—modeled entirely on the Prussian.... The French are in universal disrepute—even the Russians do not want to have anything to do with them." And their American counterparts? They "hold aloof from the other nationalities. They do not make a bad impression as soldiers, but as individuals they are very doubtful customers and there are apparently a great many adventurers among them." He accused them of looting and declared, "When they are not with their regiments they must be regarded by the inhabitants as a scourge."[36]

Once in China, Waldersee informed the kaiser in October that an earlier decision by the generals and ambassadors to spare the occupation of the walled Forbidden City was "a very harmful one ... merely of weakness."

He also reported widespread looting by most of the troops (excepting, of course, the Germans).[37] He directed about 90 men to work constantly for ten days to restore the palace to make it habitable for his headquarters. Although he assured the kaiser that the private quarters of the dowager empress were to be left unoccupied, it did not take long for von Waldersee to abandon that position. When he was pressed to allow the return of the Imperial Court to their palaces in Peking, he recorded in a lengthy letter to the kaiser, "This is not practicable as long as Peking is occupied by the international troops. In the present condition of both the Imperial Palace in the so-called 'Forbidden City,' and of the Summer Palace, I also feel it would be scarcely possible to accommodate the Court there."[38]

It did not take long for von Waldersee to inhabit the palace himself, nor would he remain there alone, if stories can be believed about a beautiful young Chinese woman he may first have met in Berlin. Although she was known by many aliases, Sai Jinhua is the most common name by which she is remembered. She was born in 1872 and was thus slightly more than 40 years younger than von Waldersee. Forced by her father's death and the resulting family's poverty to become a prostitute at the age of 13, the next year she became the concubine of diplomat Hong Jun (sometimes translated as Hung Chang). In 1887, the Dowager Empress Cixi appointed him the Chinese envoy to several nations in Europe, including Germany. His wife did not want to accompany him to what she considered a barbaric land, so Hong Jun took a delighted Sai Jinhua, treating her legally as his official second wife. Stationed in Berlin for three years, he rarely left his official residence since he preferred reading and studying Chinese history. Sai Jinhua, who learned German from her maid, was allowed to take walks through the park as long as she was accompanied by a servant, but he would not allow her to attend official diplomatic functions where men and women interacted. It also would have been painful for her to attend dances, as her feet had been bound since childhood in the Chinese custom.

It is alleged that Sai Jinhua met von Waldersee while living in Berlin but the evidence is scant as to when and where. By one account, he saw her during one of her walks and returned to find her at the same time on another day.[39] Author Dewei Wang was certainly of the opinion that a physical relationship began at that time between von Waldersee and Sai Jinhua.[40] It seems highly unlikely that von Waldersee, a man of professed religious piety, would have taken a lover. It seems even more unlikely that his wealthy and religious wife, who was widely regarded as the person who was so instrumental in the rise of his career, would have tolerated it had she known. Yet in the voluminous correspondence of his mother-in-law are several calling cards sent to her American cousin so that she might vicariously enjoy the social and political life of Berlin. There, in a letter sent on February 21, 1890, she enclosed those of the chancellor and of Prince Leopold of Prussia, whose wife was Empress Dona's sister, as well as that of Sai's husband, so the count and the Chinese envoy certainly were familiar with one another.[41] Interestingly, the cards were glued into a scrapbook opposite those of the Prince of Wales (later Edward VII) and his son, Prince George of Wales (later George V), who arrived unannounced at the von Waldersee home on March 21, 1890, but left cards when they did not find the count at home.[42]

One writer (whose veracity in some matters has already proven to be highly suspect) contends that Sai had a daughter by von Waldersee in 1890 whose "skin was almost white, its features more occidental than oriental."[43] She was named Te-Kuan (sometimes translated as Deguan). Within a year of the birth, Sai's husband was recalled to Peking and, according to the same sketchy source, von Waldersee was at the Berlin train station to see them off with "tears in his eyes as he waved good-by to a downcast Sai, who held little Te-Kuan up for him to see."[44]

In all probability, the unlikely story, even if somewhat embroidered, would have ended there had not von Waldersee been posted to China a decade later. By then Sai's life had spiraled downward into poverty once again after her diplomat husband died three years after their return to China and his family refused to support her. Leaving her little daughter with number one wife to be reared as her own, Sai had little choice except to return to a life of prostitution, even though her clientele was no longer as upper class as it had been when she was a fresh teenager.

Reduced to rags, she and her fellow residents of Peking's slums had to endure the systematic looting and raping inflicted by bands of roaming soldiers. They pretended to be searching for hidden Boxers but actually took anything of value left in what passed as residences. One day in October there was a knock at the door where Sai lived with several others and a German squadron entered the hovel to begin searching. Their leader was surprised, to say the least, when a still-attractive woman spoke to him in German. She told him of her deprivations, and, when he asked where she learned to speak German, she spoke of her years in Berlin and her friendship with Count Alfred von Waldersee, who had been kind to her. The young officer was astounded and told her that the count was then in Peking as commander in chief of the Allied Forces. He called off the search of the house and told her he would let von Waldersee know of her situation.

As the story goes, the next day a carriage came to the door and Sai was taken to the Imperial Palace, where she was reunited with her old friend. He could see that the last few years had not been kind to her so he gave her money and new clothes. Soon her daily trips were no longer necessary as she moved into the palace. The two rode their horses every day and were hailed by the locals. "Even the tiny children knew her name, and it was a common saying that Waldersee was acting Emperor and she was his Empress, as they were living together in the palace, and making use of all the objects of imperial luxury, even to the great Dragon Bed of the Dowager."[45]

Soon she was to be of great benefit to the general. She told him of the deprivations being imposed upon poor Chinese by the military officers and later was pleased that she had been able "to moderate the harsh treatment of Beijing residents."[46] Even American newspapers reported that the count had given orders to cease "hostilities against the Chinese."[47]

More importantly, she would be of service in another way. The American-born and newly widowed Baroness von Ketteler was demanding as recompense for her husband's murder that the dowager empress be personally imprisoned in addition to the heavy financial penalties to be paid by China. Such an affront to one who was considered a deity was impossible, yet the baroness would not relent. Sai decided that she was in a better position to speak to her as a woman and asked that von Waldersee schedule a meeting for the two of them. Recognizing that his negotiations with the baroness were at a standstill, he decided that Sai's intervention could not hurt.

After listening to the young woman's expressions of grief and outrage, Sai told her that the dowager empress was not even in the city at the time of von Ketteler's death and certainly could not be personally held responsible. She then suggested a different remedy, proposing that a memorial arch be erected at the site of his murder. "From the Chinese point of view, nothing will vindicate the memory of your husband more than the erection of a beautiful arch at the place where he lost his life, with an inscription by the Emperor himself to say that the Baron sacrificed himself for the sake of Germany. In this way, your husband's name would not only be inscribed in the history of your own country but would be remembered forever in China."[48]

The young American, finally realizing that this was the best she could hope for, agreed to Sai's suggestion. In September of 1901, the 18-year-old Ziafang, Prince Chun, later the father of the infant Pu Yi, who would serve as China's last emperor, was sent to Berlin as his family's personal representative to deliver sincere regrets to the kaiser for von Ketteler's death.

12. Command in the Boxer Rebellion 149

(Prince Chun caused a minor diplomatic crisis when he refused to kneel in front of the kaiser.)[49] The arch was erected on the exact spot of von Ketteler's murder, and a peace accord was signed within a year.

In this version of the story, if von Waldersee thought he could keep secret his relationship with Sai Jinhua even when he was seen riding with her daily, he was mistaken. In fact, the two horses they rode had been ordered directly from Lexington, Kentucky, and were shipped via San Francisco.[50] Everything they did was reported. One night, while the two shared the great bed, they were awakened by shouts; the apartment was on fire. They barely had time to pull clothes over their bodies before escaping the flames while guards worked futilely for hours to extinguish the fire. One decorated general, Gross von Schwartzkopf, who was von Waldersee's chief advisor, died in the conflagration, and both American and German newspapers reported the event in full detail. Surely someone with Mary's excellent sources at court would have heard the stories, including the indignity that "Waldersee and Sai had to flee from the Dragon Bed in their night clothes."[51] After a tense period of waiting, Mary received a telegram from her husband reading only, "I am well. Most of my property is burned," and she learned that von Waldersee had moved into the Winter Palace to establish his new headquarters.[52]

The count wrote a lengthy letter to the kaiser reporting that the fire involved "no question of incendiarism on the part of the Chinese." He assured his master, "After hurriedly dressing, and after my staff had got away some of my clothes and underwear safely, I myself had to escape out of the window of my house."[53] In his own diary he lamented the loss of his favorite clothes, including "a very smart khaki rig-out made for me out of English material by the regimental tailor of the Bengal Lancers and a pair of riding-boots made by a Chinese boot-maker."[54] Not surprisingly, there is no mention of Sai Jinhua even if there had been any truth to the story.

Evidently Mary was still hoping that her husband would send for her. David Lee, Mary's only brother, was visiting her in Germany when he wrote to their American cousins that she could not accept their invitation to visit them in the United States because, "This is Mary's first separation from her husband and it is very hard ... she can make no plans till she hears from Alfred—he may wish her to join him in China."[55]

Only a few months later, Mary wrote to the same cousins,

> I have greatly missed my loved husband, but I had as often as possible good news from him—as he wrote *every day*, and sent, as opportunity presented. Then I had many visits, from kind members of his family, and my own—and the Lord gave me work to do,

for Him, which is ever a joy and so the winter passed away—and now I am living in the glad expectation of meeting my dear absent one, the first week in August—at Hamburg where the Emperor telegraphed to me, that my husband and the Ober Kommando would disembark.... You will, I know, join your prayers to mine that our faithful Lord will grant a safe and prosperous voyage home.... The Lord was *very good* to preserve him to me and to all who love him—and I cannot praise Him sufficiently for so *great a mercy*—and how faithfully the Lord watched over him in that distant Land.[56]

Surely Mary would not have put in writing any unfavorable reports she had heard about her husband's service. In fact, in the same letter, she assures her cousins, "It is very gratifying to me, to read the acknowledgments of my husband's services in China, from the various governments, and to know that they *trusted* and appreciated him."[57] Writing six months later, Mary gives only a hint of what the experience had taken out of her. "I want here to say to the glory of God how faithfully He supported me, through the trials of the past year, fulfilling literally His promise to be *our strength*. In my own strength, I could not have held out, but *His* strong Arm upheld me, and He carried my burden for me."[58]

It is at that point in her life that her American-born friend Romaine, Baroness von Overbeck, might have offered the most empathy and support. Her husband had fathered an entirely separate family by a native woman in Hong Kong. If, in fact, there had been even untrue rumors that Alfred had been unfaithful to her, Mary's deep-seated religion would have been the only thing to sustain her. With no one else to turn to, it would have been a great comfort to have the ear of a woman whose husband had betrayed her.

When trying to decide whether to give any credence to von Waldersee's supposed infidelity, it is useful to consult another source. In her biography of the Empress Dowager Cixi, the historian Jung Chang has written with skepticism about the story of the field marshal and Sai Jinhua:

> The local people found this [the occupying troops' newly generous treatment] so unexpected that they credited a courtesan who claimed this was due to her wheedling pillow-talk with Count von Waldersee. The woman ... had gone with her husband to Berlin when he was posted there in the 1880s. After they returned home and he died, she picked up her old profession. During the Allied occupation, she made use of her past as the minister's consort and the little German she had learned, and did brisk business with German officers, with whom she was often seen out riding through the streets of Beijing. She persuaded the German officers in her circle to take her into the Sea Palace to Count von Waldersee's quarters, clearly hoping to be introduced to him or at least to catch his eye. Whether or not she succeeded is unclear. But her claim of having "saved the people of Beijing" by enchanting the German Field Marshal caught the popular sentimental imagination, and [she] has become a household name, regarded by many as something of a tragic heroine.[59]

Meanwhile, the vital service in China von Waldersee was accomplishing for the kaiser necessitated a steady flow of letters between them. In one, the kaiser referred to the widespread looting by soldiers of different nationalities as "Museum-stocking," and assured the count that all sources he had within China confirmed for him "how famously you have managed to handle the different people and how brilliantly you carried things ... instilling enthusiasm into everybody."[60] While von Waldersee professed to oppose the extensive looting of a nation's cultural patrimony, he could not help recording, "What is a Commanding Officer to do when he sees how round him the troops of all other nations are robbing and plundering with the sanction of their officers, and, when, indeed, the latter are appropriating the best things for themselves. How could individual soldiers be prevented from breaking loose and satisfying their greed for booty?"[61]

The much-decorated Count Alfred von Waldersee (author's collection).

Von Waldersee later rationalized some of the looting by explaining, "The troops which England has here are with a few exceptions Indians, and therefore heathens or Mohammedans, and the strong Japanese contingent also is made up of heathens."[62] And what did he think of the natives who were having their treasures stolen as they watched? "Executions make very little impression upon the Chinese public. Life is held very cheap here…. It is inexplicable with what serenity the Chinaman, who is normally a coward, meets his death. In all the countless executions I have witnessed I have never seen a Chinaman betray any sign of fear or emotion."[63]

As von Waldersee moved toward reparations and spoils for the conquering armies, he reminded himself, "If I were to handle conflicts unskillfully here, I should be doing damage to the Emperor's policy, which in all circumstances is a thing to be avoided. That an old soldier like myself would ever be called upon to play a star-part in diplomacy would have seemed incredible to me six months ago!"[64] He kept the kaiser informed of his actions, always going out of his way to place himself in the best light possible. By February of 1901, he was recording in his diary, "In the course of the last month I have been repeatedly asked from Berlin whether the ironclad squadron could not now return home. I have replied strongly in the negative and the Kaiser has supported me."[65]

By late March, he was telegraphing the kaiser that financial negotiations had bogged down completely, mainly due to the British contingent, urging that his ministers must quicken their pace. He warned of the impending heat and illness that much higher temperatures would bring, also admitting that the morale of the men would flag. Venereal disease was beginning to spread throughout his troops. Looking forward to the end of his assignment, von Waldersee delighted in the Japanese emperor's invitation for him to visit on his way home, promising that he would reside in a Shogun Palace previously used by Prince Henry of Prussia.

Finally financial details were agreed upon, with the Chinese paying exorbitant reparations. A disgusted von Waldersee wrote, "The world needs a Bismarck. If he were alive things here would wear a different complexion."[66] He was mightily pleased with himself on his way home, however, writing onboard the *Hertha* en route to Kobe, Japan, "I have been able not merely to maintain my really high position right to the end but also to enhance it…. I must therefore, have succeeded in taking the right tone…. [The Chinese] bow only before superior strength…. I know that they are sorry to part with me, although they cannot, of course, love me exactly."[67]

And what of Sai Jinhua, whom he left behind? She spiraled downward despite marrying again and, addicted to opium, died destitute in 1936 at the age of 62. Her life was adapted into several films and plays, and she is considered a heroine in some circles. Sometimes described as a cross-cultural courtesan, a Chinese historian has written, "Regardless of whether Sai Jinhua's role in China's foreign relations may have been exaggerated and despite the controversies surrounding her conduct and affairs, she lived a tough and spectacular life that has assured her a place in the modern history of China."[68] In the 1976 Hong Kong movie, *The Boxer Rebellion*, von Waldersee (portrayed by American Richard Harrison) is married to a Chinese woman who saves his life when threatened by two Chinese men. It is particularly interesting to note Jung Chang's mention that when a play about Sai Jinhua was written in the 1930s, Madame Mao Zedong (an actress and the last wife of the Chinese Communist chairman) expected to be given the lead role but was overlooked. The actress who got the part was later imprisoned by Madame Mao and died in jail.[69]

On June 5, 1901, the kaiser received the widowed young Maud, Baroness von Ketteler, whom Sai Jinhua had supposedly counseled, accompanied by her mother-in-law. As she gave a firsthand account of her husband's death and the ensuing siege in Beijing, "The Empress, who was present at the audience, often interrupted with questions, evincing the highest regard for the widow's courage, and subsequent nursing of the sick and wounded. Her Majesty, at the Emperor's request, pinned the insignia of the highest class of the Louise Order to the widow's breast." That evening the two women dined with their host and hostess. The report continued, "The widow has not yet recovered from the attack of nervous prostration from which she has been suffering."[70] The *Philadelphia Inquirer* had earlier reported (incorrectly) that Maud was to be appointed Mistress of the Robe to the empress.[71] She continued to be held in great esteem for years, as *Town & Country* reported in 1909, "The Baroness is very high in favor at the German Court, and a palace was presented her in Berlin, where she spends her winters, returning to her father's home in Detroit yearly."[72] She purchased a villa in Tuscany after the First World War and died in Connecticut in 1960.[73]

Although Mary Lee was one of the first American women to marry a titled German husband, she certainly was followed by many more than just Maud. In fact, at the time hostilities were rapidly leading to the First World War, many top-ranking German diplomats had American wives, most of whom were heiresses. In 1902, a Berlin court case reported the practice of financial agents who collected lucrative commissions for finding wealthy American wives to wed somewhat-impoverished titled German husbands. Baron Burkhard von Münchhausen (1867–1940), whose family had been ennobled in 1587, married in 1898 a wealthy widow, Martha Washington Beckel (her sister was the Baroness Hugo von Asten),[74] and they later lived on his estate at Schwöebber near Hanover, which was greatly enhanced by her American dollars until a disastrous fire in 1908. The Berlin lawsuit alleged that three German men had formed a syndicate for the baron to go to America to find a rich wife. He reportedly agreed to give the syndicate a fee of five percent of his wife's fortune and signed a promissory note in the amount of $375,000. However, once the baron arrived in America the proposed wife in Louisiana refused to go through with the marriage as she was Catholic and he was Protestant. The baron insisted that, through his own efforts, he then met Martha Washington Beckel, who, though not as rich as the targeted woman, was still moderately wealthy.

Upon their return to Germany as a married couple, the syndicate members demanded their payment, and two accepted relatively small amounts while another refused to do so, preferring instead to threaten the baron, who then sued for blackmail. Although they were acquitted of the charge, details were necessarily made public.

Back in the United States, news of the lawsuit in Germany reached the newly married baroness. Speaking from her father's home, she was described as "a handsome woman, dignified, and with a profusion of hair verging on warm red." She insisted that her husband, like many army officers, merely borrowed money in order to travel and see the world, a practice that had to be kept hidden since army officers were forbidden to borrow large sums, thus giving the lender a tight control to hold over the borrower. As she explained about the agents' introduction to the heiress and his subsequent payment, "But when the plan was broached to my husband on his second tour here he revolted and said he would rather face the world with his debts and pay them than consent to the humiliating proposals." She was then in the United States so that her aging father might meet his little grandson, and insisted to the reporters, "Contrary to most international marriages mine is an exceedingly happy one. I am proud of my husband and proud of our boy."[75] So many of these trans-Atlantic marriages happened that the U.S. Congress in 1917 passed the Alien Property Custodian Act to seize many of their millions of dollars to use in the fight against their newly adopted country.

Beginning in 1903, the German ambassador to the United States was art connoisseur Baron Herman Speck von Sternburg, called "Specky" by his friends. He had married in London in 1900 American heiress Lillian May Langham. Her father, Charles, was a wealthy mine owner in Idaho, but she was reared as a ward of her wealthy uncle, Arthur Langham of Louisville, Kentucky, president of the Providence Life Assurance Company. He died in a freak accident in 1909 when a July Fourth celebration firecracker exploded in his hand (one must assume he was adequately insured). Shortly after the marriage Baron von Sternburg was posted to Calcutta, but, in 1903, Lillian returned to her own country as the ambassador's wife. In 1908, they went to Germany seeking a cure for his advanced case of lupus, but he died there in Heidelberg. After Lillian's husband's death she married in Berlin, in 1920, Alfred Pavenstedt, a German banker based in New York. In 1904, Lillian's sister, Ivy, married Viscount Gontran de Faramond, then lieutenant commander in the French Navy and naval attaché at the French embassy in Washington. The ceremony was attended by President and Mrs. Roosevelt as well as the secretary of state and the secretary of the Navy.

12. Command in the Boxer Rebellion

Von Sternberg's replacement as German ambassador to the United States was Count Johann Heinrich von Bernstorff, son of one of the most powerful politicians in Prussia. The father served as foreign minister but overplayed his hand in a dispute and offered to resign. The emperor called his bluff by accepting his resignation, thus clearing the way for Bismarck to ascend to the post from which he brilliantly mastered the empire's diplomacy. The son was born in England, where his father served as Prussian ambassador to the Court of St. James, and thus the son spoke English fluently. His great-grandmother, Amerika Riedesel, Baroness zu Eisenbach, was born in 1780 in New York, where her father was a general in the Saratoga Campaign during the American Revolutionary War.

In 1887, von Bernstorff married Jeanne Luckemeyer, daughter of wealthy New York cotton and silk merchant Edward Luckemeyer, who left an estate of $2.5 million to his widow and only daughter. The United States government would eventually seize more than one million dollars of stocks and bonds in her name in U.S. banks as "alien property," although a U.S. court finally decreed in 1921 that the funds belonged to Countess von Bernstorff before her marriage and thus were not generated in nor held by German interests and released the money to her. The countess is specifically mentioned by Mary's cousin as one of her friends.[76]

The von Bernstorffs' only son, Count Christian Gunther, married in Berlin in 1917 Marguerite Vivian Burton Thomason of Burlington, New Jersey. She was born to parents who were stage actors and so gave up Marguerite and her sister to wealthy adoptive parents. Marguerite's foster father was treasurer of a major Philadelphia insurance company. He enrolled her in the Van Rennselaer Seminary, where she told her classmates that she would one day be a countess. Having inherited $100,000 from her late foster mother, Marguerite married and divorced her first husband before wedding Baron Walter von Roedick, an attaché at the Germany embassy in London. She later brought suit for divorce basing her claims on cruelty. Her husband testified that he received a letter from her while he was fighting on the front in which she asked for a divorce. He went home immediately to confront her, and when he followed his wife he saw her enter the apartment of young Count Christian von Bernstorff. When he knocked he heard his wife tell the count to place his revolver in his pocket before answering the door. Upon entering, von Roedick slapped von Bernstorff, took his revolver, tore off one of his epaulets, and challenged him to a duel before reporting to his military superior officer what had taken place. General von Moltke told him he would take no action in the matter. Two days later von Bernstorff came to von Roedick asking him to grant his wife a divorce so the two could marry. Sixteen prominent Germans were called to testify in the ensuing divorce trial, including Prince Albert, later Duke of Schleswig-Holstein. The divorce was granted in favor of the groom and Marguerite was free to marry von Bernstorff. They, too, eventually divorced and she married three more times.

During the July diplomatic crisis of 1914 immediately following the assassination of Archduke Franz Ferdinand, Prince Karl Max Lichnowsky, the German ambassador in England from 1912 to 1914, was the only German diplomat who raised objections to Germany's efforts to provoke an Austro-Serbian war, arguing that Britain would intervene in a continental war. On July 25, he implored the German government to accept an offer of British mediation in the Austro-Serbian dispute, following up two days later with a cable arguing that Germany could not win a continental war. The second cable was not shown to Kaiser Wilhelm II. The next day he relayed an offer from King George V to hold a conference of European ambassadors to avoid general war. Finally, on July 29 a cable to the German foreign office stated simply, "If war breaks out it will be the greatest catastrophe the world has ever seen."[77] Lichnowsky's warnings went unheeded, and by the time the final cable reached Berlin, Austrian troops were already bombarding Belgrade. On Britain's declaration of war on August 4, 1914, Lichnowsky returned to Germany, where he was highly regarded by the military command. Although Lichnowsky did not marry an American wife, his son, Count Max von Lichnowsky, did so, marrying in 1932 Mildred Withstandley Volck.

Perhaps the most striking example of those marriages of German diplomats to American heiresses is that of the parents of Count Hermann von Hatzfeldt-Wildenburg, who was appointed in 1906 as first secretary of the U.S. embassy in Washington. He was the only son of Helen Moulton of Albany, New York, who married Count Paul Hatzfeldt, long-time German ambassador in England. Unfortunately, Count Hatzfeldt's wife, Helen, was not socially acceptable at court, as the parents of her American mother, Cesarine, were Caesar Metz, a musician and "dancing master" who instructed many young New Yorkers (including "the" Mrs. Astor) as they prepared for their first social season, and his wife, Susan LeRoy, who was an amateur actress.

Helen Moulton had first met Count Hatzfeldt, who was 20 years her senior, when he was serving as private secretary to Prince Otto von Bismarck. They were married in 1863 and had three children as she accompanied him to his posts in several European capitals, including Madrid and Constantinople. Bismarck then wanted to appoint his protégé as foreign

12. Command in the Boxer Rebellion

secretary in Berlin, but he was very aware that he and his wife would often be expected at court and therefore she must be acceptable to royalty. An American whose lineage was as suspect as hers simply would not do, so Bismarck urged young Hatzfeldt to divorce his wife (it was said that Bismarck "disliked the Countess as being altogether too French in her sympathies and too American in her ideas").[78] He reluctantly did so, but the two remained very close, and Bismarck eventually had funds drawn from the Guelph Fund for the maintenance of the former wife and their children. The crash of 1873 had wiped out what was left of the Moulton fortune, and the Hatzfeldts were deeply in debt. Bismarck tried to force Hatzfeldt to marry the daughter of the wealthiest of German bankers, the Jewish Baron Bleichröder, who was Bismarck's personal financial advisor. Bleichröder was willing to pay Hatzfeldt's outstanding debts in exchange for wedding his daughter, Else, but Hatzfeldt refused (Else would instead suffer a very unhappy series of marriages). Having divorced his wife, Hatzfeldt declined to make yet another sacrifice by marrying the young woman. Back in Berlin, Hatzfeldt had great success as secretary of state for foreign affairs before transferring to London as Germany's ambassador. His two surviving children often stayed with him in London when they were not at their mother's home in Wiesbaden. Their mother knew better than to appear in London as a divorced woman, although she often joined her former husband on holiday at Brighton. She was said to have been privately received by Queen Victoria at Windsor.

After Bismarck's fall, the two Hatzfeldts were happily remarried in October of 1889 in the presence of their children and the former Empress Vicky, who was greatly involved in the courtship of the Hatzfeldt's only son, Paul, to the very wealthy Marie von Stumm, daughter of yet another American mother, Pauline von Hoffman, whose sister was the Marquise de Mores. There was a very good reason for the timing of the parents' remarriage. Their other daughter, Helene, was engaged to marry Max, Prince zu Hohenlohe-Oehringen, but it was not possible for him to marry the daughter of divorced parents. Therefore they married three months before their daughter. The Hatzfeldts' grandson, Franz, eventually inherited his cousin's princely title of Fürst von Hatzfeldt and Duke von Trachenberg with the style of "Serene Highness," but he was killed in action in 1941 having never married.[79]

On the other side of the Atlantic, the U.S. ambassador to Germany was John G. A. Leishman, former president of the Carnegie Steel Company. In 1897, he had accepted President McKinley's appointment as ambassador to Switzerland, then was ambassador to Turkey and to Italy before accepting, in 1911, an appointment as ambassador to Germany. His daughter, Martha, had already married Count Louis de Gontaut-Biron. In 1913, his younger daughter, Nancy, became engaged to the 13th Duke of Cröy, head of one of Europe's oldest noble houses, whose members had frequently married royal partners. In fact, the Cröys predated Germany's royal family, the Hohenzollerns, by more than a century. The kaiser refused to give his permission, and the duke's family formally announced its disapproval. His very imperious aunt, Princess Isabella, was married to Archduke Friedrich the Austrian Duke of Teschen (two of his sisters were queens) and supreme commander of the Austro-Hungarian army during World War I. She led the family's outrage at the proposed marriage.[80]

Nancy Leishman and the duke were married anyway in Geneva in 1913, and his family took the unprecedented step of announcing in the *Almanach de Gotha*, the bible of royalty, that the union "is not a marriage of equal birth."[81] Thus she was not entitled to any recognition by the kaiser's court or any other royal courts in Germany. Her handsome and very wealthy husband, who became duke at the age of 17 upon his father's death, was an officer in the German army. Eventually, the marriage was recognized and Nancy's son became the 14th duke. She and her husband divorced in 1922 and he married another wealthy American, Helene Lewis.

At the end of John Leishman's term as the U.S. ambassador to Germany in 1913, President Wilson appointed James W. Gerard to replace him. Gerard's wife, Mary, was a daughter of wealthy American copper king Marcus Daly, owner of the Anaconda mine, often referred to as "The Richest Hill on Earth." Mary's sister, Harriot, married, in March of 1910, Count Anton Sigray von Febre of Hungary. He was one of the groomsmen at the 1908 marriage of Count Lazlo Szechenyi to Gladys Vanderbilt. He was also a groomsman at the Scotland wedding of Anita Stewart to Prince Michael de Braganza, Duke of Vizeu. Sigray von Febre became a proponent of the Hungarian legitimist movement in World War I and was a leader of the effort to restore the Habsburgs to the Hungarian throne. He was arrested in 1921 and later released, but in 1943, before the Nazis occupied Hungary, he was a member of parliament. He was eventually taken prisoner by the Nazis at Mauthausen but was freed by American troops in 1945.

American diplomatic wives were obviously intimately aware of relations between Germany and their country of birth. Certainly intelligence and rumors could easily be passed among them, whether beneficial to either country. One newspaper reported in 1904,

> The leading conservative newspaper of Berlin denounces the marriage by diplomats of American wives, saying that this tends to democratize Europe and that such wives are

really political agents of the United States. On the same day we learn by dispatches that Countess Waldersee is credited with the overthrow of Bismarck; that Madame Bakmatieff [American Mary Beale, daughter of Gen. Edward Fitzgerald Beale; she eventually returned to Washington as the wife of the Russian ambassador to the United States], wife of the Russian envoy at Sofia, has great influence with Prince Ferdinand and is protecting the Americans there, and that the Duchess of Marlborough [the enormously wealthy American, Consuelo Vanderbilt] is so greatly in favor at King Edward's court that her husband's rapid advance is credited to her.[82]

While there is scant mention of most of the American wives of German diplomats in Mary von Waldersee's correspondence, she would have seen many of them at court and in her limited forays into society. No doubt she would have tried to enlist their help in her religious philanthropies. Had they been recruited in an attempt at averting war between their countries, perhaps history might have been different. As it happened instead, much of the vast wealth they brought to their marriages was confiscated by the United States to employ against their adopted country.

Chapter 13

Alfred's Return from China

Mary lost her greatest friend and companion, her mother, on March 30, 1899, at the age of 96. She sent a telegram to her Connecticut cousin, Mrs. Hoppin, who had been her mother's faithful correspondent, "Dearest mother went to heaven yesterday." The newspaper in her family's hometown referred to her as "remarkable, above all, for the firmness of her religious character, which partook of the constancy of the older faith. Amid all the earthly changes this remained immovably fixed…. Of excellent Connecticut lineage and the widow of a gentleman of honorable standing…. She was herself in youth beautiful, and retained her charm through life."[1] What the article did not say was that she had been almost completely deaf in her last decades and, having broken her right hand in a fall in her 80s, she taught herself to write with her left hand and thus was able to continue her detailed and witty letters home. Without them there would be very little documentation of her daughter's life. She also sent dried flowers, calling cards, dinner menus, seating charts, and diagrams of their official home in Berlin, but often reminded her cousins not to make public anything she wrote or sent to them. She was also diplomatic when it was needed. Several years earlier, when much was being written about tensions at court, Mrs. Lee answered her cousin, "You ask about Empress Frederic—when, as Crown Princess, she lived at Berlin, she was always pleasant for Mary and so she was for me—but I've not seen her since she was Empress."[2] The statement was not true but it averted any unpleasant rumors.

After her mother's death, Mary sent home to Mrs. Hoppin several gifts of her mother's personal items, reminding her, "She loved you very, very dearly—till the last, and such Christian love will certainly be renewed in Heaven…. You are right, that she has left us a bright example for her life brought forth rich fruits of the Spirit."[3]

Although Mary was not nearly so diligent a correspondent, she did

13. Alfred's Return from China

try to keep her American cousins informed after her mother's death. In a letter written from Sylt ("one of the northernmost islands of the North Sea," she explained), which she asked they circulate among themselves, Mary told of being summoned by the empress, whose mentor she had been. "The Empress gave me an audience one evening which lasted 2 hours. We were quite alone over a cup of tea—and the Empress recounted to me, with deep emotion, the last illness and death of her mother—the Duchess of Schleswig-Holstein in Dresden."[4] Only a few days later, she continued, "The Emperor paid us a visit and was bright and animated, as he always is, in intimate circles. The day following, he took my husband with him to his yacht the 'Hohenzollern,' for a week. We met again on 28th June and went together with many kind friends, to Hamburg to the launch of the 'Victoria Louise' [a cruiser built for the German Imperial Navy] which their Majesties had deputed me to baptize."[5] Obviously she took pains to present the relationship between herself and her husband with "their Majesties" to be as close as it had been in the past.

Whether or not Mary knew about any rumor of her husband's supposed relationship with Sai Jinhua in China, she believed that his health had been seriously compromised by his service there. She wrote to her American cousin after his return, "Although his health has very long suffered from the reaction of the long strain upon mind and body, still we are again united, thank the Lord!"[6] The kaiser telegraphed her about plans for her to join her husband at Hamburg upon his return.[7] She was to go onboard the steamship *Gera* to welcome him, but "all the projected festivities have been declared off, with the exception of the military reception at the City Hall,"[8] due to the death of the kaiser's mother, the dowager empress, on August 5, 1901, of inoperable breast cancer that spread to her spine. She was 60 and died less than seven months after the death of her mother, Queen Victoria. The subdued homecoming would be yet another disappointment for Count von Waldersee, who expected a hero's return.

He and Mary immediately accepted an invitation from Prince Guido Henckel von Donnersmarck to recuperate at his palatial castle, Schloss Neudeck (sometimes called the "Small Versailles"), in Silesia (now Poland).[9] One of the richest men of his day with vast mining interests, his first wife had been Esther Lachmann, a Russian Jewish courtesan known as "La Païva," referred to by one society observer as "the queen of kept women, the sovereign of her race."[10] Another said she was "the one great courtesan who appears to have had no redeeming feature."[11] She was the model for the traitorous spy, Césarine, in Dumas's play, *La Femme de Claude*.

It is doubtful that Mary and her husband would have accepted an invitation from such a notorious woman, but she had died in 1884 at the age of 64, and von Donnersmarck married a more traditional wife, Katharina "Rina" Slepzóv, three years later. Formerly a count, he was created Fürst von Donnersmarck by Wilhelm II in 1901 with the style "Serene Highness." Their descendants are currently the head of that house.

For the marriage to his second wife, von Donnersmarck commissioned a tiara for her composed of 11 particularly rare Colombian emerald pear-shaped drops weighing more than 500 carats. They were widely reported to have belonged to the collection of the Empress Eugénie, and the von Donnersmarck family's famed jewelry collection was reputed to equal or even exceed those of several European royal families. Sotheby's sold the tiara in Switzerland in 2011 for $12.76 million (£7.8 million), said to be the most expensive tiara ever sold on the open market.[12]

Mary was particularly pleased with their stay, writing,

> We have been visiting the Prince and Princess Donnersmarck for several weeks at their splendid castle of Neudeck in Silesia, where my Alfred was surrounded by every care and where everything possible was done to conduce to health and the Lord so blessed the sojourn there that he is now restored to health—and our hearts are filled with gratitude. Alfred went out constantly, on shooting expeditions with the Prince—while the Princess and I visited her charitable institutions in the neighborhood, where she does a great deal of good. Their enormous estates are close to the Russian frontier, and it interested me much to cross over, and drive through the Prince's woods in *Russia*, where I never expected to be. My dear husband stopped for a few days in Berlin—on leaving Schloss Neudeck to take part in the Chapter of the Black Eagle Order.[13]

Their stay had its desired effect, as less than six months later she wrote from the Swiss Alps, "You kindly asked about the health of my good husband and I am thankful to say that he has recovered from the ill effects of his China expedition entirely and looks bright and well again. The Lord has been, and ever is, very good to us. Praised be His holy name!"[14]

Her husband was chosen to travel to England representing the army for the 1902 coronation festivities of King Edward VII, but, as she wrote afterwards, the trip's "chief object, the King's coronation, remained unfulfilled. What a solemn word God spoke in the midst of the national festivities, well nigh turning the coronation into a funeral." The coronation was scheduled for June 26, and three nights before the planned event the new king gave a lavish dinner for more than 70 visiting royal guests, including his niece, the tsarina of Russia. On the night before he was to take the throne, he suffered a severe abdominal abscess requiring immediate surgery. The operation was performed on a table in the music room of Buckingham Palace. Although the king insisted that a planned dinner for 500,000 of the nation's poor proceed as planned, the coronation ceremony had to be postponed, and a majority of visiting royalty and foreign delegations returned to their homes, many having attended a prayer service at St. Paul's Cathedral before their departure.

Before the cancellation, von Waldersee and his fellow officers were entertained at a dinner given by Field Marshal Lord Roberts who was among the most successful of 19th century military commanders. In giving a toast that evening, von Waldersee said, "We German soldiers know how difficult was the task the British army had to accomplish in South Africa and that this task was accomplished with bravery, humanity, and the utmost devotion to the country." In his reply toast, Lord Roberts complimented von Waldersee for his distinguished services in China and thanked him on behalf of the British army for his praise of the work of the British army in South Africa. Just before calling for a toast to Emperor Wilhelm and the German army, Roberts said, "I can assure your Excellency that we soldiers are deeply sensible of the kindly feeling which prompted you to speak of the army in such appreciative terms."[15]

What was not publicly known at the time was the intense negotiations invested in what von Waldersee was to say in his toast. It was submitted beforehand to Lord Roberts, who in turn vetted it with Lord Lansdowne, the secretary of state for foreign affairs. Evidently the sticking point was the word "humanity," as von Waldersee reported,

> For it has clearly embittered the English most of all that people should accuse them of waging war in an inhuman fashion. It was a peculiar sensation for me, having to deliver such a speech, as I am convinced that the English Army was guilty of acts of inhumanity and brutality. But when the Kaiser asks me in the interests of the State so to express myself, I cannot but do so, and I must suffer the malignant remarks that will be thus brought down on me at home to pass quietly over my head.[16]

The rescheduled coronation ceremony was held on August 9 at Westminster Abbey, and most countries were represented by their diplomatic envoys rather than their royal families. The elderly and very infirm archbishop of Canterbury, Frederick Temple, insisted on conducting the service despite his many mistakes. At one point he had to be helped to his feet by the new king and even settled the crown backwards on the monarch's head. Queen Alexandra then had placed upon her head a new crown that included the magnificent Koh-i-Noor diamond of more than 105 carats.

Returning home to Germany after the failed coronation, von Waldersee must finally have realized that his often-delayed dreams of becoming chancellor would never come to fruition. Although he would accompany the kaiser on another mission to visit the Vatican and the Italian court, he was not impressed. In fact, he found King Victor Emmanuel III (who was

Von Waldersee returns from China to his decorated home in Hanover (Wikimedia Commons).

barely five feet tall) and Queen Elena "have not yet that complete self-assurance in manner and conversation which one looks for in them, and I think, moreover, that they were made uncomfortable by the intellectual superiority of the Kaiser; but, apart from that a certain coldness emanated from their entire being."[17]

For someone who had often expressed dislike of Roman Catholics, it seems ironic that von Waldersee was also chosen to accompany the kaiser to pay his respects at the Vatican, where he found "the Kaiser and the Pope outdid each other in courtesies and assurances of mutual esteem.... The whole resources of the Vatican were employed to make the reception imposing and the entire *personnel* of the Papal Court were obliging in the extreme." Even von Waldersee must have been impressed when Pope Leo XIII "greeted me as a worthy successor to Moltke, and thanked me for what I had done in China for the Christians, especially for the Catholic Missions." Two days later he was back at the Vatican again with the entire traveling party of "some sixty Protestants," all received again by the pope, who "stretched out his hand, which was kissed; he then gave them his blessing and promised to pray for them and for their families."[18] In a meeting with the general of the Jesuits, he learned that the pope wanted to bestow on him the Supreme Order of Christ, but at von Bulow's suggestion he was instead given the lower-ranked Order of Pius IX usually given to ambassadors. During the trip he had already collected from the king of Italy the Grand Cross of the Military Order of Savoy. What might the late Mrs. Lee, his anti–Catholic mother-in-law, have made of it all?

Von Waldersee realized the many shortcomings of the man he had followed—and sometimes led—for decades. He entrusted to his diary the serious misgivings about the kaiser.

> I have come to the conclusion that we are in a crisis the outcome of which no mortal can foresee. Will the Kaiser lead the German Empire forward in a straight line or will he run it aground? That is the question which is troubling not me only but many others. Our ruler, who is endowed with so many rich gifts and the best intentions in the world, has begun too many things altogether but he has brought nothing yet to completion, unfortunately; he has only set up an entanglement the way out of which appears to be undiscoverable.[19]

Only a few months before confiding those concerns, von Waldersee had reason to take stock of his own life when he turned 70 years old. "What a rich life, and how conspicuously blessed by Providence, lies behind me!" Never one to shy away from extolling his own virtues, he continued, "A military career of a brilliancy such as it has been given to few to achieve, an honored position far above that of any of the men around me of my own class—I may say without conceit above that of any in the whole world." Not forgetting the woman who had made much of it possible, he wrote, "And my happiness crowned for eight-and-twenty years past by a wife, noble-minded, pious, capable, and universally esteemed. I am inclined to believe that such a height of good fortune has never before been attained. Assuredly there are very few men who have so much on the whole to be thankful for as I."[20]

Chapter 14

The Long-Delayed Visit to America

Mary often expressed a fervent wish to return to the United States for a visit, as it had been almost 50 years since she was there. She longed to show her husband, Count von Waldersee, where she had lived as a girl. As early as 1900 she wrote to her cousins, "In America—where we hope to come God willing in the Spring of 1901. We had to postpone it—as this year, on 27th April, my dear husband will celebrate, if spared, the 50th anniversary of his military service."[1] Mary wrote a few months later to her American cousin, "How kind you are, to wish us to come to you. The meeting with you will be one of the brightest spots in our American trip."[2]

Their journey was scheduled to take place with passage on the *Graf Waldersee* of the Hamburg America Line and had already been announced. The kaiser, however, decided they might overshadow a visit by his brother, Prince Heinrich, so the von Waldersee's journey was cancelled. The prince's trip was planned for February and March 1902 with far-reaching aims of securing the U.S. acceptance of a German sphere of influence in southern South America. "Waldersee and Mary were forbidden to travel to the States at the same time since that might detract from the hoped-for impact of Heinrich's visit."[3] Count von Waldersee later wrote to his wife's American cousins, "We had hoped to see you this spring, but found it necessary to postpone our trip to America for next year God willing."[4] It was yet another disappointment at the hands of the man they had once both revered, and the count would never see America.

In 1903, Mary decided to travel with her sister, Josie, to America to see their brother, David, who was nearing 70 and reportedly ill. She would not be able to show her native land to her husband in his advancing years, but at least she could visit family and friends. She and Josie booked passage

14. The Long-Delayed Visit to America

Mary, right, and her sister, Josie, at the graves of their two brothers in Connecticut, 1903 (Harvard's Houghton Library, MS Am 994–996, von Waldersee-Lee collection).

on the *Graf Waldersee* but, when it was delayed for several days, switched to the same line's *Moltke*. Mary was understandably excited at the prospect of seeing her brother but also the opportunity to visit her native land after almost 50 years. Tragically, while she and Josie were en route their brother died of cancer of the intestines in a local hospital. He was reported to have taken his usual afternoon stroll only the day before.[5] Their cousin, Charles L. Rockwell, president of the First National Bank of Meridien, Connecticut, met them at the quarantine area so he could personally deliver the news of their brother's death.[6]

"When they sailed the sisters had reason to think that their brother would survive a severe operation he had undergone ... and yesterday when the *Moltke* arrived in Quarantine, and they were informed of Mr. Lee's death last Tuesday, both were deeply grieved."[7] The same article dispensed the surprising news that "when Mr. Lee died it was the general opinion among his intimate friends that he had never been married, and as a result when the news was received from abroad that a woman had turned up in Paris who claimed to be his wife, their astonishment was great and few of them gave any credence to the story."

It was left to Mary to clear up the situation once she arrived. She explained, via a statement released by her brother's doctor, that David had been married abroad in 1895 and, for a year, the couple lived with her in Germany. The *New-York Tribune* evidently had an inside source, as they reported a personal conversation with Mary in which she answered, when asked whether she would receive her sister-in-law, "There is no reason why we should not do so. We were always friendly with her in Europe. Of course, we had a little feeling against her on account of her refusal to accompany her husband to America. Every one sympathized with Mr. Lee in the matter. However, the death has, of course, removed any hard feeling."[8] At the time, her brother's "confidential secretary," Miss Addie Samson, who was said to be "intimately acquainted" with the deceased, said she was completely unaware her employer had ever been married. She did concede, however, "if this person's claims are legitimate, I have not the slightest doubt that she will be welcomed by the family.... The Lees are not the kind of people to have any unpleasantness in their family affairs. They are too high born and noble minded."[9]

Although the couple remained separated, they were never divorced and had not remained in contact during the intervening years. Within a week, David's elusive wife arrived in New York City and was met by "a heavily veiled woman, who was said to be the Countess von Waldersee."[10]

Mary's return to America elicited coverage by the *Times*, which found her "a splendidly preserved and a very handsome woman," but was full of errors:

> When she stepped ashore yesterday afternoon it was nearly fifty years since the Countess von Waldersee, as a girl, had left America, during all the intervening years of which she has never revisited her native land. The Countess was a girl in her teens when she left America, and was only sixteen years old [*sic*] when she became the wife of Prince Frederic of Schleswig-Holstein. The Prince was an old man when he married her, and lived only a few years [*sic*], and when he died he left her a fortune estimated at several million dollars. In 1874 she married Count von Waldersee, then a young officer in the Prussian Army. Their union has always been spoken of as an ideal one, while the

influence of the Countess in the highest circles of German life is a subject that is often made a subject of comment.[11]

David Lee had lived mostly abroad in his last years but always returned to the U.S. for about a month each summer when he stayed at the Union Club. When their mother died in 1899, there was "some difference between them [Mary and her brother] in the arranging of family matters after the death of Mrs. Lee."[12] Mary and her sister, Josie, who stayed at the Park Avenue Hotel, understandably decided to cut short their visit and soon made plans to return home earlier than they had hoped. She wrote to her cousins from her hotel, "The funeral of our beloved brother will take place, D. V. [Deo Volente, "God willing"], on Thursday, September 3 and we come to ask if you both would be able to assist at it and if Cousin James would be one of the honorary pall bearers? I need not add that this would give us great pleasure if it is not too much for you ... we will gladly come to you later on."[13] Two weeks later Mary made plans to visit the Connecticut cousins in New Haven from October 17 to the 24th. She wrote that the sad duties attending her brother's death were at an end. "Yesterday took place the final interment of our loved brother, in Woodlawn, together with our father and grandmother and little brother Georgie. These had to be removed from the marble cemetery here and they are now resting side by side."[14]

Mrs. Lee had been buried in Germany when she died in 1899. She left the bulk of her estate to her son, David, but he was only to enjoy the income while the corpus was left to her two surviving daughters, Mary and Josie. At his death it amounted to $51,000, and there were rumors that his doctor and his confidential secretary had greatly diminished the corpus. According to his will it was evenly split between his two sisters and there was no mention of his wife. One item that was revived was the surprising news that, in 1899, Mary had sued her brother for a loan of $20,000 she had made to him. As he never repaid any of it, she sued for the full amount plus $16,543 in interest.[15]

The joyous homecoming Mary had planned for years did not materialize. Not only was she denied the anticipated reunion with her brother, but she had to face questions about the existence of a sister-in-law and how she might share in any family inheritance. There is every reason to believe she must have arrived at some financial arrangement with her erstwhile sister-in-law, and those funds would have come from Mary rather than from her brother's relatively small trust estate. The old story of her financial difficulty with her brother was revived just when she was paying her last farewell to him and to the life they had known in their youth. It was not an America she recognized anyway. The old gentility of Union Square had been all but obliterated as the city marched northwards. She and Josie boarded their ship knowing that they were no longer Americans. Their lives—at least what was left of them—lay across the ocean. Josie's husband, Baron Waechter, had died at Lautenbach on August 3, 1879,[16] and Mary knew that her own elderly husband was waiting for her in Germany.

Back in 1884, Count Alfred von Waldersee had suffered a serious illness. As his mother-in-law wrote at the time, "The Crown Prince [later Emperor Frederick], Prince William [later Wilhelm II], the Duke of Connaught [Queen Victoria's third son], and other scions of Royalty found themselves by his bedside. Moltke and the principal officers were often here. Prince Bismarck could not come, but wrote his sympathy himself.... This writing for Bismarck, Alfred said, was a wonder, for he knew he rarely wrote to anyone."[17] In fact, when the then crown prince finished visiting with Alfred, he came down and sat with Mary. As Mrs. Lee wrote, "He recognized at once the portrait of our dear Prince [Noer, Mary's late husband], said it was perfect; that he knew him well, and what a noble man he was."[18]

In what was to be von Waldersee's last illness, the visits were not repeated. Upon his return from Berlin on February 19, 1904, only months after Mary's return from America, "he did not feel himself, although he rode out on horseback with his nephew, Count Franz Waldersee, and shared in our family life, as usual," wrote Mary. On the 24th, he asked to visit the graves of his two brothers, who died within 13 months of one another, the general and the admiral, whom he missed terribly. After his return he wrote to several friends, "saying it now appeared evident his generation should make way for the next and that he himself should be prepared for the journey." He was so ill on the 26th that a doctor was summoned, and, on the 28th, "he came down to dinner for the last time, tasted hardly anything and looked so ill I advised him to go to bed, which he did, and only six days later [March 5] he passed into Eternity!"[19]

The medical issue, according to Mary, was "the intestines, which manifested a torpor of action, in great measure caused, as the physicians believe, by the hot climate and great fatigue of the China expedition, and this, as a true patriot he had gladly undertaken!"[20] In her mind, then, her husband's death was directly attributable to his service in China and he had died as a result of his soldierly duties. As she wrote to her friends, Mary received "over a thousand letters—400 or 500 telegrams and about 800 floral offerings" as expressions of sympathy.[21] And what was the final judgment of his own life by this decorated soldier who had so often had his dreams yanked back at the last second by the man who had promised them? According to his nephew, Lieutenant General George Count von Waldersee, his uncle's last entry in his diary, written the night before he died, was "I pray to God that I may not have to live through what I see coming."[22]

Pages and pages of newspaper coverage both in Europe and the United States documented von Waldersee's life while reporting his death. Below sub-headlines such as "Moltke's Successor in German Army and Generalissimo of Allies in China Was 72," in all capital letters, was printed, "MARRIED AN AMERICAN."[23] The weekly news digest, "The Searchlight," seemed to encapsulate both von Waldersees' lives in its entire entry:

> Field Marshall Count von Waldersee, whose death occurred in Germany on Saturday, March 5, was best known to the American public by his appearance on the international stage when he became generalissimo of the allied forces in China during the Boxer uprising. He was von Moltke's successor as Chief of Staff of the German Army, and such was his eminence that much surprise was manifested when von Caprivi was chosen to succeed Bismarck as Chancellor instead. The Countess von Waldersee was an American.[24]

Mary received a telegram from Kaiser Wilhelm II stating, "In hearty sympathy I and the Empress feel for you in your bitter loss, for we know what you have possessed and have now lost in him who has gone to God. My grief is shared by the army, which looked up to him as the chosen warrior in times of serious war. In him I lose an old and cherished friend. May God comfort and strengthen you."[25]

The prolific German writer Wolf von Schierbrand, who published the collected speeches of the kaiser, penned a lengthy obituary of von Waldersee that focused upon the count's frustration at having been three times denied the chancellorship he believed he so richly deserved. The article's lead paragraph insisted of von Waldersee, "Himself an able man married to an American wife generally credited with even more brain power and beyond question more ambitious and fertile in resources than he, it has been the wonder of millions inside and outside of Germany how it came about that Waldersee never reached the goal he was striving for with all his heart and mind."[26] Explaining that the reasons for the failure were of "intrinsic interest," von Schierbrand then spent hundreds of column inches recounting von Waldersee's successful military career.

Similarly, Ella Gilbert Ives, a popular writer and one of the few syndicated women at the time, wrote an extended article for the *Boston Evening Transcript* about von Waldersee's death in which Mary's role was prominently featured. In fact, the sub-headline was "How His Marriage to an American Woman Influenced His Character and Career."[27]

Mary described in great detail the pomp and circumstance of her husband's funeral. She wrote of her "one great comfort" in her grief, that of "my Alfred's beautiful prayer on his dying bed, testifying to his firm faith in his Redeemer ... my dear husband in a weak voice but in full consciousness began also to pray in German, which I here translate, 'My Lord Jesus, whatever comes is right. I believe that I belong to thee—in Thy Hands I commit my spirit—only to be still. Amen.'" After she assured him that Jesus had cleansed his sins, Mary said to her husband, "Auf Wiederschen [till we meet again]," and he repeated it to her. "This was our parting greeting until we meet above. I believe that the Lord Jesus was with us, as there was perfect peace and no struggle.... He died as he had lived, a Christian here." Only then did Mary allow herself the luxury of tears.[28]

The day after his death von Waldersee's body was brought down to the salon of his home where he was embedded with flowers while a military honor guard with drawn swords stood around his body throughout the next three days. Mary opened her door to the "thousands of Hanoverians" who wished to pay their respects as they filed past the body. On the day of the funeral, March 9, the crown prince personally came to pay his respects and to deliver handwritten letters from both his parents. As Mary wrote to her family, "The Emperor deputed the Crown Prince to represent him as to his very sincere regret he was not well enough to be present himself."[29]

The crown prince then went to wait at the door of the church so he could escort Mary into the service and sit with her next to her husband's bier. They were joined there by Prince Heinrich of Prussia (the kaiser's younger brother, whose trip to the United States had prevented the one Mary had hoped for with her husband), the Prince Regent of Brunswick (the von Waldersees' long-time friend, Prince Albert of Prussia), and the reigning Prince of Bückeburg (Georg, Prince of Schaumburg-Lippe). After an impressive service the family proceeded to the train station, where they departed with the body for Neverstorff, the von Waldersee estate in Holstein then owned by the nephew of Mary's husband. Mary could not help noticing on the journey the "crowds of people whose hush of respectful affection for the great dead was most marked. The street lanterns were lighted and wreathed with crape and greens, and the flags at half mast."[30] They had brought von Waldersee's favorite horse (the same one that had been purchased in Kentucky and shipped to him in China), which was led behind the hearse. The crown prince walked with Mary while her husband's nephews, several in uniform, walked behind them.

Mary, still accompanied by the crown prince, and her party were met

14. The Long-Delayed Visit to America

Mary's final home in Hanover which she purchased after Alfred's death and left as a charitable institution (Wikimedia Commons).

at the station of Lütjenburg, in Holstein (about 30 kilometers east of Kiel), by von Waldersee's nephew, Count Franz, and, a short while later at Ploën, as Mary wrote, by "the 3rd, 4th, and 5th sons of the Emperor, and deputed by the latter to represent him on this occasion." If he didn't attend, at least he would be sure that no one could fault him for not paying the proper respect to his late friend. As Mary related to her American cousins, "This closed the earthly career of one much beloved and who had fulfilled faithfully the duties which the Lord gave him to do."[31]

Mary's life now was to be one of pious retirement and Christian good works. She took the train to Berlin every month to monitor her philanthropies there, usually accompanied by her assistant, Maria. The empress reportedly visited her several times in her declining years. She told her cousins, "I now continue my *lonely* way looking to the dear Lord for daily grace and strength to glorify Him under the cross, until He re-unites us above, in the happy Heavenly home where partings are no more." Afterward, her "dear sister remained with me 6 weeks which was an unspeakable comfort to me. Then her duties called her home but she intends coming back to me, God willing, next month. I have bought this house [in Hanover], so endeared to me by sacred memories."[32]

Chapter 15

Death and Solitude

Only a few months after Count von Waldersee's death, one of his maternal cousins created headlines in New York. Baron Arthur von Hünerbein became engaged to a young actress, Daisy Croker Warren, who was then appearing in the Broadway production of *The Southerners*. She was a niece of Tammany chief Richard Croker, formerly a New York City alderman and coroner of New York County and then New York City fire commissioner (he died at his castle in Ireland, leaving an estate of almost $5 million). While the two were riding on a trolley in Greenwich, Connecticut, the actress and the baron suddenly decided to be married right away and walked into a judge's office. The blushing bride was "unattended and in her walking suit, Miss Warren presented an unusual appearance" when the two asked for a marriage license. As the *New York Times* reported, "The ceremony lasted less than a minute."[1] Although she was referred to as "Miss," Daisy had previously been married. In fact, she had been adjudged the guilty party in a divorce only months before while appearing in *The Yankee Consul*. Her husband, Perry Morgan, who had been her violin teacher when they met, was awarded custody of their nine-year-old son.[2] By 1915, no longer the fresh young ingénue but still married to Arthur von Hünerbein, Daisy opened a voice studio at her home in Elmhurst.[3] Their marriage was not the kind of publicity that would have pleased the widowed Mary or her late husband.

As a widow, Mary was described by "Augustus," writing for the *New York Observer*:

> Yet with all her work for the poor, in the slums and in the hospitals, in chapel and in church, Countess Waldersee never forgets what is due to her high position. She is still beautiful, with a smooth and radiant complexion, silver white hair of wonderful brilliancy, an erect and dignified carriage, and always adorned with dress and jewels becoming her rank and station. That her virtuous and useful life may be extended for many years to come, is a wish, I am sure, all my readers will join.[4]

15. Death and Solitude

Mary continued her widespread philanthropy, often sending support without being solicited. The University of Wooster, a Presbyterian institution in Ohio, received a generous check of $100 from Mary and it was noted there that "the Countess was formerly a Presbyterian in New York City, but has lived in Germany almost all her life."[5] Mary had been friends for decades with the Rev. John H. W. Stuckenberg and his wife, Mary Gingrich Stuckenberg. The German-born Stuckenberg emigrated to America to receive his education then returned to the University of Halle for further studies. Back in the U.S., he volunteered as a chaplain in the Union army then met and married his wife, and in 1880 the Stuckenbergs returned to Germany for what they thought would be a short visit but remained there for 14 years. They eventually founded what would become the American Church in Berlin and were befriended by the von Waldersees. Returning to America in 1894, Mary and Mrs. Stuckenberg maintained their relationship by correspondence. In November of 1901, they met again to lay the cornerstone of the American Church in Berlin. After the Rev. Stuckenberg's death in 1903, his widow returned to America and was often in contact with Mary to seek support for mission work.

Widowed Mary at Hanover, 1910 (*Von Klarheit zu Klarheit*).

In December of 1906, when Mary was solicited once again for funds, she replied (in a letter she did not complete until January 7, 1907), "My strength for working is naturally diminishing with years and I can only pray the Lord will help to fulfill my many duties now laid upon me for it may be my few remaining years on earth." Mrs. Stuckenberg wanted Mary to finance a seminary for women, but she politely declined, writing, "We have, alas, no Carnegie here. Perhaps you may have thought that I could be responsible for this work, but that is impossible. My fortune is not sufficient for such large outlays and it is so taken up by engagements of all kinds, besides my own religious work."[6]

In her last years at her home in Hanover,

> the Empress visited her there sometimes, and the two ladies kept up a correspondence which was as affectionate as it was frequent. The Countess was often consulted by her niece on various family questions, such as the fits of independence indulged in by the Princess Victoria Louise, and her romance with Prince Ernst of Brunswick, and she invariably succeeded in smoothing the differences which arose between mother and daughter on this as well as on other questions.[7]

Finally, in July of 1914, after ten years of widowhood, Mary began to follow her beloved Alfred on the path that would reunite them. Her sister, Josie, Baroness de Waechter, always stayed with Mary in Hanover in October and then was her hostess during the summer months at what she called "my country place" at Lautenbach in the district of Ortenau in Baden-Württemberg. In June of 1914 Josie received news that Mary had been ill but had not curtailed her activities. "She had been going about, attending conferences, paying visits, apparently enjoying a trip to Hamburg-Blankensee at a friend's house, she had even made plans to go to Switzerland for several weeks, intending to start for there on July 2." Unfortunately, just after her return from Hamburg, Mary "was laid up with a severe attack of fever and inflammation of the lungs, the high temperature weakening her very much. She often fell into unconsciousness, in other moments she was clear and through the whole illness she proved to be the noble Christian praising the Lord for His goodness and being asked how she felt, answered: 'Peace, perfect peace!'"[8]

Josie sat with her sister in her last days. On those occasions when Mary awoke and recognized her, "She smiled, put her arm around my neck, kissed me looking so happy to see me. Now and then we, in a low voice, sang some hymns she loved so much: 'Saved by grace…. Then I shall see Him face to face and tell the story of His grace!'" Josie never left her post until, finally, "shortly before the end, the dear eyes opened wide as if they looked far beyond into purer heights, into the land of light and glory, she breathed gently once and again and her soul had escaped to be with her Saviour, to join the chorus of many angels round about the throne."[9] She died at 76 on July 4th, a holiday she had always celebrated despite her long absence from the United States.

The person who summoned Baroness Waechter to her sister's side was Mary's longtime faithful servant, Maria Wiehe. She wrote from Hanover to Mary's American cousins, apologizing for her poor English, to tell them of the countess's last days.

Mary at Lautenbach only months before her death, 1913 (*Von Klarheit zu Klarheit*).

I had promised her, still years ago, that I would quite openly tell her, when she should become so ill that we thought she could die; and so I told my beloved mother, as she wanted me, already since some time to call her—that perhaps the Lord would come to fetch his dear child to Heaven. Oh how she beamed, when she heard that! Do you really think, she asked me, that I will soon go to Him? Oh! I shall see Him. And from that moment her heart was filled with such a heavenly joy, which I cannot describe.... Wednesday in the night she put her dear hand on my head, while I was kneeling at her bedside and there she blessed me and prayed that the Lord would bless me and give me the spirit of love and strength and comfort and wisdom.[10]

Mary's body was brought to the same salon where Alfred's had rested ten years earlier. Josie could not help noting of Mary in her open coffin, "A heavenly smile on her face, looking many years younger, a picture of peace. I loved to sit at her side, to look at her, to thank God for every blessing He had given me so abundantly through my beloved departed sister."[11]

One of Mary's favorite pastors in Hanover held a memorial service in the house then her body was taken by carriage to the train station. The family group stayed overnight in Hamburg before continuing to Stoess-Neverstorff, where Mary was placed with Alfred in their impressive private mausoleum overlooking the sea. The many flowers and telegrams included those from "their Majesties who thought so much of my sister," as Josie recalled. There was no need for the public display of ostentation that Wilhelm had exhibited at Alfred's death. Josie returned to Mary's "empty house with a wounded heart, with a feeling of loneliness and yet comforted, knowing that our separation will not last too long, that we shall meet again at the river of water of life, bright as crystal, proceeding out of the throne of God and of the Lamb. May we all find the way there through the Grace of our Lord Jesus Christ."[12]

The *New York Sun*'s reporting of Mary's death covered two pages with her photo prominently displayed. The sub-head read, "Former Mary Lee Only American Who Was Princess in Her Own Right." Although Alfred's talents were certainly acknowledged, the story claimed that "the Countess wielded great influence at the German court. Many of the honors bestowed upon her late husband by the present Kaiser were attributed to the influence of the Countess."[13]

Another American newspaper headlined its story "Woman Feared by Bismarck Laid to Rest at Hanover." Its opening paragraph proclaimed, "Miss Lee made the most brilliant foreign marriage of any American woman, having wedded a royal prince on equal terms, and being a wife in no sense morganatic." Referring to the valuable items of Danish crown jewels left to her by her first husband, the story claimed, "It is believed that she has bequeathed them to the German Empress, her niece by marriage." As to her friendship with the empress, who, the story continued, "made her a confidante and often asked her advice on political affairs. The two together worked against Bismarck and it is said that Countess Waldersee was the only woman Bismarck was ever really afraid of." There was also the claim that Mary had a great deal to do with the 1913 marriage of the emperor's only daughter, Viktoria Luise, to the Duke of Brunswick, claimant after his father to the kingdom of Hanover[14] (where Mary lived and was very popular).

Perhaps the most interesting quote in the article, however, is one from Mary's late husband, Alfred. When asked by an American friend what he thought of the increasing trend of titled Europeans taking American wives, Count Alfred von Waldersee responded, "We have been very happy. Yet I realize that there are recesses in her brain that I have never penetrated and that there are thoughts of mine which must always be a sealed book to her. On the whole, it is better that people should marry those of their own race and training."[15]

Mary took an opposite view when she wrote the only article about herself that was ever published.

> The subject of the international marriage of the American girl is one upon which my opinion is often asked. Americans do not seem to think that such marriages are happy, as a rule. It is true that there have been a large number of unhappy marriages between American girls and foreign noblemen, but most of these have been, I think, where one was a Protestant and the other a Catholic, in which case a great gulf was put between them at the beginning. Then, of course, a marriage merely for position with a foreigner, on the one hand, and for the money of the American girl, on the other can never be a guarantee for happiness. But in a marriage for love between two of the same religion—and this I consider most important—there is no reason why happiness should not result from these international marriages. The independent character of the American girl is not a great drawback; it depends upon her ability to make these qualities respected in her husband's eyes.[16]

She went a bit farther in the only interview she ever granted, declaring, "What superb creatures the American girls are after all! I can always pick them out from other nationalities. There is a swing and independence about them that stamps them as Uncle Sam's daughters."[17]

Although thousands of column inches had been devoted to Mary and her position at court, she never sought publicity. Even in death, however, she could not escape newspaper reports of her estate worth $755,000. When she wrote her will in German, in July of 1910, her attorneys advised her to execute a separate document in English because she still possessed about $189,000 worth of assets in the United States. She had it witnessed by two friends, American diplomat James M. Bowcock and a German, Georg Lenzburg. At the time her will was to be probated in Hanover in 1915, Bowcock was serving as vice consul at Leghorn, Italy, and was easily contacted to attest to his signature. Lenzburg, however, was a German soldier fighting on the front at the time but could not be found and was assumed to have been killed or captured. Bowcock testified that he had seen Lenzburg sign the will and that he had been competent at the time. Had she not written the German document she was urged to execute, her entire estate would have been settled many months earlier.

Mary had a trust fund still worth $189,000 left to her by her father. She had it divided into fifths and left two shares to her niece, Baroness Blanche von Palm (Josie's daughter), with directions to give each of her three daughters 100,000 marks, and one-fifth each to her husband's three nephews, Colonel Count Georg von Waldersee, Captain Count Franz von Waldersee, and Major Count Gustav von Waldersee, with instructions to give a portion to another nephew, Count Chamberlain Leopold von Waldersee.[18] Count Georg would become quartermaster-general in the Great General Staff in 1914 and was assigned to Helmuth von Moltke (often referred to as "the younger," nephew of the late field marshal), where he was "a powerful voice for war. Critics of Wilhelm II mocked that he needed to have a Moltke and a Waldersee in charge of the army, just as his grandfather had in 1870."[19]

The *New York Times* recounted yet again in reporting the will that her first husband "relinquished his rank as a Prince of Schleswig-Holstein to make her his wife. After his death the Emperor of Austria made her a Princess to compensate her for the fact her husband had had to surrender his title to wed her."[20] Although Mary had been extremely generous to the church and to her many charities over the years, and had borne all the costs expected of Alfred's professional career, of her original $4 million inheritance from her first husband, at her death she still had $575,000 (approximately $13 million in current currency).[21] She left all her personal effects to her sister, Josie. Her substantial home in Hanover and all its contents, including portraits of her and her husband, were given to a German association with instructions to establish a women's aid home "for the service of the Evangelical Home and Foreign Missions." It was to be called "the Waldersee Institute." As the *New York Times* headlined its report of her estate, "American Fortune Goes to Germans." The story asserted with no supporting evidence, "She was a warm advocate of international marriage, having often said that European husbands were the best in the world."[22]

As Maria Wiehe recalled in her letter, "My Countess has left her home to a bible school for young ladies, where they are educated to be missionaries. Schwester [Sister] Maria and I remain here and continue the work in the house, but what will it be without our sunbeam?"[23] Maria was instructed to move into the countess's bedroom while the other Sister Maria was to live in the adjoining dressing room. The faithful Maria Wiehe, who was often seen accompanying Mary when she distributed religious pamphlets, received a financial bequest in addition to a life estate in the home. Several philanthropic organizations were also remembered, including the Hanover YMCA, the Berlin YMCA, and four other local charities.[24] Perhaps Mary might have received some satisfaction knowing that her long-faithful servant and friend would be there to keep alive both her memory and her devout faith.

Eugen Richter, the German politician who was a strong advocate for liberalism as well as an outspoken critic of anti–Semitism, was once asked his opinion of the late Count Alfred von Waldersee. He replied, "Without his wife he would be what William I would have been without Bismarck."[25]

Epilogue

Certainly Mary von Waldersee had her critics. Author and historian Cecil Lamar refers to her as the "witheringly pious" Countess Waldersee who was "a woman of unrelieved monotony."[1] Even Kaiser Wilhelm's mother's judgment of her could not afford a compliment without a criticism, calling her "a very good woman but violently low church."[2] Fortunately, Mary's death in mid–1914 prevented her from seeing her dearly loved Germany and her native country enter the conflagration of the Great War.

In Mary's last week on her deathbed she may have heard of the June 28, 1914, assassination at Sarajevo of the Archduke Franz Ferdinand and his greatly loved but equally shunned wife, Sophie, Duchess of Hohenberg.[3] Perhaps it is kinder to hope that the news was kept from Mary. It seems somewhat merciful that she was already in her grave by the time Austria-Hungary delivered, with Wilhelm II's encouragement, its demands to Serbia, which were impossible to accept. On July 28, 1914, Austria-Hungary declared war on Serbia, and, two days later, Russia ordered its troops to mobilize against Germany.[4]

Wilhelm II wrote to his first cousin's husband, Tsar Nicholas II, asking Russia to suspend its mobilization against Germany. He also wrote to the government of France asking them not to support Russian efforts to defend Serbia. Finally, on August 1, Germany declared war on Russia, attacked Luxembourg on August 2, and declared war against France the next day. When Belgium refused to permit German troops to cross its borders into France, Germany declared war on Belgium on August 4 and, on the same day, Great Britain declared war against Germany.[5] At the time, Great Britain's king was George V, a first cousin not only of Wilhelm II but also of Tsar Nicholas II. In fact, George V and Nicholas II looked so much alike (their mothers were sisters) they were often mistaken for one another.[6]

Meanwhile, the United States tried desperately to avoid entering the war. In May of 1915, however, a German U-boat sank the British liner *RMS Lusitania*, killing 128 Americans. President Woodrow Wilson responded that the U.S. was "too proud to fight" but demanded an end to attacks on passenger ships. Germany complied but American sentiment was becoming increasingly bellicose. Wilson was barely reelected in 1916 running on his record of not entering the war while former President Theodore Roosevelt was vocal in his denouncement of German "piracy."[7]

Germany knew when it resumed submarine warfare that it would force the U.S. into the fight. Germany's foreign minister sent to the government of Mexico a telegram inviting its government to join Germany in fighting the United States. Their reward upon victory was to be the return of Texas, New Mexico, and Arizona. Great Britain, who desperately wanted the United States to enter the war, intercepted the telegram and gave it to the U.S. ambassador in London, who, in turn, sent it to the president in Washington. After seven U.S. merchant ships were sunk by Germany and the telegram to Mexico was made public, the formerly pacifist Wilson called for war and Congress complied on April 6, 1917.[8] After passing the Selective Service Act, 2.8 million men were drafted and 10,000 soldiers per day were being shipped off to France.[9]

Could Mary have interceded with the kaiser if she were still alive and in his good graces? Almost certainly not. He had, in November of 1908, suffered what is now considered to have been a mental breakdown, although its severity is somewhat in question. "The man who once denied having a little cold because everything about him had to be great, nevertheless only had little breakdowns."[10]

The background for this particular episode had its origins as early as 1902 while Mary and her husband were both still alive. Perhaps that is one reason that Count von Waldersee's last journal entry in 1904 recorded his prayer that he "not have to live through what I see coming."[11] The immensely wealthy Friedrich Krupp, "the Cannon King," whose family factories armed Germany, lived in his palace near Essen but spent much of his time at his villa in Capri, a very popular destination for aristocratic gay men at the time. When Krupp visited Berlin he stayed at the Bristol Hotel, where he was always accompanied by teenaged boys from Capri. The hotel owner became increasingly concerned about Krupp since he made little effort to keep his actions secret, even housing his wife and their two daughters at a different hotel when they visited Berlin.[12]

Although Italy at the time had no law against homosexuality, the fact that Krupp's young men were minors caused him to be banned from Italy in the spring of 1902 by order of King Victor Emmanuel III. Krupp's wife received by mail photos of her husband participating in all-male orgies in Capri, and she went immediately to their friend, Wilhelm II, to ask that he prevent any publicity. The kaiser was outraged that she took such a bold step to involve him, and, when she returned to her home, he had her seized and placed in an insane asylum to silence her.[13] Italian newspapers reported the Krupp story and *Vorwärts*, the official SPD magazine in Germany, reprinted it. Krupp considered bringing a libel action against the German publisher, but when his assistant met with police officials they cautioned him to advise his employer that Krupp should not risk perjuring himself on the witness stand.

Krupp was a member of the Prussian upper house and had also sat in the Reichstag. Knowing that he could not stop the publicity, a week after the German article was published and a day before he was to have a private meeting with his friend, the kaiser, Krupp took his own life. Not only did the kaiser attend Krupp's funeral, he gave remarks blaming his friend's "heart failure" on the Social Democratic Press and insisted they had lied about Krupp's sexual orientation.[14] During the next few years, his widow often had to contend with blackmailers who demanded large amounts of money to suppress the damning evidence they held about her late husband.[15]

The kaiser's 1908 breakdown incident came after the public trial of his closest personal friend, Philip, Prince zu Eulenburg (who had been a count until raised to princely rank in 1900 by Wilhelm II, who also named him a hereditary peer in the Prussian House of Lords). An avowed racist and anti–Semite, he and Wilhelm had been very close since first meeting in 1886 on a hunting trip. Although Wilhelm was 12 years younger, they became the best of friends, with Wilhelm writing of his "boundless love" for Eulenburg.[16] One of the other attendees at the hunting trip where the two met was the French ambassador in Berlin, Raymond Lecomte,[17] whom the Berlin police commissioner called "the king of the pederasts."[18]

Upon Wilhelm's accession to the throne, he wished to appoint Eulenburg as the Prussian ambassador to Bavaria but Bismarck blocked the appointment, later writing to his own son that there were aspects to the Eulenburg-Wilhelm relationship that he did "not wish to commit to paper. I will not write down very much that I want to talk to you about."[19] Bismarck's son, Herbert, wrote to his father, "H. M. [His Majesty] loves Ph. Eulenburg more than any other living being."[20] Eulenburg was instead sent as envoy to the less-important Duchy of Oldenburg. Although he became adept at behind-the-scenes politics as he climbed the diplomatic ladder to other posts (Stuttgart in 1891 and Munich in 1892), his great love was music, and Bismarck accused him of "operetta politics," asking, "What else can one expect from one who sings?"[21]

When von Caprivi was appointed chancellor instead of Alfred von Waldersee, Eulenburg's influence only intensified to a degree that would not have been possible had Mary's husband been given the promised post. Eulenburg was appointed ambassador to Vienna from 1894 to 1902 "where he was shadowed by the secret police, not in order to incriminate him but to keep blackmailers away from him."[22] That level of scrutiny, however, did not prevent a bathhouse attendant from extracting 60,000 marks from Eulenburg in exchange for his silence (a fee Eulenburg tried to have reimbursed).[23] Relying upon his newly-found influence, Eulenburg wrote to Wilhelm in 1894, advising that von Caprivi be fired as chancellor and his close friend Bernhard von Bülow (called "Bernhard the Obliging," as he would never disagree with the kaiser) be appointed in his place.[24]

In 1907, in what came to be known as the Harden-Eulenburg scandals, a newspaper publisher printed an article alleging that von Bülow had been blackmailed for engaging in homosexual practices. He and Eulenburg and their friends often used feminine pronouns to describe one another, and Eulenburg was called "Philine," the feminine version of his name (Moltke was "Tutu"), while they often referred to the kaiser as "Liebchen [Darling]."[25] Von Moltke's wife, Lily whom he had married with the kaiser as a witness, saw her husband at the embassy in Vienna kissing Eulenburg. She later testified in a sealed affidavit for divorce in 1898 that her husband was more interested in having sex with Eulenburg than with her.

At the newspaper publisher's subsequent trial for libel, von Bülow took the stand to deny that he had ever engaged in any homosexual practices but testified that he had heard Eulenburg sometimes did.[26] When Eulenburg took his turn, he went a step too far, testifying not only that this particular charge was false but also asserting he had never engaged in any same-sex activities. He also testified that he thought homosexuality was a "disgusting evil" that should be stamped out. He later claimed he was maliciously targeted by a "rascally Jew"[27] and on another occasion insisted it was a Catholic plot because he was the defender of the "Protestant Empire" that the Jesuits wanted to destroy.[28] His blanket denial about his sexual history proved to be a serious strategic error even though the newspaper publisher was found guilty and imprisoned.

In a second libel trial tied to the first, in April of 1908 two Bavarian lake fishermen testified under oath in a Munich courtroom that they both had been sodomized by Eulenburg when he vacationed there in the 1880s.

They were not casual acquaintances, as one of them had been hired as Eulenburg's personal valet for five years.[29] Their sworn statements led to Eulenburg's indictment for perjury since they directly contradicted his earlier testimony.[30] The statute of limitations on their sexual activity having expired, they were brought from Bavaria to testify in Prussia that Eulenburg had perjured himself.

The police commissioner and several assistants (including a physician) visited Eulenburg at his estate giving him one last opportunity to admit his perjury. Instead he gave them his "word of honor as a Prussian prince" that he had never participated in homosexual activities (the commissioner later said he had never met a bigger liar).[31] The next day Eulenburg was arrested but claimed he was too ill to stand trial. Not surprisingly, he was immediately cut off from all his friends at court and subsequently returned the decorations he had been awarded. Wilhelm, who had been his closest friend, wrote Eulenburg a very cold letter saying he wanted no homosexuals at his court and that he never wanted to see him again.[32] Another friend wrote a letter which he, mercifully, did not send to Eulenburg suggesting that he should commit suicide to spare the kaiser's embarrassment.[33]

Eulenburg claimed at the trial that he meant by his earlier testimony that he had never taken part in any "punishable depravities," clearly trying to claim a very thin line between various sexual acts. However, it was no longer possible to do so since he was on trial for perjury rather than for homosexuality.[34] Several witnesses, including a steward on the kaiser's yacht, testified that Eulenburg had made sexual advances to them.[35] As the days wore on, Eulenburg collapsed and had to be taken to a hospital. The judge convened court by his bedside until, slightly better, Eulenburg was allowed to return home temporarily. When his next court appearance took place he collapsed and was said to be medically unable to continue. For the next ten years he was examined by doctors twice each year but was always deemed to be medically unfit for trial.[36]

Eulenburg finally died in 1921 having been completely shunned by all his former friends and associates.[37] One of his present-day descendants (he had eight children) is HRH Sophie, Hereditary Princess of Liechtenstein. By an odd twist of fate, at the death of her childless uncle Franz, Duke of Bavaria, Sophie will be the Jacobite claimant to the thrones of England, Scotland, Ireland, and France.[38] Jacobites who recognize the Stuart claim to those thrones would then recognize her as queen of the country Wilhelm loathed.

Another in the cascade of calamities faced by the kaiser in 1908 was a casual interview with a British friend who then wrote him asking permission to publish in London's *Daily Telegraph* an article based upon their conversation. The friend included in his correspondence the article as well as all the kaiser's direct quotes. Although it was submitted to Germany's foreign office for review, no one bothered to read it, and the ensuing article when published greatly insulted the British (he said the English were "mad as March hares"), Japanese, French, and Russian sensibilities. His own subjects were offended because he falsely took credit for aiding the British with military strategy during the Second Boer War (many Boers were of German ancestry).[39] Amid much finger-pointing Reich Chancellor von Bülow offered to resign but the kaiser did not accept.

Finally, in November of 1908, Dietrich, Count von Hülsen-Haeseler, chief of the German Imperial Military Cabinet, died at the estate of Max Egon II Fürst zu Fürstenberg of a heart attack while on a hunting trip honoring the kaiser. At the time of his death he was wearing a woman's ballet tutu while dancing for the kaiser.[40] Ottokar von Czernin, an Austro-Hungarian diplomat who was also there, remarked, "In Wilhelm II, I saw a man who, for the first time in his life, with horror-stricken eyes, looked upon the world as it really was."[41] Von Hülsen-Haeseler had most recently been assigned to cover up any adverse publicity about the Eulenburg incident. The accumulated stress of the Eulenburg affair, the *Daily Telegraph* article, and von Hülsen-Haeseler's almost comical death were too much for the kaiser. His 1908 breakdown was the "most serious" one he suffered and caused his diminished activity for quite some time.[42]

It was certainly no secret within the aristocracy that the upper military staff included many homosexuals, although Wilhelm would not allow Jews to have careers in the army and the diplomatic corps.[43] As that knowledge became more widely disseminated to the public, concerns increased. Maximilian Harden, the journalist who precipitated the Eulenburg publication, proclaimed, "To clear ourselves of shame and ridicule, we will *have* to go to war soon, or face the sad necessity of making a change of imperial personnel on our own account, even if the strongest personal pressure had to be brought to bear."[44] It seemed as though Germany would have to march stridently to war in order to regain its masculine sense of power. "It is indeed disturbing to reflect that the generals, who took Germany and Europe into the Armageddon of 1914, not infrequently owed their career to the kaiser's admiration for their height and good looks in their splendid uniforms."[45]

One has to ask, then, since the men "who in the 1890s stood at the very centre of the political stage in the kaiser's Germany were indeed homosexual ... this raises the question of where to place the Kaiser on the 'heterosexual-homosexual continuum.' If he ever did have anything approaching a homosexual experience, it almost certainly occurred in the mid–1880s, in the same period, that is, as his numerous extra-marital affairs with women."[46] Harden, the publisher who was responsible for the libel actions, personally interviewed the Bavarian fisherman who testified against Eulenburg in 1908, and "became convinced that he was in possession of evidence which, if laid before the Kaiser, would suffice to cause him to abdicate."[47]

Surely had Count Alfred von Waldersee still been alive, he would have been eager for war but also would have been outraged at what had happened to his beloved army in its most recent years. His increasing doubts about his kaiser would have been confirmed. Could that have been one of the reasons that the kaiser so often promised him the chancellorship but then reneged on his offer? Did he suspect that von Waldersee would have kept such officers from rising to leadership positions? One can only speculate. But for a man Wilhelm may have considered a father figure, it would not have been information he would be eager to share. Surely Wilhelm included von Waldersee in entanglements of his affairs with women (it is easy to imagine jocular boasting between the two about women), but this would have been entirely different.

And what about his wife, Mary? There is no doubt that the kaiser had warm feelings for her even if for no other reason than her expert mentoring of an unsure and inexperienced young Dona. Even in later years, after he had several times denied her husband the chancellorship, he continued his public displays of friendship, such as asking her to hold his baby grandson during a christening, having Mary officially launch a ship as his representative, and making her the first nonroyal recipient of the Wilhelm Order.

Though there is scant documentation, it seems logical to assume that Mary and the kaiser parted ways later in their friendship, most probably the second or third time he reneged on offering her husband the chancellorship (Mary actually counseled von Waldersee not to seek it the first time, as she thought him still too inexperienced for the post).

Of course, her access to Wilhelm had engendered jealousy within the court. Her detractors would have been eager to use his well-developed ego against Mary by claiming that she reveled in her position. "It is natural that the influence exercised over William and his wife by the countess should have given rise to the utmost jealousy."[48] It seems likely of those envious courtiers "little by little they played upon it, and persuaded the Emperor that his friends were boasting of their intimacy with him, as well as of their relationship with the Empress. They were openly saying, so the fiction ran, that their opinions would prevail over any others with the Sovereign."⁴⁹ According to this version, the person who took the rumors to the Emperor was the very person to whom Mary had been so devoted.

> The Empress was the first to hear about them. She simply smiled, but thought it well to mention the malicious tittle-tattle to her husband. William II became furious, though, strange to say, his anger fell, not on the people who had been silly enough to invent this stupid calumny, not against the Countess Waldersee, but against Count Waldersee himself, who, rightly or wrongly, he believed, made too much of the freedom which his Sovereign had allowed him, and of having promulgated the feeling that his opinions were adopted by William II in all questions concerning the army. He had long been dissatisfied with the Count, whom he had found too imperious and inflexible, and he seized with alacrity this opportunity to punish him.⁵⁰

It is easy to imagine Mary's reaction when he returned home and told his wife about the altercation with Wilhelm. She had proven her loyalty to the royal couple beyond any doubt, but she was, first and foremost, the wife of General Count Alfred von Waldersee to whom she owed her primary allegiance. It did not take long for the kaiser to bring the issue directly to Mary.

> He went to see the Countess, and reproached her bitterly for what he called the proud independence of her husband. A violent scene took place between the two friends of years, and William II told his wife's aunt quite distinctly that he would not allow his decisions to be discounted by his Chief of Staff, whose duty ended with the instruction of the army, and any meddling with politics was unwelcome. This sounded the knell of friendship between the young Emperor and the Countess Waldersee. Their relations became strained; and though outwardly nothing appeared to be changed, as William II still attended the receptions that were given by the Countess, yet he no longer came in to have a quiet cup of tea with her, as he had done almost daily before this episode.⁵¹

If, in fact, Mary von Waldersee had actually been a scheming adventuress who desired to be the power behind the throne, as her detractors claimed, there is no evidence of her having sought any advancement for herself. Surely she would not have joked with the kaiser and his wife about being the "commander in chief" nor shown them the letters calling her that title. Unlike the Countess von Wedel, who sought a lucrative military contract in addition to asking Wilhelm directly for money, Mary had no financial need. It is certainly true that her husband's career owed a great deal to her tact and to her purse, but she had recognized him as a rising star, and, out of many possible suitors, she chose him to be her husband. There is more than a bit of truth in the opinion of the *New York Observer*, which Mary and her mother subscribed to all their lives:

> Some public writers have ascribed political and social movements to her influence, but the Countess is no politician, no power behind the throne—only a good Christian

woman. It is true that she directed the first steps of Princess Augusta Victoria, but as soon as the pupil had become a royal majesty, her friendly guide and teacher, with consummate tact, withdrew from the court and devoted herself to her domestic and charitable duties.[52]

Those who claimed that she dictated policy to Wilhelm and chose his advisors did not know the breadth of his ego.

> Kaiser Wilhelm II is emphatically not a man to be led or swayed by any one; least of all has he ever permitted any woman, old or young, beautiful or the reverse, to influence his political conduct or the action of his government. True, Countess Waldersee is a woman of quite remarkable cleverness, and was in her youth extremely good-looking; moreover, neither Emperor William nor Empress Augusta-Victoria has ever forgotten the affection and motherly tenderness which she displayed towards her sometimes so forlorn young kinswoman, during those first years at Potsdam, and they treat her as a much-valued relative. But her alleged boundless influence over the Heir Presumptive, and subsequently over the Emperor, never existed except in endless and very theatrical press reports.[53]

If Wilhelm II had been a different person, he might have been able to retain Mary's real friendship in their later years rather than settling for her public loyalty. If so, perhaps she might have been able to steer him away from some of his worst decisions. A private conversation over a cup of tea had served him well in his earlier years, but his ego would not have permitted it later during his reign.

The empress never crossed him in any way, having learned her lesson as a young and dutiful wife. It is instructive that she visited Mary in Hanover while there is no positive record of Mary's visits to court in her later years. Wilhelm II was forced to abdicate in 1918, later writing that his abdication was the "deepest, most disgusting shame ever perpetrated by a person in history, the Germans have done to themselves … egged on and misled by the tribe of Judah.… Let no German ever forget this, nor rest until these parasites have been destroyed and exterminated from German soil."[54] One of his earlier biographers wrote of him, "Wilhelm never changed, and throughout his life he believed that Jews were perversely responsible, largely through their prominence in the Berlin press and in leftist political movements, for encouraging opposition to his rule."[55]

Having given her husband six sons and a daughter, an exhausted Dona died in 1921 not long after her husband's exile to the Netherlands (whose government refused to extradite Wilhelm to Germany to stand trial for war crimes). She had also been devastated by the subsequent suicide of her youngest son. The new Weimar Republic allowed her remains to be brought back to Germany, but her husband could not accompany her beyond the border. Unable to live alone, the next year Wilhelm II married, despite the grumblings of monarchists and some of his own children, the widowed Princess Hermine Reuss of Greiz, who already had five children by her late husband, Prince Johann von Schönaich-Carolath. Wilhelm was 53 and she was 34; they were fifth cousins through their descent from George II of Great Britain. She was to prove a faithful companion throughout his last years despite her less-than-stellar royal lineage. In 1945, she fled the advancing Red Army and, at the end of the war, was held under house arrest then imprisoned in an internment camp. She died in 1947 at the age of 59 in a small apartment in Frankfurt, still under strict guard by the occupation army.

Wilhelm II died in 1941 at the age of 82 only weeks before the German invasion of the Soviet Union. Hitler wanted to bring the body back to Germany for burial as a public display that the Nazi regime was the legitimate successor to the monarchy. In one important way he was correct. Wilhelm II had called for a Russian-style pogrom as the "best cure" for Jews, whom he called "a nuisance that humanity must get rid of in some way or other." In his own hand he then wrote, "I believe the best would be gas."[56] Wilhelm's authoritative biographer, John Röhl, wrote, "It seems difficult to come to any other conclusion than that from the age of twenty [after he had known Mary and her husband for a few years] to the age of eighty, Kaiser Wilhelm II, who ruled over Germany for thirty crucial years between Bismarck and Hitler, was a staunch anti–Semite, and that his anti–Semitism formed a central element of his outlook on the world."[57]

But Hitler was denied the spectacle of a public funeral he wanted since Wilhelm left specific instructions that he would not return until the crown was restored. Hitler allowed a small funeral to be held in the Netherlands and, against Wilhelm's wishes, had the Nazi swastika prominently displayed on the coffin. As far as Hitler was concerned, he was the natural heir to Wilhelm II.

By the time of Wilhelm's death, hardly anyone even remembered the American woman who had been his valued friend. Mary would have recognized neither the land of her birth nor the one she adopted and served.

> To the end of her life she remained dignified and silent as to her wrongs. The American girl who had made her way into one of the oldest royal families of Europe, and who later on had loved and married a man who had nothing but his sword and the affection he had inspired her with to plead for him; who had clung to him in prosperity as well as in adversity; defended him whilst he was alive, and kept his memory sacred after he was dead; had given to the world a splendid example of a woman's constancy. Whatever may have been the faults and the imperfections of the Countess von Waldersee, she deserved all her life the deep respect in which she was held.[58]

A subscriber to the *New-York Tribune* wrote to the editor during Mary's heyday to ask whether the Countess von Waldersee had "any influence in politics in Germany." The published answer was "She undoubtedly has had a great political influence in Germany, especially over the present Emperor while he was yet Prince William. By some she is represented as an ambitious political intriguer; by others as a humble-minded Christian philanthropist."[59] Perhaps she was neither—or both.

Chapter Notes

Preface

1. Countess Elisabeth von Waldersee, *Von Klarheit zu Klarheit!* (*From Clarity to Clarity*) (Stuttgart: Buchhandlung des Deutschen Philadelphia-Vereins, 1915).
2. Alson J. Smith, *A View of the Spree* (New York: John Day Company, 1962).
3. Countess von Waldersee, "The Story of My Life," *Harper's Bazar* 37/7 (July 1903): 605–606.
4. *San Francisco Call*, October 28, 1900, 9.
5. *Ibid.*
6. Count Alfred von Waldersee, *A Field-Marshal's Memoirs: From the Diary, Correspondence, and Reminiscences of Alfred, Count von Waldersee*, ed. and trans. Frederic Whyte (London: Hutchinson & Co., 1924; Westport, CT: Greenwood Press, 1978).
7. John C. G. Röhl, *Young Wilhelm: The Kaiser's Early Life, 1859–1888* (Cambridge: Cambridge University Press, 1993): 490.
8. Herbert B. Nichols, "Mary Lee, Princess of Noer," *Harvard Alumni Bulletin* 38/15 (January 17, 1936): 476–479.
9. *Ibid.*
10. Ann Lee to Mary Hoppin, Berlin, March 9, 1888, Harvard-Houghton Library, MS Am 994–996, Von Waldersee-Lee Collection.
11. *Ibid.*, Hanover, March 12, 1881.
12. *Ibid.*, Berlin, May 12, 1882.
13. *Ibid.*, Berlin, March 23, 1888.
14. *Ibid.*, Lautenbach, July 20, 1888.
15. *Ibid.*, Berlin, February 20, 1889.
16. *Ibid.*, Berlin, March 18, 1889.
17. *Ibid.*, Lautenbach, August 31, 1888.
18. *Ibid.*, Lautenbach, September 11, 1875.
19. *Ibid.*, Berlin, October 21, 1882.

Introduction

1. Matthew White, "Source List and Detailed Death Tolls for the Primary Megadeaths of the Twentieth Century," http://necrometrics.com/20c5m.htm. Accessed January 2016.
2. David Canandine, *The Decline and Fall of the British Aristocracy* (New Haven: Yale University Press, 1990): 189.
3. Frederick James Gregg, "The British Aristrocracy and the War: The Doubtful Future of the House of Lords," *Vanity Fair* (March 1916): http://www.oldmagazinearticles.com/WW1_British_Aristocracy-Nobility_during_World_War_One-pdf. Accessed March 2016.
4. The Commonwealth War Graves Commission (CWGC) Annual Report 2009–2010; Heeres-Sanitaetsinspektion im Reichskriegsministeriums (1934). Sanitaetsbericht über das deutsche Heer (deutsches Feld- und Besatzungsheer, im Weltkriege 1914–1918. Berlin. 3/1): 12–14.
5. Charles Spencer, "Enemies of the Estate," *Vanity Fair* (January 2010): http://www.vanityfair.com/news/2010/01/english-aristocracy-201001. Accessed January 2016.
6. John W. Chambers II, ed., *The Oxford Companion to American Military History* (Oxford: Oxford University Press, 1999): 849.
7. Crown Prince Wilhelm to Eulenburg, 12 April 1888, in John C. G. Röhl's *Philipp Eulenburgs Politische Korrespondenz*, vol. I (Boppard am Rhein, 1976): No. 169. See also English translation *Kaiser Wilhelm II*, ed. John C. G. Röhl and Nicolaus Sombart (Cambridge: New Interpretations, 1982): 33.
8. According to John C. G. Röhl's authoritative book *Young Wilhelm: The Kaiser's Early*

Life, 1859–1888 (Cambridge: Cambridge University Press, 1993), the kaiser's recollection of Hinzpeter's brutality as a riding instructor was not true.

9. Otto von Bismarck, *Die Gesammelten Werke, Berlin 1923–1933*, vol. 15 (Berlin: Stollberg, 1935): 553, quoted in English in Röhl's *Young Wilhelm*, 115.

10. Charles Kingston, *Famous Morganatic Marriages* (London: S. Paul & Co., 1919): 212.

11. *Boston Evening Transcript*, January 26, 1895, 16.

12. Marquise de Fontenoy, *Secret Memoirs of the Courts of Europe: William II, Germany; Francis Joseph, Austria-Hungary*, vol. 1 (Philadelphia: George Barrie & Sons, 1900). Countess Marguerite Cunliffe-Owen, daughter of Jules de Godart, Count du Planty de Sourdis, writing as the Marquise de Fontenoy, chapter 2. Her father-in-law was Sir Philip Cunliffe-Owen, KCB, whose wife was Baroness von Reitzenstein. The Cunliffe-Owens lost their fortune in 1885 and came to America, where he became an editor of the *New York Tribune*.

13. Marquise de Fontenoy, *The Marquise of Fontenoy's Revelation of High Life Within Court Palaces* (Philadelphia: Edgewood Publishing, 1892). Countess Marguerite Cunliffe-Owen, daughter of Count Jules du Planty de Sourdis, writing as the Marquise de Fontenoy.

14. *The* (Batavia, NY) *Daily News* (1894): 3. Harvard-Houghton Library, MS Am 994–996, Von Waldersee-Lee Collection.

15. *Geneva Daily News*, June 2, 1902, 7.

16. Marion Watts, "My Visit to the Countess von Waldersee," *San Francisco Call*, October 28, 1900, 9.

17. Edward Legge, *The Public and Private Life of Kaiser William II* (London: Eveleigh Nash, 1915): 45.

Chapter 1

1. All information on the early years of David Lee not otherwise attributed to his widow's correspondence is from Alson J. Smith, *A View of the Spree* (New York: John Day Company, 1962). Smith was a maternal descendant of the Lee family.

2. Through his father, Prince Ernst August was a first cousin of Prince Bernhard, consort to Queen Juliana of the Netherlands. Through his mother he was a descendant of George III of the United Kingdom and thus in the line of succession to the throne.

3. Joseph A. Scoville, *The Old Merchants of New York City*, vol. 4 (New York: G. W. Carleton, 1866): 45.

4. Scoville, *Old Merchants*, 46.

5. *Valentine's Manual of Old New York*, vol. 5, "Old Grocery Houses" (New York: Valentine's, 1919): 201.

6. Scoville, *Old Merchants*, 47.

7. Partner Daniel G. Miller was the father of Helen Day Miller, who became the wife of railroad baron Jay Gould. Their youngest daughter, Anna, achieved notoriety by her marriages to Count Boniface de Castellane and, after their divorce, to his cousin, the Prince de Sagan. The Goulds' granddaughter, Helen, became the wife of the 5th Baron Decies in 1911. After her death he married another American heiress, Elizabeth Wharton Drexel.

8. Ann Lee to Mary Hoppin, Berlin, November 20, 1890, Harvard-Houghton Library, MS Am 994–996, Von Waldersee-Lee Collection.

9. Inflation calculator: http://www.westegg.com/inflation/. Accessed February 2016.

10. "The All-Time Richest Americans," forbes.com, September 14, 2007. http://www.forbes.com/2007/09/14/richest-americans-alltime-biz_cx_pw_as_0914ialltime_slide.html. Accessed January 2016.

11. Smith, *View of the Spree*, 10.

12. Bolton Priory was purchased in 1883 by one of its graduates, the very wealthy Adele "Daisy" Livingston Sampson Stevens, who left her husband and children to marry in 1887 the 4th Duc de Dino. Her dowry was reported to be $3 million. On June 14, 1885, Mary Waldersee wrote a condolence letter to Nanette Bolton's sister, Adele, at Nanette's death. Emmett Family Papers, Archives of American Art.

13. Mary Waldersee to Mary Hoppin, Lautenbach, August 31, 1888, Harvard-Houghton Library, MS Am 994–996, Von Waldersee-Lee Collection.

14. Burke's Peerage, 1913.

15. Mary Waldersee to Hoppin, Lautenbach, August 31, 1888.

16. Winfield Scott, *Memoirs of Lieut.-General Scott, LL.D.* (New York: Sheldon & Company, 1864).

17. Smith, *View of the Spree*, 21–22.

18. Ann Lee to Hoppin, Berlin, July 19, 1889.

19. L. de Hegermann Lindencrone, *In the Courts of Memory* (New York: Harper & Brothers, 1911): 28–29.

20. Mrs. Burton Harrison (Constance Cary Harrison), *Recollections Brave and Gay* (New York: Charles Scribners' Sons, 1911): 251.
21. Elisabeth Kehoe, *The Titled Americans: Three American Sisters and the British Aristocratic World into Which They Married* (New York: Atlantic Monthly Press, 2004).
22. Countess von Waldersee, "The Story of My Life," *Harper's Bazar* 37/7 (July 1903): 601.
23. Count Maurice Fleury, *Memoirs of the Empress Eugenie* (New York: D. Appleton & Co., 1920): 341.
24. Smith, *View of the Spree*, 22.
25. Blanche's children were Renata, who married Bernhard, Baron of Schlotheim; Irene, who married Karl, Baron of Saint André; Blanche, who married Bruno, Baron Stockhorner von Starein, then Friedrich, Baron Cotta von Cottendorf; Eberhard, who inherited the barony and married Lydia Biesinger; and Alfred, who married Verena Hoffman then Gertrud Otto.
26. New York Genealogical and Biographical Record, vol. 81.
27. Ann Lee to Hoppin, Berlin, October 31, 1882.
28. *Ibid.*, October 21, 1882.
29. Philip Guedalla, "Is it a girl? No. Is it a boy? No. But, then, what is it?" in *The Second Empire* (New York: G. P. Putnam's Sons, 1922): 260.

Chapter 2

1. Hugh Chisholm, ed., "Schleswig-Holstein Question," in *Encyclopædia Britannica*, 11th ed. (Cambridge: Cambridge University Press, 1911).
2. Lytton Strachey, *Queen Victoria* (New York: Harcourt Brace, 1921).
3. Danish Military History, "The Schleswig-Holstein Rebellion," http://www.milhist.dk/trearskrigen/outbreak_uk.htm. Accessed May 7, 2012.
4. Heinrich von Treitschke, *History of Germany in the Nineteenth Century*, vol. 7 (New York: Robert M. McBride & Co., 1919): 371.
5. Elise C. Otté, *Scandinavian History* (London: Macmillan, 1894): 365.
6. *Ibid.*
7. C. F. Wraxall, *Life & Times of Her Majesty Caroline Matilda, Queen of Denmark & Norway*, vol. 1 (London: Wm. H. Allen & Co., 1864): 345–346.
8. See the simplified genealogical chart.
9. Alson J. Smith, *A View of the Spree* (New York: John Day Company, 1962): 25.
10. *Ibid.*
11. Charles Kingston, *Famous Morganatic Marriages* (London: S. Paul & Co., 1919).
12. Smith, *View of the Spree*, 26.
13. Allan Nevins, *The War for the Union: The Improvised War 1861–1862* (New York: Scribners, 1959).
14. *New York Times*, September 23, 1862.
15. Desmond Seward, *Eugenie: The Empress and Her Empire* (London: Sutton Publishing, 2004).
16. *The American Almanac, Yearbook, Cyclopedia, and Atlas* (New York: American and Journal, 1903); Edward Legge, *The Comedy and Tragedy of the Second Empire: Paris Society in the Sixties* (New York: Harper & Bros., 1911).
17. F. E. Johanet, *Autour du Monde Millionnaire Américain* (Paris: Callman-Levy, 1898): 155. One of their two sons would become an early race-car driver and enthusiast.
18. Seward, *Eugenie*, 53. Their daughter, Alice, married Count Amédée d'Audebard de Férussac (1817–1897).
19. Smith, *View of the Spree*, 27.
20. *Ibid.*
21. Ann Lee to Mary Hoppin, Paris, June 26, 1863, Harvard-Houghton Library, MS Am 994–996, Von Waldersee-Lee Collection.
22. *Ibid.*
23. *Ibid.*
24. Von Waldersee-Lee collection of correspondence, Harvard-Houghton Library, MS Am 994–996.
25. *Memoirs of Ernst II, Duke of Saxe-Coburg-Gotha*, vol. II (London: Remington & Co., 1888): 77.
26. Kingston, *Famous Morganatic Marriages*, 204.
27. *Ibid.*
28. Ann Lee to Hoppin, Berlin, November 20, 1890. Princess Caroline Matilda was the youngest child of Frederick, Prince of Wales. She was queen of Denmark and Norway, 1766–1775.
29. Smith, *View of the Spree*, 29–30.
30. Frederick A. Noër, *The Emperor Akbar, A Contribution Towards the History of India in the 16th Century* trans. Gustav von Buchwald (Calcutta: Thacker, Spink & Co., 1890): ii.
31. *Ibid.*
32. Graf von Noër, *Kaiser Akbar: Ein Versuch über die Geschichte Indiens im sechzehnten*

Jahrhundret (Leiden: E. J. Brill, 1885); later trans., Richard von Garbe, *Akbar, Emperor of India* (Redding, CA: Gilman Press, 2010), originally published in 1909.

33. *The Mercury*, Hobart (Tasmania), October 11, 1870, 2.

34. Trubner's American and Oriental Literary Record (London: Trubner & Co., 1881): 163.

35. Kingston, *Famous Morganatic Marriages*.

36. Mary Waldersee to Mary Hoppin, Lautenbach, August 31, 1888, Harvard-Houghton Library, MS Am 994–996, Von Waldersee-Lee Collection.

37. Countess von Waldersee, "The Story of My Life," *Harper's Bazar* 37/7 (July 1903): 602–603.

38. *Geneva Daily News*, June 2, 1902, 7.

39. On June 10, 1869, in the royal chapel of Pena Castle, King Fernando II of Portugal married morganatically the American-born opera singer Elise Hensler immediately after the groom's brother, the Duke of Saxe-Coburg, created her the Countess of Edla. There was also discussion of a possible morganatic marriage between Britain's King Edward VIII and his American mistress, Wallis Simpson, later Duchess of Windsor.

40. Kingston, *Famous Morganatic Marriages*, 205.

41. Noër, *The Emperor Akbar*, ii.

42. The 1887 *Almanach de Gotha*, section 1, p. 41, lists the later date; the 1897 and 1904 *Almanach de Gotha*, 3rd section, p. 393 and p. 426 list the earlier date (Gotha: Justus Perthes).

43. Letter of October 19, 1960, to Alson J. Smith (*A View of the Spree*, New York: John Day Company, 1962) in *Stadt-Stuttgart Kulturamt* (Stuttgart); subsequent issues of the *Almanach de Gotha*; Edward E. Salisbury, *Family Histories & Genealogies*, vol. 3, privately printed, 1892.

44. Charles Kingston, *Famous Morganatic Marriages* (London: S. Paul & Co., 1919): 206.

Chapter 3

1. Charles Kingston, *Famous Morganatic Marriages* (London: S. Paul & Co., 1919): 208.

2. Mary Waldersee to Mary Hoppin, Lautenbach, August 31, 1888, Harvard-Houghton Library, MS Am 994–996, Von Waldersee-Lee Collection.

3. Richard Jay Hutto, *Crowning Glory: American Wives of Princes and Dukes* (Macon: Henchard Press, 2007), 11.

4. Alson J. Smith, *A View of the Spree* (New York: John Day Company, 1962): 34.

5. "Sovereigns and the Holy Land," *Putanga* (New Zealand) *Evening Post*, February 5, 1898.

6. Von Waldersee-Lee collection of correspondence, Harvard-Houghton Library, MS Am 994–996.

7. Ann Lee to Mary Hoppin, Berlin, July 18, 1889, Harvard-Houghton Library, MS Am 994–996, Von Waldersee-Lee Collection.

8. Charles Kingston, *Famous Morganatic Marriages* (London: S. Paul & Co., 1919): 206.

9. Ann Lee to Hoppin, Lautenbach, November 16, 1865.

10. *Ibid.*

11. Countess von Waldersee, "The Story of My Life," *Harper's Bazar* 37/7 (July 1903): 603.

12. Smith, *View of the Spree*, 38.

13. Mary Waldersee to Mary Hoppin, Lautenbach, August 31, 1888, Harvard-Houghton Library, MS Am 994–996, Von Waldersee-Lee Collection.

14. *New York Times*, December 31, 1865.

15. Ann Lee to Hoppin, Lautenbach, November 16, 1865.

16. Mrs. Lee's lengthy letter describing the funeral was written from Lautenbach on November 16, 1865.

17. Smith, *View of the Spree*, 41.

18. *Ibid.*

19. *Ibid.*

20. *Ibid.* Princess Karoline Amelie, 1826–1901, was named for her aunt, the queen of Denmark. She never married.

21. "Writings of Graf von Noer," *Calcutta Review* 169 (July 1887): 113.

22. Smith, *View of the Spree*, 40–41.

23. Ann Lee to Hoppin, Berlin, March 11, 1887.

24. *Ibid.*, Lautenbach, November 16, 1865.

25. Smith, *View of the Spree*, 40.

26. *Ibid.*, 41.

27. Ann Lee to Hoppin, Lautenbach, November 16, 1865.

28. Mrs. Lee's lengthy letter describing the funeral was written from Lautenbach on November 16, 1865. One of those "sweet little children," Augusta Viktoria, only six years old, would become the wife of Kaiser Wilhelm II with the help of her great-aunt Mary.

29. It was an honor widely reported in many sources, e.g., *Ashburton* (New Zealand) *Guardian*, July 3, 1888, 3; *Traveler's Record* 24/6 (September 1888): 3; *Munsey's Magazine* 20 (January 1, 1899): 327; *The Literary Digest* 21 (October 20, 1900): 476; *New York Times*, April 23, 1899; *The* (San Francisco) *Argonaut*, September 3, 1900, 7; *New York Tribune*, March 6, 1904, 11; *New York Sun*, July 5, 1914.
30. *New York Tribune*, March 25, 1888.
31. Ann Lee to Hoppin, Berlin, August 31, 1888.
32. Undated and unattributed newspaper clipping in von Waldersee-Lee correspondence, Harvard-Houghton Library, MS Am 994–996.
33. Hutto, *Crowning Glory*.
34. Inflation calculator: http://www.westegg.com/inflation/. Accessed February 2016.
35. Smith, *View of the Spree*, 42.
36. Queen Victoria to the crown princess of Germany, February 27, 1882: Roger Fulford, ed., *Beloved Mama* (London: Evans Brothers, 1981): 115.
37. They have at least two descendants still living, brothers Bernard Louis Laur and Eric Laur. Both are listed (very far down the list) as heirs to the British throne through their descent from Caroline Matilda, queen of Denmark and Norway, who was born a princess of Great Britain as a daughter of Frederick Prince of Wales. As Roman Catholics, they do not have dynastic rights.
38. Ann Lee to Hoppin, Lautenbach, August 2, 1875.
39. *Truth* (weekly journal, London) vol. 63 (January 7, 1886): 2.
40. By the 1897 and 1904 *Almanachs* she was still listed but had been moved to the third section. When she was sent by the *Almanach* a form to update her information, she changed her father's occupation from "grocer" to "banker."
41. Harvard-Houghton Library, MS Am 994–996, Von Waldersee-Lee Collection.
42. *Ibid.*, letter to Elizabeth Hoppin.
43. November 16, 1865; Harvard-Houghton Library, MS Am 994–996, Von Waldersee-Lee Collection.
44. Countess von Waldersee, "Story of My Life," 603.
45. Countess von Waldersee, "Story of My Life," 601.
46. David Blackbourn, *History of Germany, 1780–1918: The Long Nineteenth Century* (New York: Oxford University Press, 1998): 261–263; Mary Fulbrook, *Piety and Politics: Religion and the Rise of Absolutism in England, Wurttemberg and Prussia* (Cambridge: Cambridge University Press, 1983): 52.
47. *New York Observer*, June 8, 1905.

Chapter 4

1. Marlene A. Eilers, *Queen Victoria's Descendants* (Rosvall Royal Books, 1997): 90.
2. Paula Bartley, *Queen Victoria* (Oxford: Routledge, 2016): 189–190.
3. *Ibid.*
4. *Ibid.*, 90–91.
5. Jerrold M. Packard, *Victoria's Daughters* (New York: St. Martin's Press, 1998): 111.
6. Princess Victoria (Vicky) to her mother, Queen Victoria, April 18, 1865, in *Letters of the Empress Frederick*, ed. Frederick Ponsonby (London: Macmillan, 1930): 57.
7. *Ibid.*, 91.
8. They would become known to modern royal observers as Princess Helena Victoria, who never married, and Princess Marie Louise, who wrote one of the best royal memoirs, *My Memories of Six Reigns* (London: Evans Brothers, 1956).
9. Countess von Waldersee, "The Story of My Life," *Harper's Bazar* 37/7 (July 1903): 603.
10. Desmond Seward, *Eugenie: The Empress and Her Empire* (London: Sutton Publishing, 2004): 52.
11. *New York Times*, April 23, 1899. Lady Arthur Paget, born Minnie Stevens in New York, was almost certainly paid for introducing the 9th Duke of Marlborough to his eventual wife, the enormously wealthy Consuelo Vanderbilt, who remembered being assessed by Lady Paget's "pair of hard green eyes." Consuelo Vanderbilt, *The Glitter and the Gold* (New York: St. Martin's Press, 1953).
12. Alson J. Smith, *A View of the Spree* (New York: John Day Company, 1962): 49.
13. *New York Tribune*, quoted in the *Otago Witness*, June 15, 1888, 31.
14. Smith, *View of the Spree*, 49.
15. Edward Legge, *The Public and Private Life of Kaiser William II* (London: Eveleigh Nash, 1915): 45.
16. *New York Times*, April 23, 1899.
17. *Ibid.*
18. *New York Observer*, March 30, 1899, 1. The *Observer* was the favorite American newspaper of Mary, her mother, and her sister,

and they remained subscribers throughout their decades in Germany.
19. http://genealogy.euweb.cz/ascania/ascan6.html. Accessed May 19, 2012. Leopold IV, Duke of Anhalt-Dessau (1794–1871), took the title Duke of Anhalt in 1863 after the extinction of all other lines of the house. He married in 1818 Friederike Princess of Prussia (1796–1850), a granddaughter of King Frederick Wilhelm II. Due to her mother's later marriages, Frederica would have many half-siblings, including King George V of Hanover.
20. *Boston Evening Transcript*, January 26, 1895, 16.
21. Smith, *View of the Spree*, 52.
22. Walter Goerlitz, *History of the German Staff* (New York: Praeger, 1956): 104.
23. Smith, *View of the Spree*, 53.
24. *Ibid.*, 50.
25. Countess von Waldersee, "Story of My Life," 603.
26. Harvard-Houghton Library, MS Am 994–996, Von Waldersee-Lee Collection.
27. Paris, April 1870, Count Alfred von Waldersee, *A Field-Marshal's Memoirs: From the Diary, Correspondence, and Reminiscences of Alfred, Count von Waldersee*, ed. and trans. Frederic Whyte (London: Hutchinson & Co., 1924; Westport, CT: Greenwood Press, 1978).
28. Smith, *View of the Spree*, 54.
29. Ann Lee to Mary Hoppin, Berlin, May 16, 1879, Harvard-Houghton Library, MS Am 994–996, Von Waldersee-Lee Collection.
30. *Ibid.*, May 12, 1882.
31. Mrs. David Lee to Mary Hoppin, Paris, February 18, 1874, Harvard-Houghton Library, MS Am 994–996, Von Waldersee-Lee Collection.
32. Wade Trosclair, *Alfred von Waldersee, Monarchist: His Private Life, Public Image, and the Limits of His Ambition, 1882–1891*, Masters thesis, Louisiana State University (May 2012): 17.
33. Trosclair, *Waldersee, Monarchist*, 17.
34. Smith, *View of the Spree*, 55.
35. Margaret Cunliffe-Owen writing as the Marquise de Fontenoy, *The Marquise of Fontenoy's Revelation of High Life Within Court Palaces* (Philadelphia: Edgewood Publishing, 1892): 390.
36. Smith, *View of the Spree*, 57.
37. They were the great-grandparents of Millicent Fenwick, an American fashion editor who served two terms in the U.S. House of Representatives as a moderate Republican before being defeated for the U.S. Senate. Her father, Ogden H. Hammond, served as U.S. ambassador to Spain.
38. Charles W. Nicholls, *The Ultra-fashionable Peerage of America* (New York: G. Harjes, 1904): 32.
39. Smith, *View of the Spree*, 58.
40. Ann Lee to Hoppin, September 11, 1876. Harvard-Houghton Library, MS Am 994–996, Von Waldersee-Lee Collection.
41. Ann Lee to Hoppin, Lautenbach, November 16, 1865.
42. *Ibid.*

Chapter 5

1. Charles Kingston, *Famous Morganatic Marriages* (London: S. Paul & Co., 1919): 211.
2. Alson J. Smith, *A View of the Spree* (New York: John Day Company, 1962): 63.
3. John Röhl, email message to author, December 17, 2015. Heinrich O. Meisner, ed., *Waldersees Denkwürdigkeiten*, vol. 1 (Stuttgart: Deutsche Verlags-Anstalt, 1922).
4. Prince Wilhelm to his mother, April 6, 1875, AdHH Schloss Fasanerie.
5. John C. G. Röhl, *Young Wilhelm: The Kaiser's Early Life, 1859–1888* (Cambridge: Cambridge University Press, 1993): 335–336.
6. Crown princess to Prince Wilhelm, May 28, 1879, GStA Merseburg, BPHA Rep. 52T/13.
7. Kaiser Wilhelm II to his grandson Prince Wilhelm of Prussia, March 30, 1931, GStA Berlin, BPH Rep. 53/32.
8. John Röhl, email message to author November 15, 2015.
9. *Ibid.*
10. Queen Victoria to Kaiserin Augusta, May 20, 1879; Queen Victoria to Crown Prince, May 20–21, 1879; quoted in Röhl, *Young Wilhelm*, 343.
11. Crown prince to crown princess, May 10–11, 1880, *Ibid.*, 359.
12. Röhl, *Young Wilhelm*, 343.
13. *Ibid.*, 345.
14. Patrica H. Fleming, "The Politics of Marriage Among Non-Catholic European Royalty," *Current Anthropology* 14 (June 1973): 231–249.
15. Quoted in crown prince to Stockmar, July 12, 1879, AdHH Schloss Fasanerie. In a letter to her mother, the crown princess conceded that Calma had a more beautiful face than Dona, but that the latter had the better figure. Crown princess to Queen Victoria, June 3, 1880, RA Z34/28.

16. Bismarck to Kaiser Wilhelm I, August 18, 1879; Bismarck to crown prince, August 18, 1879; Friedberg to crown prince, August 20, 1879; Kaiser Wilhelm I to crown prince, August 21 and 22, 1879; Kaiserin Augusta to crown prince, August 22, 1879, RA Kaiser Frederick III's papers on the marriage.
17. Crown prince to crown Princess, January 1, 1880.
18. *Ibid.*, January 21, 1880.
19. Röhl, *Young Wilhelm*, 349.
20. *Ibid.*, 455–456. Prelude in Alsace; Emilie Love to Waldersee, April 17, 1889, GStA Meresburg, Rep. 92, Waldersee Papers, B I no. 42.
21. Otto von Bismarck to Herbert Bismarck, November 24 and 25, 1888. Quoted by Röhl, *Young Wilhelm*, 459.
22. Mary, Countess Alfred Von Bothmer, *The Sovereign Ladies of Europe* (London: Hutchinson & Co., 1899): 208. Born in England in 1859 as Mary Collingwood Taylor, she married Alfred Felix, Count von Bothmer (1859–1934) and died at Lauterberg, Harz, in 1939. She evidently had superb access to European courts and wrote several books. Her husband translated some books into German and the two wrote a volume of poetry together.
23. E. F. Benson's account disagrees in his publications that Vicky chose Willy's wife, but Röhl's research is authoritative.
24. The crown princess did not hesitate to blame Bismarck for the duke's death. Bismarck was "his murderer," she declared when she received the news of the death. He had died, she said, of a broken heart. The crown prince also believed that Bismarck carried the duke's death on his conscience. On the way to the funeral he wrote, "I feel as if I could not atone enough for all the heartache poor Fritz suffered at the hands of Prussia." Crown prince to crown princess, January 15 and 20, 1880. Röhl, *Young Wilhelm*, 881.
25. Crown prince to crown princess, January 15, 1880, Röhl, *Young Wilhelm*, 358.
26. *Ibid.*, January 21, 1880, Röhl, *Young Wilhelm*, 352.
27. Jerrold M. Packard, *Victoria's Daughters* (New York: St. Martin's Press, 1998): 210.
28. John C. G. Röhl, *Kaiser Wilhelm II, New Interpretations: The Corfu Papers* (Cambridge: Cambridge University Press, 2005): 45; she was a daughter of Admiral the Hon. Victor Montagu and a granddaughter of the 7th Earl of Sandwich.
29. Smith, *View of the Spree*, 65.
30. Virginia Cowles, *Gay Monarch* (New York: Harper & Brothers, 1956): 180.
31. Frederick Ponsonby, ed., *Crown Princess Victoria to her mother, Queen Victoria*, February 18, 1880 in *Letters of the Empress Frederick* (London: Macmillan, 1930).
32. Edward Legge, *The Public and Private Life of Kaiser William II* (London: Eveleigh Nash, 1915): 43–44.
33. Crown Princess Victoria to her mother, Queen Victoria, March 26, 1880, in Ponsonby, *Letters of the Empress Frederick*.
34. Countess Marguerite Cunliffe-Owen writing as "La Marquise de Fontenoy," *Secret Memoirs of the Courts of Europe: William II, Germany; Francis Joseph, Austria-Hungary* (Philadelphia: George Barrie & Sons, 1900): 13.
35. March 12, 1881, Berlin. Harvard-Houghton Library, MS Am 994–996, Von Waldersee-Lee Collection.
36. Catrine Clay, *King, Kaiser, Tsar* (London: John Murray, 2006): 82.
37. *Ibid.*, 83.
38. Smith, *View of the Spree*, 67.
39. Legge, *Kaiser William II*, 44.
40. *Ibid.*, 68.
41. *Ibid.*, 69.
42. *Epoch Magazine*, December 26, 1890, 330.
43. Ann Lee to Mary Hoppin, Berlin, May 12, 1882, Harvard-Houghton Library, MS Am 994–996, Von Waldersee-Lee Collection.
44. Kingston, *Famous Morganatic Marriages*.
45. Margaret Cunliffe-Owen writing as the Marquise de Fontenoy, *Within Royal Palaces* (Philadelphia: Edgewood Publishing, 1892): 390–391.
46. Harold Frederic, *The Young William II, Emperor of Germany: A Study in Character Development on a Throne* (New York: Putnam's, 1891): 127–128. Frederic was a novelist and the Berlin correspondent for the *New York Times*.
47. *Ashburton* (New Zealand) *Guardian*, July 3, 1888, National Library of New Zealand.
48. Count Alfred von Waldersee, *A Field-Marshal's Memoirs: From the Diary, Correspondence, and Reminiscences of Alfred, Count von Waldersee*, ed. and trans. Frederic Whyte (London: Hutchinson & Co., 1924; Westport, CT: Greenwood Press, 1978): xvi–xvii.
49. http://www.bbc.co.uk/bitesize/higher/history/nationalism/consc/revision/3/. Accessed January 2016.

50. Smith, *View of the Spree*, 77.
51. Prince Bernhard von Bülow, *Memoirs of Prince von Bulow*, vol. 1 (New York: Boston, Little, 1931): 306.
52. Countess Marguerite Cunliffe-Owen writing as "La Marquise de Fontenoy," *Secret Memoirs of the Courts of Europe: William II, Germany; Francis Joseph, Austria-Hungary* (Philadelphia: George Barrie & Sons, 1900): 131; a daughter of Count Jules du Planty de Sourdis, she married Frederick Cunliffe-Owen (whose mother was Baroness von Reitzenstein), who became an editor of the *New York Herald Tribune* in 1889.
53. Legge, *Kaiser William II*, 44–45.
54. Mabell Percy Haskell, "The Countess von Waldersee," *The Woman's Home Companion* (May 1901): 15.
55. *Boston Evening Transcript*, January 26, 1895, 16.
56. *New York Tribune*'s Berlin correspondent, quoted in *The Brisbane* (Queensland) *Courier*, June 5, 1888, 6.
57. Henry William Fischer, *Private Lives of Kaiser William II and His Consort*, vol. 3 (New York: Fred de Fau & Co., 1909): 17. Fischer used the pseudonym of "Ursula, Countess von Eppinghoven," but stated in his introduction that, while that was a fictitious name, the book was written with the assistance of "a countess of a very distinguished family."
58. Baroness von Larisch (pseud.), *Behind the Scenes With the Kaiser* (New York: Hertag Publishers, 1922).
59. Isabel V. Hull, *The Entourage of Kaiser Wilhelm II, 1888–1918* (Cambridge: Cambridge University Press, 1982): 358, n. 14.
60. *Boston Evening Transcript*, January 26, 1895, 16.
61. Countess Marguerite Cunliffe-Owen writing as "La Marquise de Fontenoy," *Secret Memoirs*, 13.
62. Harvard-Houghton Library, MS Am 994–996, Von Waldersee-Lee Collection, March 19, 1886.
63. Smith, *View of the Spree*, 79.
64. Henry William Fischer (writing as the Countess von Eppinghoven and/or as the Baroness von Larisch), *Behind the Scenes with the Kaiser, 1888–1892*, vol. II (New York: The World Publishing Co., 1909) 321; quoted in *Pittsburgh Post-Gazette*, March 7, 1919, 11.
65. Legge, *Kaiser William II*, 45.
66. Count Axel von Schwering (pseud.), *The Berlin Court Under William II* (London: Cassell & Co., 1915).

Chapter 6

1. Martin Brecht, *Martin Luther* (Minneapolis: Fortress Press, 1985–1993): 336.
2. Jacob Rader Marcus, *The Jew in the Medieval World*, 198, cited in Robert Michael, *Holy Hatred: Christianity, Antisemitism, and the Holocaust* (New York: Palgrave Macmillan, 2006): 110.
3. Friedrich Ferdinand Graf von Beust, *Aus drei Viertel-Jahrhunderten*, vol. 1 of 2 (Stuttgart: J. G. Cottaschen, 1887): 178.
4. D. A. Jeremy Telman, "Adolf Stoecker: Anti-Semite with a Christian Mission," *Jewish History* 9/2 (Fall 1995).
5. J. F. Dickie, *In the Kaiser's Capital* (New York: Dodd, Mead, 1912): 112–113.
6. Smith, *View of the Spree*, 60.
7. Countess Marguerite Cunliffe-Owen writing as "La Marquise de Fontenoy," *Secret Memoirs of the Courts of Europe: William II, Germany; Francis Joseph, Austria-Hungary* (Philadelphia: George Barrie & Sons, 1900): 14.
8. Alson J. Smith, *A View of the Spree* (New York: John Day Company, 1962): 60.
9. H. H. Ben-Sasson, ed., *A History of the Jewish People*. (Cambridge: Harvard University Press, 1976): 875; D. A. Jeremy Telman, "Adolf Stoecker: Anti-Semite with a Christian Mission," *Jewish History* 9/2 (1995): 93–112.
10. Jehuda Reinharz and Paul Mendes-Flohr, *Jew in the Modern World* (Oxford: Oxford University Press, 2010): 278–280.
11. Albert S. Lindemann, *Anti-Semitism Before the Holocaust* (London: Routledge, 2000): 61.
12. Richard Jay Hutto, *Crowning Glory: American Wives of Princes and Dukes* (Macon: Henchard Press, 2007): 102–104.
13. Fontenoy, *Secret Memoirs*, 19.
14. *Ibid.*, 14.
15. Smith, *View of the Spree*, 88.
16. All descriptions from John C. G. Röhl, Martin Warren, and David Hunt, *Purple Secret: Genes, Madness and the Royal Houses of Europe* (London: Corgi Books, 1999): 183–184.
17. Hannah Pakula, *An Uncommon Woman: The Empress Frederick, Daughter of Queen Victoria, Wife of the Crown Prince of Prussia, Mother of Kaiser Wilhelm* (New York: Simon & Schuster, 1997): 335.
18. Vicky to Fritz, October 28, 1877, quoted in Röhl, *Young Wilhelm*, 107.

19. Röhl, Warren, and Hunt, *Purple Secret*, 182–237.
20. David Blackbourn, *History of Germany, 1780–1918: The Long Nineteenth Century* (New York: Oxford University Press): 261–263.
21. Isabel V. Hull, *The Entourage of Kaiser Wilhelm II, 1888–1918* (Cambridge: Cambridge University Press, 1982): 358.
22. Pakula, *Uncommon Woman*, 459.
23. Emil Ludwig and William Hohenzollern, *The Last of the Kaisers* (New York: Putnam's, 1927): 80.
24. *Ashburton* (New Zealand) *Guardian*, July 3, 1888, National Library of New Zealand.
25. Countess Marie von Bothmer, *The Sovereign Courts of Europe* (New York: Appleton & Co., 1891): 161–162. Mary Young, born in London in 1842, married in 1856 Major Count Hippolite von Bothmer (1812–1891), a German diplomat and one-time consul in Marseilles. They lived in Germany, and among her books was the popular *German Home Life*, which she wrote in 1876.
26. Pakula, *Uncommon Woman*, 459.
27. Kaiser Wilhelm II, marginal note on Schweinitz's report of May 24, 1891.
28. "The German War on the Jews," *New York Times*, November 24, 1880, reported in John C. G. Röhl. *The Kaiser and His Court: Wilhelm II and the Government of Germany* (Cambridge: Cambridge University Press, 1995): 135.
29. Bernard Miall, *Suppressed Letters by the Kaiser and New Chapters from the Autobiography of the Iron Chancellor* (New York: Harper Brothers, 1921): 13.
30. Miall, *Suppressed Letters*, 18.
31. Margaret Cunliffe-Owen writing as the Marquise de Fontenoy, *Within Royal Palaces* (Philadelphia: Edgewood Publishing, 1892): 393.
32. *Ibid.*, 394.
33. November 22, 1880; address in the Prussian Diet by Eugen Richter.
34. Emil Ludwig, *The Moral Conquest of Germany* (New York: Doubleday, Doran & Co., 1945): 89.
35. *Ibid.*
36. Robert Melson, *Revolution and Genocide: On the Origins of the Armenian Genocide and the Holocaust* (Chicago: University of Chicago Press, 1996).
37. Daphne Bennett, *Vicky: Princess Royal of England and German Empress* (New York: St. Martin's Press, 1971): 315.
38. John C. G. Röhl, *The Kaiser and His Court: Wilhelm II and the Government of Germany* (Cambridge: Cambridge University Press, 1995): 197–198.
39. John C. G. Röhl, *Young Wilhelm: The Kaiser's Early Life, 1859–1888* (Cambridge: Cambridge University Press, 1993): 405.
40. Ivo N. Lambi, *Canadian Journal of History* 34/3 (December 1999): 455–458.
41. "I spent months in East Germany working through the original diaries of Count Waldersee himself. The published version must be one of the greatest scandals in historical scholarship, as not only was the published text altered for effect (e.g., by omitting Waldersee's dreadful antisemitism) but the manuscript itself was badly mauled by the editor." Email message to author, November 14, 2015.
42. John C. G. Röhl, *Young Wilhelm*, 490.
43. "Rivals Cause Friction" and "American Women Marry Abroad," *The Annals of Iowa* 30/4 (Spring 1950): 263–264.
44. J. F. Dickie, *In the Kaiser's Capital* (New York: Dodd, Mead, 1912): 111.
45. *Ibid.*, 111.
46. Smith, *View of the Spree*, 62.
47. *New York Observer*, March 30, 1899.
48. Vicky to her mother, Queen Victoria, July 19, 1889, *Letters of the Empress Frederick*, ed. Frederick Ponsonby (London: Macmillan, 1930): 382.
49. Röhl, *Young Wilhelm*, 365, attributing Prince Bernhard von Bülow, *Memoirs of Prince von Bulow*, vol. 1 (Boston: Little, Brown, 1931): 259.
50. Bülow, *Memoirs*, 259.
51. Smith, *View of the Spree*, 90–91.
52. *Ibid.*, 93–94.

Chapter 7

1. *Cosmopolitan* 5 (March–October 1888): 145.
2. Michael Balfour, *The Kaiser and His Times* (Boston: Houghton Mifflin, 1964): 70.
3. Anonymous, *The Empress Frederick: A Memoir* (London: Dodd, Mead, 1914): 299.
4. Alson J. Smith, *A View of the Spree* (New York: John Day Company, 1962): 100. One wonders, however, how Smith could have known about such an intimate moment since the family correspondence makes no mention of it.
5. *Letters of the Empress Frederick*, ed. Frederick Ponsonby (London: Macmillan, 1930): 286.

6. *Ibid.*, 287.
7. Count Alfred von Waldersee, *A Field-Marshal's Memoirs: From the Diary, Correspondence, and Reminiscences of Alfred, Count von Waldersee*, ed. and trans. Frederic Whyte (London: Hutchinson & Co., 1924; Westport, CT: Greenwood Press, 1978): 117.
8. *Ibid.*, 118–119.
9. *Ibid.*, 119.
10. *Ibid.*
11. *Ibid.*, 121.
12. *Ibid.*, February 2, 1885, 121–122.
13. Ann Lee to Mary Hoppin, Berlin, March 4, 1885, Harvard-Houghton Library, MS Am 994–996, Von Waldersee-Lee Collection.
14. Mary von Waldersee to Ann Lee, Copenhagen, May 30, 1885, Harvard-Houghton Library, MS Am 994–996, Von Waldersee-Lee Collection.
15. Von Waldersee, *Field-Marshal's Memoirs*, 123.
16. *Ibid.*, December 6, 1886, 125.
17. *Ibid.*, February 15, 1887, 125–126.
18. *Ibid.*, May 15, 1887, 126.
19. *Ibid.*, June 6, 1887, 126.
20. *Ibid.*, June 6, 1887, 127.
21. *Ibid.*, November 7, 1887, 127–28.
22. *Boston Evening Transcript*, January 26, 1895, 16.
23. Von Waldersee, *Field-Marshal's Memoirs*, November 26, 1887, 128.
24. *Ibid.*, February 10, 1888, 128.
25. *Ibid.*, March 2, 1888, 129.
26. *Ibid.*, March 10, 1888, 133.
27. *Ibid.*, March 11, 1888, 135–136.
28. *Ibid.*
29. Hannah Pakula, *An Uncommon Woman: The Empress Frederick, Daughter of Queen Victoria, Wife of the Crown Prince of Prussia, Mother of Kaiser Wilhelm* (New York: Simon & Schuster, 1997): 459.
30. Von Waldersee, *Field-Marshal's Memoirs*, 137.
31. *Ibid.*
32. Ponsonby, *Letters*, 287.
33. Julius H. M. Busch, *Bismarck: Some Secret Pages of His History*, vol. 3 (London: Macmillan, 1898).
34. Ponsonby, *Letters*, letter from Emperor Frederick to Bismarck of March 12, 1888, 289–291.
35. *Ibid.*, letter from Empress Frederick to her mother Queen Victoria, March 16, 1888, 292–293.
36. John Stoddard, *John L. Stoddard's Lectures*, vol. 6 (Boston: Balch Brothers, 1898) 104.

Chapter 8

1. Trichinella is the genus of parasitic roundworms of the phylum Nematoda that cause trichinosis.
2. Myron Schultz, "Rudolf Virchow," *Emerg Infect Dis* 14/9 (2008): 1480–1481. doi:10.3201/eid1409.086672. PMC 2603088. http://www.pubmedcentral.nih.gov/articlerender.fcgi?tool=pmcentrez&artid=2603088. Accessed January 2016. Isaac Asimov, *Treasury of Humor* (New York: Mariner Books, 1991): 202.
3. "Authentic German Liberalism of the 19th Century," Ludwig von Mises Institute, http://www.mises.org/daily/1787. Accessed March 2016.
4. Ann D. Lee to John A. Kasson, Berlin, March 8, 1889, "Rivals Cause Friction," "American Women Marry Abroad," *The Annals of Iowa* 30/4 (Spring 1950): 263–264.
5. Several letters between January and June 1888 in *Letters of the Empress Frederick*, ed. Frederick Ponsonby (London: Macmillan, 1930).
6. *The Bookman* XL (September 1914–February 1915): 213; also quoted in the anonymously written *The Empress Frederick: A Memoir* (London: Dodd, Mead, 1914): 299.
7. Empress Frederick to Princess Charlotte of Meiningen in Giles McDonough, *The Last Kaiser: The Life of Wilhelm II* (New York: St. Martin's Press, 2001): 117.
8. Fürst Otto von Bismarck, *The Man and the Statesman*, vol. 2 (London: Smith, Elder & Co., 1898): 330.
9. *The Bookman*, 216.
10. Von Waldersee diary entry for March 11, 1888, in *A Field-Marshal's Memoirs: From the Diary, Correspondence, and Reminiscences of Alfred, Count von Waldersee*, ed. and trans. Frederic Whyte (London: Hutchinson & Co., 1924; Westport, CT: Greenwood Press, 1978).
11. *Ibid.*, March 17, 1888.
12. *Ibid.*, March 23, 1888.
13. Lee to Kasson, *Annals of Iowa*, 264.
14. Ann Lee letter, March 19, 1896.
15. Von Waldersee, *Field-Marshal's Memoirs*, diary entry for April 13, 1888.
16. McDonough, *Last Kaiser*, 117.
17. Von Waldersee, *Field-Marshal's Memoirs*, diary entry for March 13, 1888.
18. McDonough, *Last Kaiser*, 118.

19. *Ibid.*, 119, quoting Michael Balfour, *The Kaiser and His Times* (Boston: Houghton Mifflin, 1964): 70.
20. Von Waldersee, *Field-Marshal's Memoirs*, diary entry for April 24, 1888.
21. McDonough, *Last Kaiser*, 120.
22. Ann Lee to Mary Hoppin, Berlin, April 17, 1888, Harvard-Houghton Library, MS Am 994–996, Von Waldersee-Lee Collection.
23. McDonough, *Last Kaiser*, 122.
24. *Ibid.*, 123.
25. Julius H. M. Busch, *Bismarck: Some Secret Pages of His History* vol. 3 (London: Macmillan, 1898): 187.
26. *Letters of the Empress Frederick*, ed. Frederick Ponsonby (London: Macmillan, 1930): 303.
27. Empress Frederick to Queen Victoria, April 27, 1888, in Ponsonby, *Letters*, 305.
28. Ponsonby, *Letters*, 304.
29. Asa Don Dickinson, ed., *The Kaiser: A Book about the Most Interesting Man in Europe* (New York: Doubleday, Page & Co., 1914): 30.
30. Marie, Queen of Romania, *The Story of My Life*, part 4, *Saturday Evening Post*, January 6, 1934.
31. John C. G. Röhl, *Wilhelm II: The Kaiser's Personal Monarchy, 1888–1900* (Cambridge: Cambridge University Press, 2004): 642.
32. Royal historian Katie Tice, email message to author, January 11, 2016.
33. Röhl, *Personal Monarchy*, 643.
34. *New York Times*, November 13, 1929.
35. Stephanie Groueff, *Crown of Thorns: The Reign of King Boris III of Bulgaria* (New York: Madison Books, 1987): 26.
36. Fürst Otto von Bismarck, *The Man and the Statesman*, vol. 2 (London: Smith, Elder & Co., 1898): 330.
37. Von Waldersee, *Field-Marshal's Memoirs*, diary entry for March 17, 1888, 139.
38. *The Bookman*, 215; *Empress Frederick: A Memoir*, 307.
39. *The Bookman*, 217; *Empress Frederick: A Memoir*, 313.
40. Von Waldersee, *Field-Marshal's Memoirs*, diary entry for May 25, 1888, 143.
41. *Ibid.*
42. *Ibid.*, May 30, 1888.
43. Ponsonby, *Letters*, 317.
44. Johannes Lepsius, Albrecht Mendelssohn-Bartholdy, and Friedrich Thimme, *Die grosse politik der europäischen kabinette, 1871–1914*, vol. 6 (Berlin: Deutsche veragsgesellschaft für politik und geschichte, 1922): 326.
45. Emil Ludwig, *Kaiser Wilhelm II* (London: Putnam, 1926): 54.
46. *The Bookman*, 218; *Empress Frederick: A Memoir*, 314.
47. Empress Frederick to Queen Victoria, June 15, 1888, in Ponsonby, *Letters*, 315–316.
48. Röhl, *Personal Monarchy*, 34.
49. Daphne Bennett, *Vicky: Princess Royal of England and German Empress* (New York: St. Martin's Press, 1971): 294.
50. *Ibid.*, 294–295.
51. Edward Legge, *King Edward in His True Colors* (London: Eveleigh Nash, 1972): 58.
52. Röhl, *Personal Monarchy*, 173–174, Wilhelm II, quoting von Waldersee's diary entry for July 5, 1888.

Chapter 9

1. John C. G. Röhl, *Young Wilhelm: The Kaiser's Early Life, 1859–1888* (Cambridge: Cambridge University Press, 1993): 490.
2. Charles Kingston, *Famous Morganatic Marriages* (London: S. Paul & Co., 1919): 212.
3. *Ibid.*
4. Ulrich Feldhahn, *Die preußischen Könige und Kaiser* (Lindenberg: Kunstverlag Josef Fink, 2011): 15–16.
5. Much of the information concerning Elisabeth von Wedel-Bérard is taken from *Young Wilhelm* by John C. G. Röhl. Chapter 19 offers exhaustive research about her life as it relates to Wilhelm II and the German court.
6. Röhl, *Young Wilhelm*, 491.
7. *The Independent*, October 2, 1884, 1257.
8. Giles McDonough, *The Last Kaiser: The Life of Wilhelm II* (New York: St. Martin's Press, 2001): 84.
9. John C. G. Röhl, *Kaiser Wilhelm II, New Interpretations: The Corfu Papers* (UK: Cambridge University Press, 2005): 45.
10. Von Waldersee diary entry for December 26, 1884, GStA Merseburg, Waldersee Papers; cf. Meisner, I, 247.
11. *Ibid.*, entry for January 16, 1885, 249.
12. Röhl, *Young Wilhelm*, 493.
13. *Ibid.*
14. Countess Elisabeth von Wedel-Bérard, *My Relations With Kaiser Wilhelm II* (Zürich: Verlag von Cäsar Schmidt, 1900): 31 and 37.
15. Prince Wilhelm to Waldersee, n.d. [February 1885], GStA Merseburg, Rep. 92; Waldersee B I no. 42.

16. *Ibid.*, 28 February 1885.
17. Röhl, *Young Wilhelm*, 495.
18. Prince Wilhelm to Elisabeth Countess Wedel-Bérard, January 30, 1885, quoted from *Quick* 45 (November 10, 1956).
19. Röhl, *Young Wilhelm*, 495.
20. Prince Wilhelm to Waldersee, April 4, 1885, GStA Merseburg, Rep. 92 Waldersee B I no. 42.
21. Wedel-Bérard, *My Relations with Kaiser Wilhelm II*, 176.
22. Röhl, *Young Wilhelm*, 499.
23. Kingston, *Famous Morganatic Marriages*, 212.
24. Röhl, *Corfu Papers*, 45.
25. *West (Perth) Australian Sunday Times*, March 10, 1901, 5.
26. Elisabeth Wédel-Berard to Prince Radolin, June 25, 1902, PA AA Bonn, R 3474.
27. *New York Times*, January 24, 1901.
28. Henri de Noussanne, *The Kaiser as He Is: Or, the Real William II* (New York: Putnam, 1905): 169. The book was banned throughout Germany.
29. Consul Marshall von Bieberstein to Foreign Office, November 6, 1903, PA AA Bonn, R 3475.
30. Röhl, *Young Wilhelm*, 505.
31. Marshall von Bieberstein to Bülow, September 30, 1905, PA AA Bonn, R 3476.
32. *El Paso Morning Times*, October 7, 1913, 6.
33. *New York Times*, December 22, 1907.
34. "The poor woman was incarcerated in an asylum in Basel for several years, but when it became too expensive to keep her there she was forcibly transported to the border at Lörrach and handed over to the German authorities. The rumour was that she was then kept in Freiburg. I actually went there in 1981 and interviewed a Frau Dr. Kindt in the hope of getting confirmation, but she said there was no record (or was not allowed to tell me). One problem is that the authorities referred to her by the name of her second husband, Schlarbaum. My impression from the records in the Auswärtiges Amt was that the transfer from Basel was arranged by the state authorities, not by the family, though they may have used some family story to persuade her to come quietly." John Röhl, email message to author, January 4, 2016.
35. Röhl, *Corfu Papers*, 45.
36. John C. G. Röhl, *Wilhelm II: The Kaiser's Personal Monarchy, 1888–1900* (Cambridge: Cambridge University Press, 2004): 566.
37. Von Waldersee diary entry for February 27, 1894, in Count Alfred von Waldersee, *A Field-Marshal's Memoirs: From the Diary, Correspondence, and Reminiscences of Alfred, Count von Waldersee*, ed. and trans. Frederic Whyte (London: Hutchinson & Co., 1924; Westport, CT: Greenwood Press, 1978).

Chapter 10

1. Undated newspaper clipping 16; GstA, Nachlass Waldersee, C. I Nr. 2 (probably reprinted in the *Petit Parisien*).
2. *Ibid.*
3. Simon S. Montefiore, *The Romanovs 1613–1918* (New York: Knopf, 2016): 480.
4. Ann Lee to Mary Hoppin, Berlin, February 21, 1884, Harvard-Houghton Library, MS Am 994–996, Von Waldersee-Lee Collection.
5. *Ibid.*
6. *Ibid.*
7. Ann Lee to Hoppin, Herwarthstrasse, April 2, 1883. The Duke of Connaught's wife was Princess Louise of Prussia whose father was a nephew of the German Emperor Wilhelm I. Her mother was Princess Maria Anna of Anhalt, a cousin of Count Alfred von Waldersee.
8. Ann Lee to Hoppin, Berlin, April 24, 1885.
9. Alson J. Smith, *A View of the Spree* (New York: John Day Company, 1962): 94.
10. Gerard Noel, *Princess Alice: Queen Victoria's forgotten daughter* (London: Constable and Company Limited, 1985).
11. Stanley Weintraub, *Victoria* (London: John Murray, 1987): 462.
12. Ann Lee to Hoppin, Berlin, April 25, 1884. This letter of many pages was begun on April 25 but obviously not completed until after the wedding she described which took place on the 30th. Mrs. Lee often used this procedure.
13. Weintraub, *Victoria*, 462.
14. *Ibid.*, 463.
15. *Ibid.*
16. Ann Lee to Hoppin, Berlin, March 4, 1885.
17. *New-York Daily Tribune*, March 25, 1888.
18. *Ibid.*
19. Undated and unattributed newspaper clipping, Harvard-Houghton Library, MS Am 994–996, Von Waldersee-Lee Collection.

20. *Letters of the Empress Frederick*, ed. Frederick Ponsonby (London: Macmillan, 1930): 382.
21. Ann Lee to Hoppin, Berlin, March 8, 1888.
22. *Ibid.*, Berlin, April 17, 1888.
23. *Ibid.*
24. *Ibid.*, Berlin, June 1888.
25. *Ibid.*
26. *Ibid.*
27. Von Waldersee diary entry, January 27, 1889, in Count Alfred von Waldersee, *A Field-Marshal's Memoirs: From the Diary, Correspondence, and Reminiscences of Alfred, Count von Waldersee*, ed. and trans. Frederic Whyte (London: Hutchinson & Co., 1924; Westport, CT: Greenwood Press, 1978): 155.
28. *Ibid.*, January 2, 1890, 157.
29. *Ibid.*, March 15, 1890, 159.
30. Comment during the Congress of Berlin in 1878, as quoted in "European Diary" by Andrei Navrozov, in *Chronicles* 32 (2008).
31. Ann Lee to Hoppin, Berlin, March 22, 1890.
32. *Boston Transcript*, January 26, 1895.
33. Von Waldersee, *Field-Marshal's Memoirs*, diary entry for March 20, 1890, 161.
34. *Ibid.*, March 22, 1890, 162.
35. Mrs. Lee used the word "waiter," confirmed to be a serving tray by Mitchell Owens, decorative arts and antiques editor for *Architectural Digest Magazine*, email message to author, May 14, 2016.
36. Ann Lee to Hoppin, October 27, 1890.
37. *Ibid.*
38. Von Waldersee, *Field-Marshal's Memoirs*, diary entry for April 24, 1890, 163.
39. Ann Lee to Hoppin, Berlin, November 20, 1890.
40. *Ibid.*
41. Wade Trosclair, *Alfred von Waldersee, Monarchist: His Private Life, Public Image, and the Limits of His Ambition, 1882–1891*, Masters thesis, Louisiana State University (May 2012): 184.
42. Von Waldersee, *Field-Marshal's Memoirs*, diary entry from Pleischwitz, September 21, 1890, 167.
43. John C. G. Röhl, *Wilhelm II: The Kaiser's Personal Monarchy, 1888–1900* (Cambridge: Cambridge University Press, 2004): 417. Waldersee journal entry from October 8, 1890, not reproduced in Meisner, *Denkwürdigkeiten*.
44. Virginia Cowles, *The Kaiser* (New York: Harper & Row, 1963): 117.
45. *Ibid.*, 117.
46. Von Waldersee, *Field-Marshal's Memoirs*, diary entry for January 28, 1891, 181.
47. Ann Lee to Hoppin, Berlin, February 5, 1891.
48. *Ibid.*
49. *Ibid.*
50. *Ibid.*
51. *Ibid.*, Berlin, March 1, 1891.
52. *Ibid.*
53. *Ibid.* Prince Joachim took his own life by gunshot after his father's abdication. His grandson, Prince Franz, married Grand Duchess Maria Vladimirovna, currently the most accepted claimant to the Russian throne. Their son, Grand Duke George, is her heir.
54. Ann Lee to Hoppin, Berlin, December 19, 1890.
55. *Ibid.*
56. *Ibid.*, Berlin, March 1, 1891.
57. Undated and unattributed newspaper clipping, Harvard-Houghton Library, MS Am 994–996, Von Waldersee-Lee Collection.

Chapter 11

1. *Epoch Magazine* 8/203 (December 26, 1890): 330.
2. John Dahlgren died soon after his marriage to Elizabeth Drexel. She then married society leader Harry Lehr, who told her on their wedding night he was homosexual. After his death, she then married the 5th Baron Decies, widower of American Helen Gould, who was a granddaughter of railroad magnate Jay Gould.
3. *Biographies in Naval History*, Naval Historical Center, Department of the Navy (July 25, 2001); Alice J. Gayley, "Admiral John A. Dahlgren," *Pennsylvania in the Civil War. PA Roots*. library.syr.edu/digital/guides/d/dahlgren_ja.htm. Accessed September 26, 2015.
4. Richard Jay Hutto, *Crowning Glory: American Wives of Princes and Dukes* (Macon: Henchard Press, 2007): 78–79.
5. Information concerning the Dahlgren family is taken from http://www.colsdioc.org/Portals/0/Departments/CRS/CRS_2001_08.pdf. Accessed February 2016. The family papers and correspondence are housed at Georgetown University.
6. Madeline Vinton Dahlgren, *Memoir of John A. Dahlgren* (Boston: James R. Osgood & Co., 1882): 644.
7. Helen F. Siu, ed., *Merchants' Daughters:*

Women, Commerce, and Regional Culture in South China (Hong Kong: Hong Kong University Press, 2011): 135.
8. Alan Walker, *Hans von Bülow: A Life and Times* (Oxford: Oxford University Press, 2009): 227.
9. Walker, *von Bülow*, 228.
10. Kenneth Birkin, *Hans von Bülow: A Life for Music* (Cambridge: Cambridge University Press, 2011): 239.
11. Walker, *von Bülow*, 228.
12. Gustav Freiherr von Overbeck was appointed Maharajah of Sabah and Rajah of Gaya and Sandakan by the Sultan of Brunei December 29, 1877, and Datu Bendahara and Rajah of Sandakan by the Sultan of Sulu January 22, 1878; Eine biographische Skizze, LM, Band 28, Detmold 1959, S. 163–217.
13. *Washington Post*, April 12, 1878.
14. http://www.lawnet.sabah.gov.my/Lawnet/SabahLaws/Treaties/CommissionFromSultanOfBorneoAppointingGustavusBaronDeOverbeckMaharajahOfSabah(NorthBorneo)AndRajahOfGayaAndSandakans.pdf. Accessed January 2016.
15. Hutto, *Crowning Glory*, 160–161.
16. https://davidderrick.wordpress.com/2007/09/13/a-rough-guide-to-british-malaya/. Accessed February 2016.
17. *Von Overbeck v. Dahlgren*, 28 F.2d 936 (1928).
18. *London Times*, May 9, 1894.
19. March 11, 1887, Harvard-Houghton Library, MS Am 994–996, Von Waldersee-Lee Collection.
20. Mary to her mother, May 30, 1885, Harvard-Houghton Library, MS Am 994–996, Von Waldersee-Lee Collection.
21. Ann Lee to Mary Hoppin, Harvard-Houghton Library, MS Am 994–996, Von Waldersee-Lee Collection.
22. August 5, 1888, Harvard-Houghton Library, MS Am 994–996, Von Waldersee-Lee Collection.
23. http://manuscripts.ptsem.edu/collection/231. Accessed March 2016; the Princeton Theological Seminary's Archives and Special Collection has a handwritten postcard of encouragement from Countess von Waldersee to the young man written on August 25, 1891.
24. *Houston Daily Post*, January 20, 1896. Additionally, an undated and unattributed newspaper clipping describing the event is in the von Waldersee-Lee collection.
25. Mary von Waldersee letter, Lautenbach, September 7, 1896, Harvard-Houghton Library, MS Am 994–996, Von Waldersee-Lee Collection.
26. *The* (London) *Times*, August 9, 1901, 3.
27. *The London Gazette*, August 16, 1901.
28. Ann Lee to Mary Hoppin.
29. *Ibid.*, Berlin, April 24, 1885.
30. *Ibid.*, Berlin, January 3, 1886.

Chapter 12

1. The *New York Times* noted of their honeymoon in Ethiopia that her husband was "in high in favor with Menelek [the emperor] and the nobility of Abyssinia, and his Yankee bride will no doubt be received with all the rude honors of which the kingdom is capable" (October 13, 1907).
2. *New York Times*, October 24, 1900.
3. *Ibid.*
4. *New York Times*, February 25, 1897.
5. Larry Clinton Thompson, *William Scott Ament and the Boxer Rebellion: Heroism, Hubris, and the Ideal Missionary* (Jefferson, NC: McFarland, 2009): 7.
6. Joseph W. Esherick, *The Origins of the Boxer Uprising* (Berkeley: University of California Press, 1987) 297–298.
7. Thompson, *Boxer Rebellion*, 12.
8. *Ibid.*, 7–8.
9. Robert B. Edgerton, *Warriors of the Rising Sun: a History of the Japanese Military* (New York: W. W. Norton, 1997): 70.
10. *Ibid.*
11. Upton Close, *In the Land of the Laughing Buddha: The Adventures of an American Barbarian in China* (New York: Putnam, 1924): 267; Diana Preston, *The Boxer Rebellion: The Dramatic Story of China's War on Foreigners That Shook the World in the Summer of 1900* (New York: Walker & Co., 1999): 71.
12. *New York Times*, June 14, 1901.
13. *Baltimore Sun*, July 7, 1900.
14. *Grand Rapids Herald*, October 18, 1900.
15. Grant Hayter-Menzies, *The Empress and Mrs. Conger: The Uncommon Friendship of Two Women and Two Worlds* (Hong Kong: Hong Kong University Press, 2011): 133–134.
16. Preston, *Boxer Rebellion*, 148–149.
17. Sarah Pike Conger, *Letters from China* (Chicago: A. C. McClurg, 1910): 135.
18. Peter Fleming, *The Siege at Peking* (New York: Harper, 1959): 208.
19. Von Waldersee diary entry, August 7–25, 1900, in *A Field-Marshal's Memoirs: From the Diary, Correspondence, and Reminiscences*

of Alfred, Count von Waldersee, ed. and trans. Frederic Whyte (London: Hutchinson & Co., 1924; Westport, CT: Greenwood Press, 1978): 206–207.

20. Robert K. Massie, *Dreadnought: Britain, Germany, and the Coming of the Great War* (New York: Random House, 1991): 283.

21. *Ibid.*

22. *New York Times*, August 13, 1900.

23. *New York Times*, August 9, 1900.

24. *New York Times*, August 11, 1900.

25. Mary von Waldersee letter, Hanover, June 16, 1901, Harvard-Houghton Library, MS Am 994–996, Von Waldersee-Lee Collection.

26. Von Waldersee, *Field-Marshal's Memoirs*, August 7–25, 1900: 209.

27. *Ibid.*

28. *Ibid.*

29. *Ibid.*, 210.

30. *New York Times*, August 17, 1900).

31. *New York Times*, August 23, 1900).

32. Robert K. Massie, *Castles of Steel: Britain, Germany, and the Winning of the Great War at Sea* (New York: Random House, 2003): 3.

33. Prime Minister Winston Churchill's broadcast "Report on the War," April 27, 1941.

34. Von Waldersee, *Field-Marshal's Memoirs*, September 18, 1900: 212,

35. *Ibid.*

36. *Ibid.*, September 29, 1900, 217.

37. *Ibid.*, October 22, 1900, 218.

38. Count von Waldersee's November 3, 1900, letter to the kaiser, recorded in Von Waldersee, *Field-Marshal's Memoirs*, 228.

39. Much of the information on Sai Jinhua is taken from *That Chinese Woman*, translated from Chinese by Henry McAleavy (New York: Thomas Y. Crowell Co., 1959).

40. Dewai Weng, *Fin-de-siècle Splendor: Repressed Modernities of Late Qing Fiction, 1849–1911* (Stanford: Stanford University Press, 1997): 103.

41. Letter of February 21, 1890 and card in undated scrapbook: both Harvard-Houghton Library, MS Am 994–996, Von Waldersee-Lee Collection.

42. Letter of March 22, 1890, Harvard-Houghton Library, MS Am 994–996, Von Waldersee-Lee Collection.

43. Alson J. Smith, *A View of the Spree* (New York: John Day Company, 1962): 167–169; the Chinese historian Ch'en Chieh, in his *History of the Boxer Rebellion*, recorded an "adulterous intrigue" with von Waldersee while Sai's husband was assigned to Berlin.

44. Smith, *View of the Spree*, 169.

45. McAleavy, *That Chinese Woman*, 206.

46. Wenxian Zhang, "Sai Jinhua," in Melissa Hope Ditmore, ed., *Encyclopedia of Prostitution and Sex Work*, vol. 2 (Santa Barbara: Greenwood, 2006): 423.

47. *New York Times*, January 6, 1901.

48. McAleavy, *That Chinese Woman*, 213.

49. "The Vicissitudes of Prince Chun's Mansion," *China Heritage Quarterly* 12 (December 12, 2007).

50. *New York Times*, September 15, 1900.

51. Smith, *View of the Spree*, 254.

52. *New York Times*, January 6, 1901.

53. Von Waldersee dispatch to the kaiser of April 20, 1901, reprinted in Von Waldersee, *Field-Marshal's Memoirs*, 264.

54. Von Waldersee, *Field-Marshal's Memoirs*, April 18, 1901: 265.

55. David B. Lee letter of September 19, 1900, Harvard-Houghton Library, MS Am 994–996, Von Waldersee-Lee Collection.

56. Mary von Waldersee letter, June 16, 1901, Harvard-Houghton Library, MS Am 994–996, Von Waldersee-Lee Collection.

57. *Ibid.*

58. Mary von Waldersee letter, January 19, 1902, Harvard-Houghton Library, MS Am 994–996, Von Waldersee-Lee Collection.

59. Jung Chang, *Empress Dowager Cixi* (New York: Knopf, 2013): 295f.

60. Kaiser's letter of November 11, 1900, to von Waldersee, reprinted in Von Waldersee, *Field-Marshal's Memoirs*, 230.

61. Von Waldersee, *Field-Marshal's Memoirs*, November 12, 1900: 231.

62. *Ibid.*, 232.

63. *Ibid.*, 234. Several months later he recorded in his diary, "That many Chinese are shot is quite true; they had, however, always deserved their fate." February 12, 1901.

64. Von Waldersee, *Field-Marshal's Memoirs*, December 23, 1900: 243–44.

65. *Ibid.*, February 12, 1901, 252.

66. *Ibid.*, May 23, 1901, 268.

67. *Ibid.*, June 5–8, 1901, 269.

68. Xianchu Wan, "Sai Jinhua," in *Biographical Dictionary of Chinese Women, The Qing Period, 1844–1911*, trans. Poon Shuk Wah, ed. Lily Xiao Hong Lee and A. D. Stefanowska; ed. Clara Wing-chung Ho, Qing Period (New York: M. E. Sharpe, 1998).

69. John Röhl, email message to author, March 15, 2016.

70. *New York Times*, June 6, 1901.

71. *Philadelphia Inquirer*, December 17, 1900.

72. *Town & Country*, September 25, 1909.
73. Her papers are housed at the University of Michigan: http://catalog.hathitrust.org/Record/001986650. Accessed March 2016.
74. *Kansas City Journal*, December 10, 1898, 12.
75. *Chicago Tribune*, November 7, 1902, 1; also reported in *Owego* (NY) *Daily Record*, November 7, 1902, and *Indianapolis News*, November 7, 1902.
76. Smith, *View of the Spree*, 95.
77. Francis A. March, *History of the World War: An Authentic Narrative of the World's Greatest War* (Philadelphia: United Publishers, 1919): 68.
78. "Some European Nobles That Are Almost American," *New York Times*, March 12, 1911.
79. *Brooklyn Daily Eagle*, November 12, 1901; *New York Times*, November 11, 1905; *San Jose Evening News*, May 4, 1906; La Marquise de Fontenoy, *New York Times*, *Chicago Daily Tribune*, June 19, 1911; *Chicago Daily Tribune*, October 6, 1912; *Chicago Daily Tribune*, August 30, 1914.
80. Princess Isabella was equally outraged at the Archduke Franz Ferdinand, heir to the throne. He often visited her home, and she assumed he was courting one of her eight daughters. Instead, he was smitten with her lady-in-waiting, Countess Sophie Chotek. He refused to give her up and finally accepted a morganatic marriage against united disapproval. The countess was maliciously reminded at every court function of her lowly place of precedence, and Princess Isabella never forgave her. The assassination of the couple at Sarajevo precipitated the outbreak of World War I.
81. *New York Times*, December 11, 1913.
82. "Why Foreign Diplomats Marry American Girls," *Los Angeles Herald*, June 12, 1904.

Chapter 13

1. Undated newspaper clipping signed "J. M. H.," in Harvard-Houghton Library, MS Am 994–996, Von Waldersee-Lee Collection.
2. Ann Lee letter to Mary Hoppin, Württemberg, September 2, 1890. Harvard-Houghton Library, MS Am 994–996, Von Waldersee-Lee Collection.
3. Mary von Waldersee letter of March 8, 1900, Harvard-Houghton Library, MS Am 994–996, Von Waldersee-Lee Collection.
4. Mary von Waldersee letter, Sylt, Jul 8, 1900.
5. *Ibid.*
6. Letter of January 19, 1902, Harvard-Houghton Library, MS Am 994–996, Von Waldersee-Lee Collection.
7. Mary von Waldersee letter, Hanover, June 16, 1901.
8. *New York Times*, August 7, 1901.
9. His sister, Wanda, married in 1843 Ludwig, Fürst von Schönaich-Carolath. Friedrich von Holstein, head of the political department of the German foreign office for 30 years, wrote that the father of one of her sons was either a waiter or a coachman: "One must choose between the two."
10. Count Horace de Viel-Castel, *The Memoirs of Count Horace de Viel-Castel: A Chronicle of the Principal Events, Political and Social, During the Reign of Napoleon III from 1851 to 1864* (London: Remington and Company, 1888): 33–34.
11. Joanna Richardson, *La Vie Parisienne: 1852–1870* (London: H. Hamilton, 1971): 69.
12. http://www.telegraph.co.uk/news/worldnews/europe/switzerland/8520066/Worlds-most-expensive-tiara-sells-for-7.8m.html. Accessed February 2016.
13. Letter of January 19, 1902, Harvard-Houghton Library, MS Am 994–996, Von Waldersee-Lee Collection.
14. Letter of July 12, 1902, written from Adelboden, Berner Oberland; Harvard-Houghton Library, MS Am 994–996, Von Waldersee-Lee Collection.
15. *San Francisco Call*, 23 June 1902, 1.
16. Von Waldersee diary, "End of September, 1902," in *A Field-Marshal's Memoirs: From the Diary, Correspondence, and Reminiscences of Alfred, Count von Waldersee*, ed. and trans. Frederic Whyte (London: Hutchinson & Co., 1924; Westport, CT: Greenwood Press, 1978): 278.
17. *Ibid.*, May 1903, 281.
18. *Ibid.*, May 1903, 281–282.
19. *Ibid.*, "End of September, 1902," 278–279.
20. *Ibid.*, April 10, 1902, 276–277.

Chapter 14

1. Mary von Waldersee letter, March 8, 1900. Harvard-Houghton Library, MS Am 994–996, Von Waldersee-Lee Collection.
2. *Ibid.*, July 8, 1900.
3. John Röhl, *Wilhelm II: Into the Abyss of*

War and Exile, 1900–1941 (Cambridge: Cambridge University Press, 2014), 223–228; email message to author, December 27, 2015.
 4. Count Alfred von Waldersee letter, Hanover, June 21,1902. Harvard-Houghton Library, MS Am 994–996, Von Waldersee-Lee Collection.
 5. Undated newspaper clipping in Von Waldersee-Lee correspondence, Harvard-Houghton Library, MS Am 994–996.
 6. *New-York Daily Tribune*, August 30, 1903.
 7. *New York Times*, August 30, 1903.
 8. *New-York Daily Tribune*, August 30, 1903.
 9. *Ibid.*
 10. *New York Times*, September 6, 1903.
 11. *New York Times*, August 30, 1903.
 12. *New York Times*, August 31, 1902.
 13. Mary von Waldersee letter, Park Avenue Hotel, New York City, August 31, 1903, Harvard-Houghton Library, MS Am 994–996, Von Waldersee-Lee Collection.
 14. *Ibid.*, September 17, 1903.
 15. *New York Times*, June 28, 1899.
 16. Edward E. Salisbury and Evelyn McCurdy Salisbury, *Family Histories and Genealogies*, 3 vols. (privately printed, 1892) 73.
 17. Letter of January 18, 1884, Harvard-Houghton Library, MS Am 994–996, Von Waldersee-Lee Collection.
 18. *Ibid.*
 19. Mary von Waldersee's letter of May 5, 1904, to her American family, Harvard-Houghton Library, MS Am 994–996, Von Waldersee-Lee Collection.
 20. *Ibid.*
 21. Letter from Hanover of May 5, 1904, Harvard-Houghton Library, MS Am 994–996, Von Waldersee-Lee Collection.
 22. Von Waldersee diary, March 5,1904, in *A Field-Marshal's Memoirs: From the Diary, Correspondence, and Reminiscences of Alfred, Count von Waldersee*, ed. and trans. Frederic Whyte (London: Hutchinson & Co., 1924; Westport, CT: Greenwood Press, 1978).
 23. Undated and unattributed newspaper clipping in von Waldersee-Lee correspondence.
 24. *The Search-light: A Condensed Weekly of the News and Progress of the World* 23 (March 12, 1904): 256.
 25. Undated and unattributed newspaper clipping in von Waldersee-Lee correspondence.
 26. *Ibid.*
 27. July 5, 1914.
 28. Letter from Hanover of May 5, 1904, Harvard-Houghton Library, MS Am 994–996, Von Waldersee-Lee Collection.
 29. *Ibid.*
 30. *Ibid.*
 31. All descriptions of the funeral from Mary's letter from Hanover of May 5, 1904, Harvard-Houghton Library, MS Am 994–996, Von Waldersee-Lee Collection.
 32. Undated letter from Mary to Mr. and Mrs. Charles Rockwell after May 1904, Harvard-Houghton Library, MS Am 994–996, Von Waldersee-Lee Collection.

Chapter 15

 1. *New York Times*, June 17, 1904.
 2. *New York Times*, March 12, 1904.
 3. *The Newtown Register*, October 21, 1915.
 4. Undated page from the *New York Observer* in von Waldersee-Lee correspondence, Harvard-Houghton Library, MS Am 994–996.
 5. *New York Observer*, June 8, 1905.
 6. Mary von Waldersee to Mary G. Stuckenberg, December 6, 1906 (completed January 7, 1907), MS-093: John Henry Wilbrand Stuckenberg Papers. Special Collections & College Archives, Musselman Library, Gettysburg College.
 7. Count Axel von Schwering (pseud.), *The Berlin Court Under William II* (London: Cassell & Co., 1915) 195.
 8. All descriptions of Mary's last illness and funeral are from the letter of her sister, Baroness de Waechter, to their American cousins. Harvard-Houghton Library, MS Am 994–996, Von Waldersee-Lee Collection.
 9. *Ibid.*
 10. Maria Weihe to Lee cousins in America, Hanover, July 22, 1914, Harvard-Houghton Library, MS Am 994–996, Von Waldersee-Lee Collection.
 11. Mary's sister, Baroness de Waechter, to their American cousins. Harvard-Houghton Library, MS Am 994–996, Von Waldersee-Lee Collection.
 12. *Ibid.*
 13. *The Sun*, July 5, 1914.
 14. Their grandson, Prince Ernst August, married in 1999 as his second wife Princess Caroline of Monaco, whose mother was the American-born actress Grace Kelly.
 15. Undated and unattributed newspaper

clipping in von Waldersee-Lee correspondence.
16. Countess von Waldersee, "The Story of My Life," *Harper's Bazaar* 37/7 (July 1903).
17. Marian Watts, "My Visit to the Countess von Waldersee," *San Francisco Call*, October 28, 1900, 9.
18. *New York Herald*, September 9, 1915.
19. John Röhl, email message to author, January 4, 1916.
20. *New York Times*, September 9, 1915.
21. Inflation calculator: http://www.westegg.com/inflation/. Accessed February 2016.
22. *New York Times*, January 22, 1915.
23. Maria Weihe to Lee cousins in America, Hanover, July 22, 1914, Harvard-Houghton Library, MS Am 994–996, Von Waldersee-Lee Collection.
24. *New York Times*, January 22, 1915.
25. *New-York Daily Tribune*, August 30, 1903.

Epilogue

1. LaMar Cecil, *Wilhelm II: Emperor and Exile, 1900–1941* (Chapel Hill: University of North Carolina Press, 1996): 63f.
2. Vicky to her mother, Queen Victoria, July 19, 1889, *Letters of the Empress Frederick* (Macmillan, 1928): 382.
3. Formerly his aunt's lady-in-waiting, Countess Sophie Chotek. Despite bitter opposition, the archduke refused to give her up and finally accepted a morganatic marriage against united disapproval.
4. Pamela Dell, *A World War I Timeline*, Smithsonian War Timelines Series (Mankato: Capstone, 2013): 10–12.
5. H. P. Willmott, *World War I* (New York: Dorling Kindersley, 2003).
6. *The* (London) *Times*, July 7, 1893, 5.
7. Henry William Brands, *T. R.: The Last Romantic* (New York: Basic Books, 1997): 756.
8. "Woodrow Wilson Urges Congress to Declare War on Germany," delivered at a joint session of the two houses of Congress on April 2, 1917. Woodrow Wilson, War Messages, 65th Cong., 1st Sess. Senate Doc. No. 5, Serial No. 7264, Washington, DC, 1917; 3–8, passim.
9. "Selective Service System: History and Records," https://www.sss.gov/Old/Old_Site/hist, accessed May 30, 2016.
10. John C. G. Röhl, *Kaiser Wilhelm II, New Interpretations: The Corfu Papers* (Cambridge: Cambridge University Press, 2005):

40. The kaiser admitted to having a breakdown in 1918, but he "put himself to bed, slept for 24 hours and was as good as new."
11. Von Waldersee diary entry, March 5, 1904, in Count Alfred von Waldersee, *A Field-Marshal's Memoirs: From the Diary, Correspondence, and Reminiscences of Alfred, Count von Waldersee*, ed. and trans. Frederic Whyte (London: Hutchinson & Co., 1924; Westport, CT: Greenwood Press, 1978): 286.
12. Robert Beachy, *Gay Berlin: Birthplace of a Modern Identity* (New York: Vintage Books, 2015): 72–73.
13. William Manchester, *The Arms of Krupp: The Rise and Fall of the Industrial Dynasty That Armed Germany at War* (Boston: Little & Brown, 1968; paperback edition 1970): 276.
14. Willi Boelcke, *Krupp und die Hohenzollern in Dokumenten 1850–1918* (Frankfurt: Athenaion, 1970): 158–162.
15. Beachy, *Gay Berlin*, 73.
16. John C. G. Röhl, *The Kaiser and His Court: Wilhelm II and the Government of Germany* (Cambridge: Cambridge University Press, 1994): 36.
17. Lecomte (1857–1921) used his position to reveal to his government that Germany was bluffing in the Morocco Crisis of 1906, ending in a French diplomatic victory at the conference at Algeciras. Wayne R. Dynes, ed., *Encyclopedia of Homosexuality*, vol. 1 (Oxford: Routledge, 1990): 376.
18. Beachy, *Gay Berlin*, 122.
19. Röhl, *Kaiser and His Court*, 62.
20. *Ibid.*, 61.
21. Elena Mancini, *Magnus Hirschfeld and the Quest for Sexual Freedom: A History of the First International Sexual Freedom Movement* (London: Macmillan, 2010): 97.
22. Röhl, *Kaiser Wilhelm II: A Concise Life* (Cambridge: Cambridge University Press): 104.
23. *Ibid.*, 104.
24. Ragnhld Fiebig-von Hase, "The Uses of 'Friendship': The 'Personal Regime' of Wilhelm II and Theodore Roosevelt," in *The Kaiser*, ed. Annika Mommbauer and Wilhelm Deist (Cambridge: Cambridge University Press, 2003): 143–175.
25. Röhl, *Kaiser and His Court*, 58.
26. Vargo, *Scandal: Infamous Gay Controversies of the Twentieth Century* (New York: Routledge, 2003): 167.
27. Norman Domeier, *The Eulenburg Affair: A Cultural History of Politics in the*

German Empire (Rochester: Boydell & Brewer, 2015): 169.
  28. *Ibid.*, 188.
  29. Beachy, *Gay Berlin*, 132.
  30. Röhl, *Kaiser and His Court*, 59.
  31. Beachy, *Gay Berlin*, 134.
  32. John C. G. Röhl, *1914: Delusion or Design?* (New York and London: Elek, 1973): 57.
  33. Röhl, *Kaiser and His Court*, 60.
  34. Robert Aldrich, "Eulenburg, Philip von," in *Who's Who in Gay and Lesbian History: From Antiquity to World War II*, ed. Robert Aldrich and Garry Wotherspoon (New York: Psychology Press, 2002): 181–182.
  35. Beachy, *Gay Berlin*, 136.
  36. *Ibid.*
  37. *Ibid.*, 135–137.
  38. http://www.jacobite.ca/kings/sophie.htm. Accessed May 30, 2016.
  39. Robert K. Massie, *Dreadnought: Britain, Germany, and the Coming of the Great War* (New York: Random House, 1991).
  40. Harold James, *A German Identity: 1770–1990* (New York: Routledge, 1989): 82.
  41. James D. Steakley, "Iconography of a Scandal: Political Cartoons and the Eulenburg Affair in Wilhelmin Germany," in *Hidden from History: Reclaiming the Gay & Lesbian Past*, ed. Martin Bauml Duberman, Martha Vicinus, and George Chauncey (New York: Meridian, New American Library, Penguin Books, 1990).
  42. Röhl, *Corfu Papers*, 40.
  43. Georgiana Battiscombe, *Queen Alexandra* (London: Constable, 1960): 174.

  44. Röhl, *Kaiser and His Court*, 63.
  45. *Ibid.*, 20.
  46. *Ibid.*
  47. *Ibid.*
  48. Countess Marguerite Cunliffe-Owen writing as "La Marquise de Fontenoy," *Secret Memoirs of the Courts of Europe: William II, Germany; Francis Joseph, Austria-Hungary* (Philadelphia: George Barrie & Sons, 1900): 21.
  49. Count Axel von Schwering (pseud.), *The Berlin Court Under William II* (London: Cassell & Co., 1915): 190. Von Schwering was a pseudonym, perhaps for the kaiser's childhood friend, Prince von Fürstenberg, according to the *Literary Digest*, 52/2, quoting the *New York Sun* and the *Brooklyn Daily Eagle* (June 29, 1915).
  50. *Ibid.*
  51. Von Schwering, *Berlin Court*, 191–192.
  52. *New York Observer*, March 30, 1899.
  53. Marguerite Cunliffe-Owen, *Imperator Et Rex: William II of Germany* (New York: Harper Brothers, 1904): 99.
  54. John Röhl, *The Kaiser and His Court: Wilhelm II and the Government of Germany* (Cambridge: Cambridge University Press, 1994): 210.
  55. LaMar Cecil, *Wilhelm II: Emperor and Exile, 1900–1941* (Chapel Hill: University of North Carolina Press, 1996): 57.
  56. Röhl, *Kaiser and His Court*, 211.
  57. *Ibid.*
  58. Von Schwering, *Berlin Court*, 195–196.
  59. *New York Tribune*, January 25, 1889.

Bibliography

Aldrich, Robert. "Eulenburg, Philip von." In *Who's Who in Gay and Lesbian History: From Antiquity to World War II*. Edited by Robert Aldrich and Garry Wotherspoon. New York: Psychology Press, 2002.
"The All-Time Richest Americans." forbes.com. September 14, 2007. Accessed January 2016. http://www.forbes.com/2007/09/14/richest-americans-alltime-biz_cx_pw_as_0914ialltime_slide.html.
The American Almanac, Yearbook, Cyclopedia, and Atlas. New York: American and Journal, 1903.
"American Women Marry Abroad." *The Annals of Iowa* 30/4 (Spring 1950).
Asimov, Isaac. *Treasury of Humor*. New York: Mariner Books, 1991.
"Authentic German Liberalism of the 19th Century." Ludwig von Mises Institute. Accessed March 2016. http://www.mises.org/daily/1787.
Balfour, Michael. *The Kaiser and His Times*. Boston: Houghton Mifflin, 1964.
Bartley, Paula. *Queen Victoria*. Oxford: Routledge, 2016.
Battiscombe, Georgiana. *Queen Alexandra*. London: Constable, 1960.
Beachy, Robert. *Gay Berlin: Birthplace of a Modern Identity*. New York: Vintage Books, 2015.
Bennett, Daphne. *Vicky: Princess Royal of England and German Empress*. New York: St. Martin's Press, 1971.
Ben-Sasson, H. H., ed. *A History of the Jewish People*. Cambridge: Harvard University Press, 1976.
Biographies in Naval History. Naval Historical Center, Department of the Navy (July 25, 2001).
Birkin, Kenneth. *Hans von Bülow: A Life for Music*. Cambridge: Cambridge University Press, 2011.
Blackbourn, David. *History of Germany, 1780–1918: The Long Nineteenth Century*. New York: Oxford University Press, 1998.
Boelcke, Willi. *Krupp und die Hohenzollern in Dokumenten 1850–1918*. Frankfurt: Athenaion, 1970.
The Bookman XL (September 1914–February 1915).
Brands, Henry William. *T. R.: The Last Romantic*. New York: Basic Books, 1997.
Brecht, Martin. *Martin Luther*. Minneapolis: Fortress Press, 1985–1993.
Burke's Genealogical and Heraldic History of the Peerage, Baronetage and Knightage. Edited by Ashworth P. Burke. London: Harrison and Sons Ltd., 1913.
Busch, Julius H. M. *Bismarck: Some Secret Pages of His History*. Vol. 3. London: Macmillan, 1898.
Canandine, David. *The Decline and Fall of the British Aristocracy*. New Haven: Yale University Press, 1990.

Cecil, LaMar. *Wilhelm II: Emperor and Exile, 1900–1941*. Chapel Hill: University of North Carolina Press, 1996.
Chang, Jung. *Empress Dowager Cixi*. New York: Knopf, 2013.
Chisholm, Hugh, ed. "Schleswig-Holstein Question." In *Encyclopædia Britannica*, 11th ed. Cambridge: Cambridge University Press, 1911.
Clay, Catrine. *King, Kaiser, Tsar*. London: John Murray, 2006.
Close, Upton. *In the Land of the Laughing Buddha: The Adventures of an American Barbarian in China*. New York: Putnam, 1924.
The Commonwealth War Graves Commission (CWGC) Annual Report 2009–2010. Heeres-Sanitaetsinspektion im Reichskriegsministeriums (1934). Sanitaetsbericht über das deutsche Heer deutsches Feld- und Besatzungsheer, im Weltkriege 1914–1918. Berlin. 3/1.
Conger, Sarah Pike. *Letters from China*. Chicago: A. C. McClurg, 1910.
Cowles, Virginia. *Gay Monarch*. New York: Harper & Brothers, 1956.
_____. *The Kaiser*. New York: Harper & Row, 1963.
Cunliffe-Owen, Marguerite ("La Marquise de Fontenoy"). *Imperator Et Rex: William II of Germany*. New York: Harper Brothers, 1904.
_____. *The Marquise of Fontenoy's Revelation of High Life Within Court Palaces*. Philadelphia: Edgewood Publishing, 1892.
_____. *Secret Memoirs of the Courts of Europe: William II, Germany; Francis Joseph, Austria-Hungary*. Philadelphia: George Barrie & Sons, 1900.
_____. *Within Royal Palaces*. Philadelphia: Edgewood Publishing, 1892.
Dahlgren, Madeline Vinton. *Memoir of John A. Dahlgren*. Boston: James R. Osgood & Co., 1882.
De Hegermann Lindencrone, L. *In the Courts of Memory*. New York: Harper & Brothers, 1911.
De Noussanne, Henri. *The Kaiser as He Is: Or, the Real William II*. New York: Putnam, 1905.
De Viel-Castel, Horace. *The Memoirs of Count Horace de Viel-Castel: A Chronicle of the Principal Events, Political and Social, During the Reign of Napoleon III from 1851 to 1864*. London: Remington and Company, 1888.
Dell, Pamela. *A World War I Timeline*. Smithsonian War Timelines Series. Mankato: Capstone, 2013.
Dickie, J. F. *In the Kaiser's Capital*. New York: Dodd, Mead, 1912.
Dickinson, Asa Don, ed. *The Kaiser: A Book about the Most Interesting Man in Europe*. New York: Doubleday, Page & Co., 1914.
Domeier, Norman. *The Eulenburg Affair: A Cultural History of Politics in the German Empire*. Rochester: Boydell & Brewer, 2015.
Dynes, Wayne R., ed. *Encyclopedia of Homosexuality*. Vol. 1. Oxford: Routledge, 1990.
Edgerton, Robert B. *Warriors of the Rising Sun: A History of the Japanese Military*. New York: W. W. Norton, 1997.
Eilers, Marlene A. *Queen Victoria's Descendants*. Rosvall Royal Books, 1997.
The Empress Frederick: A Memoir. London: Dodd, Mead, 1914.
Esherick, Joseph W. *The Origins of the Boxer Uprising*. Berkeley: University of California Press, 1987.
Feldhahn, Ulrich. *Die preußischen Könige und Kaiser*. Lindenberg: Kunstverlag Josef Fink, 2011.
Fiebig-von Hase, Ragnhld. "The Uses of 'Friendship': The 'Personal Regime' of Wilhelm II and Theodore Roosevelt." In *The Kaiser*. Edited by Annika Mommbauer and Wilhelm Deist. Cambridge: Cambridge University Press, 2003.
Fischer, Henry William. *Behind the Scenes with the Kaiser, 1888–1892*. Vol. II. New York: The World Publishing Co., 1909.

_____. *Private Lives of Kaiser William II and His Consort*. Vol. 3. New York: Fred de Fau & Co., 1909.
Fleming, Patrica H. "The Politics of Marriage Among Non-Catholic European Royalty." *Current Anthropology* 14 (June 1973).
Fleming, Peter. *The Siege at Peking*. New York: Harper, 1959.
Fleury, Maurice. *Memoirs of the Empress Eugenie*. New York: D. Appleton & Co., 1920.
Frederic, Harold. *The Young William II, Emperor of Germany: A Study in Character Development on a Throne*. New York: Putnam's, 1891.
Frederick, Ponsonby, ed. *Letters of the Empress Frederick*. London: Macmillan, 1930.
Fulbrook, Mary. *Piety and Politics: Religion and the Rise of Absolutism in England, Wurttemberg and Prussia*. Cambridge: Cambridge University Press, 1983.
Fulford, Roger, ed. *Beloved Mama*. London: Evans Brothers, 1981.
Gayley, Alice J. "Admiral John A. Dahlgren." *Pennsylvania in the Civil War. PA Roots*. Accessed September 26, 2015. library.syr.edu/digital/guides/d/dahlgren_ja.htm.
Goerlitz, Walter. *History of the German Staff*. New York: Praeger, 1956.
Gregg, Frederick James. "The British Aristrocracy and the War: The Doubtful Future of the House of Lords." *Vanity Fair* (March 1916). Accessed March 2016. http://www.oldmagazinearticles.com/WW1_British_Aristocracy-Nobility_during_World_War_One-pdf.
Groueff, Stephanie. *Crown of Thorns: The Reign of King Boris III of Bulgaria*. New York: Madison Books, 1987.
Guedalla, Philip. "Is it a girl? No. Is it a boy? No. But, then, what is it?" In *The Second Empire*. New York: G. P. Putnam's Sons, 1922.
Harrison, Constance Cary. *Recollections Brave and Gay*. New York: Charles Scribners' Sons, 1911.
Haskell, Mabell Percy. "The Countess von Waldersee." *The Woman's Home Companion* (May 1901).
Hayter-Menzies, Grant. *The Empress and Mrs. Conger: The Uncommon Friendship of Two Women and Two Worlds*. Hong Kong: Hong Kong University Press, 2011.
Hull, Isabel V. *The Entourage of Kaiser Wilhelm II, 1888–1918*. Cambridge: Cambridge University Press, 1982.
Hutto, Richard Jay. *Crowning Glory: American Wives of Princes and Dukes*. Macon: Henchard Press, 2007.
James, Harold. *A German Identity: 1770–1990*. New York: Routledge, 1989.
Johanet, F. E. *Autour du Monde Milionnaire Américain*. Paris: Callman-Levy, 1898.
Kehoe, Elisabeth. *The Titled Americans: Three American Sisters and the British Aristocratic World into Which They Married*. New York: Atlantic Monthly Press, 2004.
Kingston, Charles. *Famous Morganatic Marriages*. London: S. Paul & Co., 1919.
Lambi, Ivo N. *Canadian Journal of History* 34/3 (December 1999).
Legge, Edward. *The Comedy and Tragedy of the Second Empire: Paris Society in the Sixties*. New York: Harper & Bros., 1911.
_____. *King Edward in His True Colors*. London: Eveleigh Nash, 1972.
_____. *The Public and Private Life of Kaiser William II*. London: Eveleigh Nash, 1915.
Lepsius, Johannes, Albrecht Mendelssohn-Bartholdy, and Friedrich Thimme. *Die grosse politik der europaischen kabinette, 1871–1914*. Vol. 6. Berlin: Deutsche veragsgesellschaft für politik und geschichte, 1922.
Lindemann, Albert S. *Anti-Semitism Before the Holocaust*. London: Routledge, 2000.
Ludwig, Emil. *Kaiser Wilhelm II*. London: Putnam, 1926.
_____. *The Moral Conquest of Germany*. New York: Doubleday, Doran & Co., 1945.
Ludwig, Emil and William Hohenzollern. *The Last of the Kaisers*. New York: Putnam's, 1927.

Manchester, William. *The Arms of Krupp: The Rise and Fall of the Industrial Dynasty That Armed Germany at War.* Boston: Little, Brown, 1968.
Mancini, Elena. *Magnus Hirschfeld and the Quest for Sexual Freedom: A History of the First International Sexual Freedom Movement.* London: Macmillan, 2010.
March, Francis A. *History of the World War: An Authentic Narrative of the World's Greatest War.* Philadelphia: United Publishers, 1919.
Massie, Robert K. *Castles of Steel: Britain, Germany, and the Winning of the Great War at Sea.* New York: Random House, 2003.
_____. *Dreadnought: Britain, Germany, and the Coming of the Great War.* New York: Random House, 1991.
McDonough, Giles. *The Last Kaiser: The Life of Wilhelm II.* New York: St. Martin's Press, 2001.
Meisner, Heinrich O., ed. *Waldersees Denkwürdigkeiten.* Vol. 1. Stuttgart: Deutsche Verlags-Anstalt, 1922.
Melson, Robert. *Revolution and Genocide: On the Origins of the Armenian Genocide and the Holocaust.* University of Chicago Press, 1996.
Memoirs of Ernst II, Duke of Saxe-Coburg-Gotha. Vol. II. London: Remington & Co., 1888.
Miall, Bernard. *Suppressed Letters by the Kaiser and New Chapters from the Autobiography of the Iron Chancellor.* New York: Harper Brothers, 1921.
Michael, Robert. *Holy Hatred: Christianity, Antisemitism, and the Holocaust.* New York: Palgrave Macmillan, 2006.
Montefiore, Simon S. *The Romanovs 1613–1918.* New York: Knopf, 2016.
Navrozov, Andrei. "European Diary." *Chronicles* 32 (2008).
Nevins, Allan. *The War for the Union: The Improvised War 1861–1862.* New York: Scribners, 1959.
The New York Genealogical and Biographical Record. Vol. 81. New York: New York Genealogical and Biographical Society, 1870.
Nicholls, Charles W. *The Ultra-fashionable Peerage of America.* New York: G. Harjes, 1904.
Nichols, Herbert B. "Mary Lee, Princess of Noer." *Harvard Alumni Bulletin* 38/15 (January 17, 1936).
Noel, Gerard. *Princess Alice: Queen Victoria's Forgotten Daughter.* London: Constable and Company Limited, 1985.
Noër, Frederick A. *The Emperor Akbar, A Contribution Towards the History of India in the 16th Century.* Translated by Gustav von Buchwald. Calcutta: Thacker, Spink & Co., 1890.
"Old Grocery Houses." In *Valentine's Manual of Old New York.* Vol. 5. New York: Valentine's, 1919.
Otté, Elise C. *Scandinavian History.* London: Macmillan, 1894.
The Oxford Companion to American Military History. Edited by John W. Chambers II. Oxford: Oxford University Press, 1999.
Packard, Jerrold M. *Victoria's Daughters.* New York: St. Martin's Press, 1998.
Pakula, Hannah. *An Uncommon Woman: The Empress Frederick, Daughter of Queen Victoria, Wife of the Crown Prince of Prussia, Mother of Kaiser Wilhelm.* New York: Simon & Schuster, 1997.
Ponsonby, Frederick, ed. *Letters of the Empress Frederick.* London: Macmillan, 1930.
Preston, Diana. *The Boxer Rebellion: The Dramatic Story of China's War on Foreigners That Shook the World in the Summer of 1900.* New York: Walker & Co., 1999.
Princess Marie Louise. *My Memories of Six Reigns.* London: Evans Brothers, 1956.
Reinharz, Jehuda and Paul Mendes-Flohr. *Jew in the Modern World.* Oxford University Press, 2010.

Richardson, Joanna. *La Vie Parisienne: 1852–1870*. London: H. Hamilton, 1971.
"Rivals Cause Friction." *The Annals of Iowa* 30/4 (Spring 1950).
Röhl, John C. G. *The Kaiser and His Court: Wilhelm II and the Government of Germany.* Cambridge: Cambridge University Press, 1994.
_____. *Kaiser Wilhelm II, New Interpretations: The Corfu Papers.* Cambridge: Cambridge University Press, 2005.
_____. *1914: Delusion or Design?* New York: Elek, 1973.
_____. *Philipp Eulenburgs Politische Korrespondenz.* Vol. I. Boppard am Rhein: Harald Boldt Verlag, 1976.
_____. *Wilhelm II: Into the Abyss of War and Exile, 1900–1941.* Cambridge: Cambridge University Press, 2014.
_____. *Wilhelm II: The Kaiser's Personal Monarchy, 1888–1900.* Cambridge: Cambridge University Press, 2004.
_____. *Young Wilhelm: The Kaiser's Early Life, 1859–1888.* Cambridge: Cambridge University Press, 1993.
Röhl, John C. G., and Nicolaus Sombart, eds. *Kaiser Wilhelm II.* Cambridge: New Interpretations, 1982.
Röhl, John C. G., Martin Warren, and David Hunt. *Purple Secret: Genes, Madness and the Royal Houses of Europe.* London: Corgi Books, 1999.
Salisbury, Edward E., and Evelyn McCurdy Salisbury. *Family Histories and Genealogies.* Vol. 3. Privately printed, 1892.
"The Schleswig-Holstein Rebellion." Accessed May 7, 2012. http://www.milhist.dk/trearskrigen/outbreak_uk.htm.
Schultz, Myron. "Rudolf Virchow." *Emerg Infect Dis* 14/9 (2008). Accessed January 2016. doi:10.3201/eid1409.086672. PMC 2603088. http://www.pubmedcentral.nih.gov/articlerender.fcgi?tool=pmcentrez&artid=2603088.
Scott, Winfield. *Memoirs of Lieut.-General Scott, LL.D.* New York: Sheldon & Company, 1864.
Scoville, Joseph A. *The Old Merchants of New York City.* Vol. 4. New York: G. W. Carleton, 1866.
The Search-light: A Condensed Weekly of the News and Progress of the World 23 (March 12, 1904).
Seward, Desmond. *Eugenie: The Empress and Her Empire.* London: Sutton Publishing, 2004.
Siu, Helen F., ed. *Merchants' Daughters: Women, Commerce, and Regional Culture in South China.* Hong Kong: Hong Kong University Press, 2011.
Smith, Alson J. *A View of the Spree.* New York: John Day Company, 1962.
Spencer, Charles. "Enemies of the Estate." *Vanity Fair* (January 2010). Accessed January 2016. http://www.vanityfair.com/news/2010/01/english-aristocracy-201001.
Steakley, James D. "Iconography of a Scandal: Political Cartoons and the Eulenburg Affair in Wilhelmin Germany." In *Hidden from History: Reclaiming the Gay & Lesbian Past.* Edited by Martin Bauml Duberman, Martha Vicinus, and George Chauncey. New York: Meridian, New American Library, Penguin Books, 1990.
Stoddard, John. *John L. Stoddard's Lectures.* Vol. 6. Boston: Balch Brothers, 1898.
Strachey, Lytton. *Queen Victoria.* New York: Harcourt Brace, 1921.
Telman, D. A. Jeremy. "Adolf Stoecker: Anti-Semite with a Christian Mission." *Jewish History* 9/2 (Fall 1995).
That Chinese Woman. Translated by Henry McAleavy. New York: Thomas Y. Crowell Co., 1959.
Thompson, Larry Clinton. *William Scott Ament and the Boxer Rebellion: Heroism, Hubris, and the Ideal Missionary.* Jefferson NC: McFarland, 2009.
Town & Country. (September 25, 1909).
Trosclair, Wade. *Alfred von Waldersee, Monarchist: His Private Life, Public Image, and the*

Limits of His Ambition, 1882–1891. Masters thesis, Louisiana State University (May 2012).
Trubner's American and Oriental Literary Record. London: Trubner & Co., 1881.
Truth 63 (London: January 7, 1886).
Vanderbilt, Consuelo. *The Glitter and the Gold.* New York: St. Martin's Press, 1953.
"The Vicissitudes of Prince Chun's Mansion." *China Heritage Quarterly* 12 (December 12, 2007).
Von Beust, Friedrich Ferdinand Graf. *Aus drei Viertel-Jahrhunderten.* Vol. 1. Stuttgart: J. G. Cottaschen, 1887.
Von Bismarck, Fürst Otto. *The Man and the Statesman.* Vol. 2. London: Smith, Elder & Co., 1898.
Von Bismarck, Otto. *Die Gesammelten Werke, Berlin 1923–1933.* Vol. 15. Berlin: Stollberg, 1935.
Von Bothmer, Marie. *The Sovereign Courts of Europe.* New York: Appleton & Co., 1891.
Von Bothmer, Mary. *The Sovereign Ladies of Europe.* London: Hutchinson & Co., 1899.
Von Bülow, Bernhard. *Memoirs of Prince von Bulow.* Vol. 1. Boston: Little, Brown, 1931.
Von Larisch, Baroness (pseud.). *Behind the Scenes with the Kaiser.* New York: Hertag Publishers, 1922.
Von Noër, Graf. *Akbar, Emperor of India.* Translated by Richard von Garbe. Redding, CA: Gilman Press, 2010.
_____. *Kaiser Akbar: Ein Versuch über die Geschichte Indiens im sechzehnten Jahrhundret.* Leiden: E. J. Brill, 1885.
Von Schwering, Axel (pseud.). *The Berlin Court Under William II.* London: Cassell & Co., 1915.
Von Treitschke, Heinrich. *History of Germany in the Nineteenth Century.* Vol. 7. New York: Robert M. McBride & Co., 1919.
Von Waldersee, Alfred. *A Field-Marshal's Memoirs: From the Diary, Correspondence, and Reminiscences of Alfred, Count von Waldersee.* Edited and translated by Frederic Whyte. London: Hutchinson & Co., 1924; Westport, CT: Greenwood Press, 1978.
Von Waldersee, Elisabeth. *Von Klarheit zu Klarheit!* (*From Clarity to Clarity*). Stuttgart: Buchhandlung des Deutschen Philadelphia-Vereins, 1915.
Von Waldersee-Lee Collection. Cambridge MA: Harvard-Houghton Library, MS Am 994–996.
Von Waldersee, Mary. "The Story of My Life." *Harper's Bazar* 37/7 (July 1903).
Von Wedel-Bérard, Élisabeth. *My Relations with Kaiser Wilhelm II.* Zürich: Verlag von Cäsar Schmidt, 1900.
Walker, Alan. *Hans von Bülow: A Life and Times.* Oxford: Oxford University Press, 2009.
Wan, Xianchu. "Sai Jinhua." In *Biographical Dictionary of Chinese Women, The Qing Period, 1844–1911.* Translated by Poon Shuk Wah. Edited by Lily Xiao Hong Lee and A. D. Stefanowska. Qing Period edited by Clara Wing-chung Ho. New York: M. E. Sharpe, 1998.
Weintraub, Stanley. *Victoria.* London: John Murray, 1987.
Weng, Dewai. *Fin-de-siècle Splendor: Repressed Modernities of Late Qing Fiction, 1849–1911.* Stanford: Stanford University Press, 1997.
White, Matthew. "Source List and Detailed Death Tolls for the Primary Megadeaths of the Twentieth Century." http://necrometrics.com/20c5m.htm. Accessed January 2016.
Willmott, H. P. *World War I.* New York: Dorling Kindersley, 2003.
Wraxall, C. F. *Life & Times of Her Majesty Caroline Matilda, Queen of Denmark & Norway.* Vol. 1. London: Wm. H. Allen & Co., 1864.
"Writings of Graf von Noer." *Calcutta Review* 169 (July 1887).
Zhang, Wenxian. "Sai Jinhua." in Melissa Hope Ditmore, ed. *Encyclopedia of Prostitution and Sex Work.* Vol. 2. Santa Barbara: Greenwood, 2006.

Index

Numbers in **bold italics** refer to pages with photographs.

Augusta Victoria (Dona, wife of Kaiser), Kaiserin/Empress 56–69, **57**, **64**, 74, 76, 79, 82, 100, 120–122, 188–190

Charlotte, Princess of Prussia (sister of Kaiser) 59, 74–75, 94, 100

Edward VII, King (uncle of Kaiser) 8, 63, **98**, 104, 163–165
Eulenburg affair 183–188

Frederick III (Kaiser/Emperor, father of Kaiser Wilhelm) **79**, **80**, 83–86, 88–89, 91–92, 93–95, 101–103

Ketteler, Baroness August von (Matilda Cass Ledyard) 138–140

Lee, Ann D. (mother of Mary) 12, 28–29, 39–40, 42, 46–48, 81, 119–120, 122, 133–134, **136**, 160, 169
Lee, David (father of Mary) 11, 12, 30, 35, 43
Lee, Mary (Princess von Noër, Countess von Waldersee, 1837–1914): birth and family 13–17, **18**, **19**; created princess in her own right 40; encourages marriage to Dona 60–61; engagement and marriage 51–54; establishes salon 65–66, 82; final illness and death 176–178, **177**; friction and break with Kaiser 189–190; friendship with Baroness von Overbeck 129–**135**; friendship with Rev. Stoecker 74; funeral and family reaction 36–41; growing influence 115–118, **116**, 120–128; husband at coronation activities for Edward VII 163–165; husband departs for China 145–146; husband is passed over and demoted 124–128; husband mentors Wilhelm in Berard affair 105–114, **111**; husband summoned to lead China expedition 142–143; husband's appointment as Chief of General Staff 104; husband's death 35–36; husband's death and funeral 170–173; husband's performance in China 151–152; husband's promotion and move to Berlin 63–65; husband's relationship with Sai Jinhua 146–149; husband's return from China 161; illness and death of Kaiser 86–88, 96–97; marriage and honeymoon 32–36; at marriage of Prince Henry 101–102; Mary alone 149–150; meets first husband 27; meets second husband 50; mentors Dona 67–70; mother's death 160; move to Europe 17–20; opinion of American wives of foreign husbands 179; and other American wives of German diplomats 153–159; philanthropy 71–72, 134, 173, 175–176; proposal and title 29–31; public perception 178–181, 190, 192; purchases final home in Hanover 173, **175**; receives the Wilhelm Order 134–**136**; recuperation 161–162; retrieves incriminating letters 105, 110; returns to America 42–44, 166–170, **167**; returns to Paris 46–48; Stoecker meeting at her home 75–81, **87**; suitors 25, 48, 49; will and estate 179–180

Noër, Prince Frederick von (Prince Fredrick of Schleswig-Holstein-Sonderburg-Augustenburg, Mary's first husband) 24–25, 29–30, **30**, 32–36, **34**, 35–36, 86
Noër, Princess von *see* Lee, Mary

Overbeck, Baroness Gustav von (Romaine Madelein Goddard) 129–134

Sai Jinhua 146–150, 152–153
Schleswig-Holstein-Sonderburg-Augustenburg, Frederick, Prince of (Count von Noër, Mary's step-son) 38–39, 41
Schleswig-Holstein-Sonderburg-Augustenburg, Louisa, Princess of (Princess Vlangi-Handjeri, Mary's step-daughter) 25, 41–42
Stoecker, Rev. Adolf 71–74, 75–81, *76*, 82, 96

Victoria, Kaiserin/Empress (mother of Wilhelm II) 7, 8, 9, 57–62, *79*, *80*, 83–84, 85, 91–92, 93–95, *98*, 101, 102, 119–120

Victoria, Queen/Empress (grandmother of Wilhelm II) 8, 41, 45–46, *98*, 99, 102, 104, 118

Waechter, Josie, Baroness de (Mary's sister) 15–16, *19*, 19–20, 24–25, *167*, 166–170, 176–178
Waldersee, Count Alfred Von (Mary's second husband) 49–50, *51*, 63–65, 84, 85, *87*, 88–89, 101, 102, 104, 105–114, *111*, *116*, 122, *123*, 124–126, 142–*143*, 145–146, 146–150, *151*, 161–162, 163–165, *164*, 170, 182–189
Waldersee, Countess Von *see* Lee, Mary
Wilhelm II, Kaiser/Emperor 7, 8, 9, 55–61, *64*, 67, 74, *80*, *85*, 87–88, 93–95, *98*, 103–104, *107*, 105–114, *123*, 171, 182–192

www.ingramcontent.com/pod-product-compliance
Ingram Content Group UK Ltd.
Pitfield, Milton Keynes, MK11 3LW, UK
UKHW041953140426
5217IPUK00015B/782